THE
SIX SECRETS
OF
INTELLIGENCE

THE SIX SECRETS OF INTELLIGENCE

What your education failed to teach you

CRAIG ADAMS

ICON

Published in the UK and USA in 2019
by Icon Books Ltd, Omnibus Business Centre,
39–41 North Road, London N7 9DP
email: info@iconbooks.com
www.iconbooks.com

Sold in the UK, Europe and Asia
by Faber & Faber Ltd, Bloomsbury House,
74–77 Great Russell Street,
London WC1B 3DA or their agents

Distributed in the UK, Europe and Asia
by Grantham Book Services, Trent Road,
Grantham NG31 7XQ

Distributed in the USA
by Publishers Group West,
1700 Fourth Street, Berkeley, CA 94710

Distributed in Canada by Publishers Group Canada,
76 Stafford Street, Unit 300
Toronto, Ontario M6J 2S1

Distributed in Australia and New Zealand
by Allen & Unwin Pty Ltd, PO Box 8500,
83 Alexander Street, Crows Nest, NSW 2065

Distributed in South Africa
by Jonathan Ball, Office B4, The District,
41 Sir Lowry Road, Woodstock 7925

Distributed in India by Penguin Books India,
7th Floor, Infinity Tower – C, DLF Cyber City,
Gurgaon 122002, Haryana

ISBN: 978-178578-482-8

Typeset in Gentium by Marie Doherty

Printed and bound in Great Britain by
Clays Ltd, Elcograf S.p.A.

Contents

PART III – THINKING ABOUT THINKING

PART IV – THINKING ABOUT EDUCATION

PART V – A SCHOOL OF THOUGHT

Introduction

Having emerged from the dark hardship of another day spent deep in the belly of the earth, Mr Wu sits in his living room, illuminated by a single bare light bulb. In the two-room brick house he built with his own hands, there is no sign of anything that you or I would call a luxury. Outside, there is no family car, and there never has been. Mr Wu has never seen the ocean.

And yet, after twenty years of mining coal, neither the intensity of his work nor the depth of his sacrifice has gone unrewarded. Mr Wu and his wife, who toils and saves with no less dedication, have something that's very special indeed; something that's worth more to them than a car or a holiday. What they have is a daughter who's educated.

The young Miss Wu will graduate from university soon. She's growing up in an increasingly connected world, and to find her place in it she's studying logistics: the science of distribution. Twenty years of her parents' effort and thousands of hours of her own study have led to one moment: the moment when her schooling must transform itself into a job.

Her parents have invested in the best education they could afford for their only daughter because as they grow older, they will both depend on her to take care of them. The Wu family can't afford to think about it any other way. For a miner's daughter in rural China in the early 21st century, education is about getting a job.

Deep inside the earth on the other side of the world, education is also going on. Through a dark tunnel, a tube carriage lurches from side to side, its passengers swaying to the rhythm of its journey. I've been lucky enough to find a seat, and so has the man sitting opposite me. I'm watching him with interest, and I'm not the only one.

I doubt he's doing it on purpose; in fact, he seems to be completely absorbed in his own world, but eyes are turning towards him nonetheless. My fellow watchers, I think, are sharing the emotions that I'm feeling – a mixture of admiration and guilt – because the man is doing something that most of us feel we should be doing more of: reading.

It's not just any book he's reading, though. This book is huge. It's thick. It's one of those books where the spine is so wide that your first thought is not to wonder whether it might be interesting or entertaining, but to calculate how many hours of your life you would have to sacrifice to absorb it. I subtly tilt my head to read the title on the spine: JAMES JOYCE – ULYSSES.

At eight o'clock on a Tuesday night, this sharp-suited reader with bags under his eyes and a big leather satchel at his feet is very obviously on his way home from a long day at the office. I imagine him concentrating through endless meetings, frowning at huge spreadsheets or poring over dense legal documents. Yet despite his busy day, and in contrast to all the other things he could be doing, he's giving his time, energy and concentration to a behemoth of a book that's famously difficult to read. Why?

For the man on the train, this education isn't about making money. The man on the train doesn't have his back pressed up against the wall of economic necessity. This mind-sharpening is a different sort of thing to the education of a coal miner's daughter and it seems to be meandering its way towards a destination that's difficult to put one's finger on. But wherever it's heading, it's the man who's in charge of his own journey ... just as we are.

In the Western world in the early decades of the 21st century, most of us are like the guy on the train. We arrive at school, take our seat and wait for the ride to begin; but once our schooldays are over, we get to walk in any educational direction we choose and it's completely up to us how we do it. Education, like life, is a lottery, and – in stark contrast to those whose circumstances deny them both freedom *and* opportunity – the problem most of us face today isn't a lack of choice; it's having too much.

So what do you choose? Do you visit the library or the bookshop, and if so, which books do you pick out from the shelves? Do you download apps that promise to expand your vocabulary, polish your grammar or train your brain? Do you watch lectures online, listen to podcasts, or feed your mind with a diet of museums, galleries and exhibitions?

Most of us go in for a bit of everything. School is a base coat of traditional subjects that we embellish with a combination of what's interesting, well-advertised and fashionable; but we can get so caught up in whatever is currently holding our interest that it's easy to lose sight of what we really want in exchange for all that time, money and effort. What change are we hoping to see?

When we're not educating ourselves to get a qualification that will help us to get a job or start a career, it's my contention that we're not entirely sure what we want, and that we find it hard to say exactly how our efforts to educate ourselves add up to a sharper mind. We're impressed and entertained by knowledge about everything from the history of the world to the workings of the universe. We're fascinated by all sorts of *facts* – but what we really want is something more mysterious and elusive. There is something that lives between the boundaries of any particular area of knowledge: something that's deeper than the triviality of trivia. What we're after is the thing we call *intelligence*.

One way to understand what we want is to follow the advice of Sigmund Freud and examine our fantasies. The collective intellectual dream that we see reflected back at us in the form of the characters we admire from films, on television and in books is not that of an expert in one tiny factual area, nor a master of general knowledge. Our fictional fantasies are of the flexible minds of insightful detectives and mercurial political masterminds. What we're after is the kind of mental agility that makes observations no matter the situation, and has something to say no matter the topic of conversation. We don't often fantasise about winning the local pub quiz. We want to be the person in the room who sees how everything fits together.

But what exactly is this all-round ability that we sometimes call *general intelligence*? Why is it that some people always have something to say and solutions to offer in any business meeting, political debate, family argument or philosophical discussion? How do they do it? You can't memorise a pile of facts that works in every situation: that would be impossible. Intelligence is mysterious, but understanding it starts with a simple idea: intelligence isn't what you know; *it's how you think.*

Standing at this crossroads of the mind, with our backs turned away from the limitations of facts, you might think that we'd be set on the right path – headed in the general direction of intelligence – but there's a problem. We describe intelligent people in different ways: 'perceptive', 'subtle', 'critical', 'logical', 'rational', 'analytical' or 'creative' – but what exactly do these words mean and how are they supposed to help us? We try to point out the fact that some people can do things with their brains that others can't by saying things like: 'she's got an *analytical mind*' or 'what's important is *critical thinking*' – but how can being told to be 'more analytical' or 'more critical' actually change the way we think? A collection of vague synonyms that only *describes* the fact that some people notice what others don't does not *explain* it. If we can't say much about the thinking that defines intelligent people, how can we learn to do what they do?

This is the nature of intelligence and the problem with education itself. It's easy to make grand promises and bombard the credulous with clever-sounding words that appear to explain something so elusive, but it's incredibly difficult to say something fundamental and useful about what goes on in our heads. It's difficult to say something practical that illuminates the everyday thinking of our everyday lives. In the modern age, the vague promise of a true education of the general mind is everywhere, but the concrete ideas that transform the way we see the world are not.

In the modern West – where we have so much freedom and opportunity to develop the sizzling ball of electricity that we use to make the decisions that shape every moment of our lives – we make the mistake of focusing only on the present and the future. We churn out educational platitudes centred around the meaningless trope of a '21st-century education'; we idolise our technology and we believe, with all the blind self-importance of modern man, that progress is unrelenting. But some of the sharpest minds of the modern age – indeed, some of the minds that helped create it – would disagree. Einstein said that someone who reads only today's books and newspapers is like a short-sighted person who refuses to wear glasses. Steve Jobs, the most famous technologist of the modern age, once said that technology is not what really matters, and that it can even be disposed of in favour of a good teacher. When he was asked, in 2001, about 'the classroom of the future', he gave an answer that you might not expect. He said: 'I would trade all of my technology for an afternoon with Socrates.'

I found that Socrates – despite being the father of Western philosophy and one of history's most inspiring teachers – wasn't the answer, but it was close. Less than a century after Socrates' death in Athens in the year 399 BC, another philosopher left the city after failing to get the top job at its most famous school. He eventually made his way to the Gulf of Kalloni, on the island of Lesbos, where he indulged his passion for the study of nature, but another job offer was just around the corner. A school had been specially built for one fourteen-year-old boy, and the king who built it was looking for a teacher. King Philip of Macedon wanted his son's mind and character to be shaped by the best education that money could buy, and judged by how great a mark that mind and character made on history, Philip would have been pleased with the result. Both the teacher and student would go on to eclipse the fame of the king who had brought them together: the philosopher was Aristotle and the boy became known as Alexander the Great.

With a growing collection of ideas and years of teaching experience under his belt, Aristotle returned to Athens to found his own school, and to write a collection of books (widely thought to have been lecture notes for his students) that would become the foundation of a staggering range of disciplines for the next 2,000 years. Eventually, the influence of those books waned; but in one area at least, the outline of what he wrote is just as true now as it was then. Aristotle was the first human being to describe the fundamental principles of the way we think about, argue over, explain and prove what we believe to be true. When he finally set down his lifetime of ideas, the jewel in the crown of his thought was a true marvel: a blueprint of the human mind.

Aristotle didn't just understand our powers of deduction or the thing we now call 'logic': he discovered them. He wasn't just an independent thinker who could see through the tricks of manipulative people: he was the first to be able to explain how those tricks worked. Some people claim he even invented science, and Virginia Woolf said of him that when it came to literature, he wrote 'the first and last words on the subject'. A hundred books wouldn't do justice to the influence of this great man, but it's not his influence, nor even his brilliance that interests us here. This isn't a book about smart people: it's about the ones who can make *us* smarter.

One of the greatest thinkers who ever lived achieved what no one had ever done: he managed to turn his mind in on itself and explain what went on inside it. Aristotle discovered not just the fundamental principles of the way we think, but something more important even than that: a way of explaining how those principles work. In a crowded and competitive market of teachers who were the first to recognise the power of understanding our own thought, Aristotle outdid them all by discovering the fundamental blueprint of the human mind. *The Six Secrets of Intelligence* is about how that blueprint reveals the underlying patterns of every conversation, discussion, debate, argument or theory that we've ever had, and how we can use its intuitive ideas to become both harder to manipulate, and able to think in new and different ways.

The principles of intelligence that Aristotle discovered are secrets in the sense of their being key ideas that unlock an ability: the intellectual ability that every one of us is born with by virtue of the fact that we're human. And yet ... in the

21st century, we've replaced them with a simplistic and seductive view of intelligence, education and the human mind. In spite of the fact that at the cutting edge of modern science, we are beginning to see that Aristotle was right all along, the modern age has turned its back on the ideas that reveal what's eternal and unchanging about the way we think: the fundamental and unavoidable principles of reasoning and truth. Aristotle's challenge was to condense and explain these ideas in a way that even a fourteen-year-old like Alexander could understand and put to use in daily life, and to do it with as much clarity and simplicity as he could muster. My aim is exactly the same.

So where to begin? We'll start by taking a small but necessary step backwards. The education of a toga-wearing, slave-owning people who lived thousands of years ago only interests us in so far as it gives us some much-needed perspective. By understanding where everyone's education begins, and why schools and traditional education have been both unwilling and unable to show us what's essential for a true education of the human mind, we'll come to see what's missing in our quest to sharpen it. That's Part I.

In Part II we'll plunge straight into the six fundamental principles of reasoning and truth, and apply them to some of the most common and controversial issues of the present day.

Part III explores the innate and unavoidable nature of a human mind, explains why some people notice what others don't and reveals what modern psychology teaches us about how they learned to do it.

In Part IV, we'll see why what we're taught to believe about intelligence and education is wrong, why modern education doesn't teach us to think for ourselves, and why intellectual power is built on emotional strength.

In the fifth and final part, I'll bring everything together to explain what is really worth learning, and why the ideas that matter never get old. A true education of the mind depends on a handful of fundamental ideas that we rarely discover when we seek them out alone – but thanks to Aristotle, we don't have to ...

Part I

Not Thinking

A Brief History of Not Thinking

What to Think, Not How to Think

Alexander the Great was a lucky boy, because when history rolled its dice over ancient Greece, it threw three sixes in a row. Legend has it that one young Greek was about to start a career as a playwright when he heard Socrates speak for the first time, and that his response was to burn everything he'd ever written and ask to become Socrates' student. That young Greek's name was Plato. When Plato eventually opened the doors of his own school, one of the students to walk through them was a seventeen-year-old Aristotle. Socrates taught Plato, and Plato taught Aristotle. Alexander's father may have only paid for the services of a single teacher, but what he got was three for the price of one: the distilled wisdom of the three greatest minds of ancient Greece.

Today, our world is almost irreconcilably different to theirs, and so despite their greatness, it might seem that we'd struggle to learn very much from the ancient Greeks, but that view is a mistake. Our computers and our telephones may be windows that look out onto an almost infinite landscape of facts, figures, discussions, essays, articles and information that would have been nothing but a wild fantasy in Alexander's time, and in reading these very words as printed ink in a book or as pixels on a screen, you're doing something that no Greek ever did. But ask yourself what difference it would make if these words were scratched into wax, painted on parchment or chiselled into stone. Even after 2,000 years, despite all the superficial differences in our technology, the electric dance of the human brain that turns letters into the ideas that fill our heads hasn't changed at all. So much that is fundamental about the way we think never changes, and the same is true of the first chapter of our educational lives. The education of every human who has ever lived has begun in the same way: with stories.

It's a fact of life that children get told what to do. As children, we're encouraged and punished, rewarded and chastised, and if we pay attention to both the carrot and the stick, we can work out how we're supposed to behave. This constant calibration of what's acceptable helps us to learn what we should aim for, but it's piecemeal. It happens in tiny increments, like a puzzle that we slowly piece together over the years of our childhood. Humans have always needed something stronger than the day-to-day interactions that shape us: something more consistent and more powerful. Humans have always needed stories.

For thousands of years children have been regaled with a relatively small selection of stories: those which comprise the great works of religion, and each culture's selection of myths, fables, epics, legends and tales. Over and above the direction provided by our parents we have a pantheon of story-time models to learn from. We hear of the goodness and wisdom of the heroes and heroines, and they give us something to imitate.

Alexander's favourite story was the *Iliad*, which is about the Greek war against the Trojans. The *Iliad* might not be considered appropriate for young children today because it's largely comprised of graphic descriptions of warriors getting killed in a variety of gruesome ways – but it did have what all foundational stories of a culture need: authority. When schools first appeared in Greece and children started to learn how to write, they were made to copy out a famous line about the man they believed was its author. It is a famous and somewhat terrifying sentence, and it shows just how deeply his work saturated the minds of the Greek world: 'Homer was not a man, but a god.'

What was true for Alexander then is still true for us now. Our earliest educational experiences – the stories that are repeatedly drummed into our young minds and which provide us with the values that our society is built on – aren't designed to teach us *how* to think: they're designed to teach us *what* to think.

And for good reason. Whatever ideal our culture stamps upon us, it has to do so when we're young enough to be moulded. As children, we are the freshly poured wax that society presses into shape, and no matter how much any of us complains about 'brainwashing' in education, we should remember that it's the foundation of education and has been since the dawn of humanity. When your blood boils at the unthinking absorption of ideals, remember that you only call it 'indoctrination' if you happen to disagree with the doctrine. Otherwise, you call it 'education'. Every community passes on the culture that unites it, because without it, there would be no community of which to speak.

Stories, however, are not the only tool of what is sometimes called 'social education'. When schools first appeared in ancient Greece, they also spent the majority of their time and effort in moulding children to become part of their society, and they achieved this, in large part, through sport. The poet Aristophanes' portrait of 'education in the olden days' (in his play *The Clouds*) is almost entirely made up of exercise, the gymnasium and the *pedotribe* (the ancient Greek equivalent of a PE teacher). Even after the Greeks had made advances in philosophy, mathematics, literature and a whole host of other intellectual activities, if you'd asked the surrounding tribes what it was that made the Greeks Greek, they would have told you that as far as they could tell, it was running around a gymnasium without any clothes on.

Mount Olympus was chosen as the venue for the athletic competition that united the Greek world – the Olympic Games – because it was an ancient and well-known religious site. The various Greek city-states (whose citizens otherwise spent plenty of time trying to kill each other) agreed a truce once every four years so that they could come together and compete there, under the watchful eye of a 40-foot-tall statue of the god Zeus. Today, staging an athletics event in a holy place might be considered sacrilege, but for the Greeks it was just the opposite: it was a way of uniting themselves in a form of worship. Today we sometimes say that sport is like religion, but we only mean it metaphorically. For the Greeks, sport wasn't just like religion: it *was* religion.

In the same way that religion makes use of rituals that give everyone a chance to do something together, and so create a sense of community, such was the function of sport in ancient Greece. When you add to that the *values* of a sporting culture – the honesty, fair play and moral conduct that we call *sportsmanship* – you have not just a way of behaving, but countless occasions and opportunities to instil and reinforce this behavioural code as a community.

As well as preparing to take part in the athletics that shaped Greek culture by getting thumped around the gymnasium by the pedotribe (who carried a forked stick for the purpose),

Greek boys also learned how to play the lyre and sing patriotic songs, which further reminded them of the behaviour that was expected of them. Of course, to learn songs, it helps to be able to read, and they were given lessons in reading too. But, as the historian of education Henri Marrou puts it, the teacher of literacy was 'third in order of origin and, for a long time, third in order of value too'. What he means is that Greek parents were far more concerned that their children should grow up to be *well-behaved* and able to take part in the sport and music that brought everyone together. It is an irony of educational history that we now use the word 'pedagogue' as a sexier, upmarket version of the more everyday word 'teacher' – because the original pedagogue was a slave whose job it was to accompany the children to every lesson to make sure that they behaved themselves.

It's easy to think of school as being a place where you go to learn different skills, but in the same way that few of us who learn to play a sport or an instrument at school go on to become professionals, Greek schooling was first and foremost about learning to be a part of the group. Imagine yourself sitting around a sixties campfire, where being part of the group means knowing the words and the meaning of songs – the words that express what the group believes – not being the show-off drawing individual attention by playing a technically demanding solo while everyone else is trying to sing together.

Today, we fail to recognise all of the activities that we do at school that are designed to teach us what we need to know (or know how to do) in order to become part of our societies. The drive to socially educate – to teach the values that define our society and culture, and the activities that bring us together – is still alive and well. The emphasis on sport in American universities is one example, where educational institutions in relatively small towns own stadiums that are larger than those of most European professional sports teams, and which are packed to the rafters for every game. The playgrounds full of Chinese children swaying in a unison of tai chi are another. The hymns about what's right and what's good that have been learned and sung by generations of schoolchildren in Britain, or the sportsmanship and fair play that's part of learning to play cricket are all echoes of the music, poems and sport that have been part of what goes on in schools for thousands of years. One way that an English person can express their belief that something is unjust or not the accepted way of doing things is to say that it 'just isn't cricket'. There is no school in the world where children are not lectured to in some form or another about the values that we hold dear: selflessness, charity, respect and a hundred other desirable and essential ideas. Although we don't always notice it, a great deal of what we learn at school, and what we learned from our childhood stories, has nothing to do with learning to think.

The real problem, however, with the stories, sports, music and activities that define the culture into which we are born, is not that they teach us what to believe instead of how to think. The real problem with social education is that it couldn't teach us to think even if it wanted to.

There comes a point in our lives when most of us want to exchange the simple obedience of childhood for the freedom of thinking for ourselves; and, just as this happens to us as individuals, it happened to the whole of Greek culture. Around 500 BC, the people of Athens did something remarkable that changed the world forever: they tried out something they called 'democracy'. Whether democracy was the cause or the result of other changes that were going on in the Greek world is hard to say, but as the historian Thucydides tells us: 'the Athenians were the first who laid aside arms and adopted an easier and more luxurious way of life.' A period of wars, invasions and migrations was coming to an end, and with killing on the wane and talking on the rise, the emphasis shifted from brawn to brains.

The heroes of that pre-democratic time had been more martial in character. Alexander's hero was the warrior Achilles: the protagonist of Homer's *Iliad*. Achilles is the equivalent of our modern action hero: he's not terribly bright, but he is fantastically brave, incredibly bold and extremely talented at killing his enemies. Homer's second story, however, which was a kind of sequel to the *Iliad*, reflected the changing times with a new hero. The protagonist of the *Odyssey* is the smart and wily Odysseus, who is a cross between an eloquent and inspirational wartime politician, a resourceful secret agent and a special forces operative. Here we see a culture that was in the process of becoming more like ours: a culture that has noticed that the people who get ahead in life aren't just those who know how to bash other people over the head to get their own way. Achilles is about war, bravery, blood, and fighting your way out of trouble, but Odysseus has other options too: he's able to *talk* his way out of trouble. When it comes to having intelligent things to say – Achilles, the less modern hero, had to step aside to let Odysseus show us how it's done. But – and it's a big but – it's here that we run into the real problem with the stories of traditional social education: when you read Homer, *you never get to see how it's done.*

In Homer's epic poems, the cause of almost every instance of genius or stupidity is something mysterious: a god. When the leader of the Greek army makes a terrible decision that nearly loses them the war and results in the death of many of the story's much-loved characters, he blames it on Zeus. He says that his judgement was turned upside-down by the king of the gods; that he was sent into a state of confusion. He's not just making excuses to see if he can get away with stupidity either: one of the men who suffers because of his bad decision agrees with him, saying, 'Zeus the counsellor took away his understanding'. In the same way, when Odysseus' son finds himself having nothing clever to say to a great king, the goddess Athene says to him: 'where your own intelligence fails, a god will inspire you.'

Homer simply had no way of explaining why some people can do things with their mind that others can't, and the same is true of the great works of religion that are still read today. Just as it was in the Homeric epics, the only way you get to be smart or brave is through the power of a god.

Every culture dangles dreams of a sharp mind in front of us, but stories have a fatal educational flaw: they tell us which target to aim for, but say nothing about how to hit it. Today we still tell stories and watch films and TV programmes that paint portraits of both smart and brave heroes, but even our modern fictions make no mention of how the smooth-talking characters who see the solutions that we fail to notice actually do what they do.

The stories of old, written in a distant age of gods, magic and witchcraft, had no way of showing us around the mind because they didn't have any idea what it was, how we might understand it, or how we might use it. For the majority of human history, we've believed that intelligence is a gift from a god or fate because so much of our mental world was a mystery. Without being able to talk about what goes on inside our heads it's difficult, if not impossible, to harness the power of our incredible minds.

The education that introduces us to the culture into whose embrace we are born is not an education in thinking; but it does teach us something important: that in order to become smarter, we need a way of *talking about thinking*. The first step towards changing the way you think is to realise that we need more than a finished portrait of intelligence: we need the ideas that *explain* intelligence and show us how to sharpen it.

A New World of Intellectual Possibility

The social education of classical Greek culture gradually took shape over the centuries: turning stories, sport and music into social glue just as we do today. But then everything changed. At a time when Athenian parents only wanted their kids to be well behaved and able to take their place in society, along came a group of teachers from other parts of the Greek world whose main interest wasn't manners, modesty or trying to fit in. What these foreigners offered was a course in outwitting, outfoxing and outmanoeuvring; a sharp-toothed and silver-tongued approach to education that promised not community cohesion, but individual ability.

The steady advance of democracy that had begun in the 6th century BC meant that, increasingly, you could only be truly powerful if you were as good with words as you were with a sword. Today, not much has changed: those who get ahead in life know how to persuade other people that they're right. Education adapts itself to changes in our cultural environment so that we can thrive in the inevitable competition to survive it, and when this enigmatic group of foreign teachers turned up in

Athens claiming to be able to transform anyone into an invincible machine of argument and persuasion, they found that they could charge a fortune and still attract plenty of interest. They were known as *the Sophists*, and before long they became rich celebrity figures basking in the spotlight of fame and adored by a circle of devoted pupils. But the strength of speech and the power of persuasion had long been highly valued; Homer's epic stories are full of eloquent characters and important speeches. So what exactly had the Sophists discovered that gave them the edge in the arms race of thinking?

⌒

It all starts with sounding good. When it comes to convincing other human beings to agree with you, content isn't everything. It's possible to make exactly the same point in two different ways, and somehow, one will sound convincing while another doesn't persuade at all. The Sophists weren't the first to discover that this is true, but they were the first to be able to teach others how it works.

In the year 427 BC, despite the fact that Athens had already witnessed some of the greatest orators in history, a Sicilian by the name of Gorgias arrived in town and quickly earned himself an astonishing reputation. Even Plato, who was highly suspicious of all things Sophistic, said that Gorgias was 'popularly regarded as the best speaker ever to have addressed the Assembly'. What was Gorgias' secret? It was rhetoric: the art of persuasion.

What Gorgias realised was that there are ways of saying things that make them not only more memorable, but more convincing too. Have you ever noticed how difficult it is to remember a couple of lines of text? I'd bet that you're unable

to quote much prose – say, a speech, an essay, a newspaper article or an extract from a novel – but that without much trouble,
you could remember enough song lyrics to fill a modestly sized
book. There's something about the rhythm and rhyme of poetry
that makes the words stick in our heads. What Gorgias realised
was that there's a relationship between what sounds good, what
sticks in our memory and what has the power to persuade.

But what does it mean to 'sound good'? Essentially, the
answer has to do with *patterns*. We love a bouncing rhythm of
consonants, vowels or syllables. We especially love things in
threes. There are phrases that combine patterns of all of those
things and they're so catchy that some of them are still stuck in
our minds hundreds of years after they were written. There's
Julius Caesar's '*I came, I saw, I conquered*', which sounds even better in the original Latin: '*veni, vidi, vici*'. In Shakespeare's play
about Caesar, Mark Anthony opens his speech with the immortal line: '*Friends, Romans, Countrymen*' ... and every *Tom, Dick and
Harry* knows that one should tell *the truth, the whole truth and
nothing but the truth*, as well as being aware of the advice we
should bear in mind when buying a house: *location, location, location*. But back to *education, education, education* ...

There is something about our minds that's drawn to patterns, and this is what causes particular arrangements of sounds
and ideas to be both more memorable and more persuasive.
Gorgias was a master of turning reasonable ideas into *patterned*
reasonable ideas that stuck in your mind because of the way
they sounded. He famously advertised his skills by writing
model speeches, and the best known of these is one in which
he tries to convince us that the person who was to blame for
the war that we hear about in the *Iliad* isn't a Greek queen, but
a Trojan prince:

And how would it not be reasonable for a woman
raped and robbed of her country
and deprived of her friends
to be pitied rather than pilloried?

He did the dread deeds; she suffered them.
It is just, therefore,
to pity her, but to hate him.

This short extract (here translated skilfully by the classicists Dillon and Gergel) shows off an amazing density of patterns. There are patterns of vowels, consonants, syllables and even ideas. The rhythm of *raped/robbed*, *her country/her friends*, *pitied/pilloried* and *he did/she suffered* makes an impact that we feel on a level that we're not entirely aware of and don't control. When Gorgias writes that speeches work like 'drugs over the nature of bodies', he's not only describing the power to influence the way we feel; he's also pitching himself as a doctor of persuasion. He's saying that there is a system to be understood, and in the same way that our bodies are similar enough for a doctor to learn the system and be able to help us, the same is true of our minds.

Gorgias is the great-grandfather of political soundbites, advertising slogans and slippery rhetoric. He was one of the first to draw up and teach a system of the most effective ways to sex up a speech and make it work like a Jedi mind trick – except the Jedi mind trick is a fantasy, and rhetoric is real. As if you had waved a magic wand in front of their face, people can be made to agree with things that they might otherwise have dismissed as ridiculous, and this was how Gorgias revealed something about thinking that had never really been explored. What Gorgias realised was that the mind is not a mystery; it could be examined and understood.

⌒

The power of persuasion can be subtle, but there is another ability that always leaves us staggered: memory. In the modern age, our technology allows us to carry around huge quantities of information and frees us from having to remember things like shopping lists or wedding speeches. We're especially impressed by people who can speak for an hour without a note in sight, or remember our names despite having met us only once at a party three years previously. We are enchanted by people who can easily pluck dates, facts and figures from the depths of the mind that we just can't seem to reach. But, like persuasion, memory is not as magical as we think.

In one of the books that Plato wrote about him, the Sophist Hippias is depicted as boasting that he can 'reel off fifty names after hearing them only once,' to which Socrates replies: 'You're right: I wasn't taking your mnemonic technique into account.' What Socrates is alluding to is that what Hippias is able to do is something that anyone can learn. It's simply a matter of technique; and just like Gorgias' rhetoric, it's a technique that relies on patterns.

The technique that transforms our memories was attributed by the Greeks to a man called Simonides, who, according to legend, had momentarily left a party when an earthquake struck, squashing everyone inside into an unrecognisable pulp. Being the only survivor, it fell to Simonides to try and spare everyone the ignominy of a group burial. If only he could remember exactly who was at the party *and* where they were sitting when the roof collapsed ...

Of course, I wouldn't be telling you the story if Simonides hadn't been able to do exactly that, but remember that this book isn't about smart people; it's about the ones who can make *us* smarter. Simonides' stroke of genius wasn't his feat of memory itself: it was realising that the feat had been made possible by a pattern. Had the evening been a cocktail party or a disco, Simonides would have had a problem because the guests would have been milling around in disorganised chaos. This party, however, was a banquet, and at a banquet, everyone sits in their place. What Simonides realised was that having to remember *where* everyone was sitting didn't make it harder to name everyone who was at the party; it made it easier.

Simonides used this insight to develop the idea of the 'memory palace': an imaginary space that we know inside out and which we can use to help us 'place' things in a pattern that helps us to remember them. The colours of the rainbow seem to us to be seven unconnected words – red, orange, yellow, green, blue, indigo and violet – until we organise them into something simpler: a sentence or phrase that sticks in our mind as a single and complete unit rather than seven separate ones. In the United States this is the fictional character Roy G. Biv, and in England, the sentence/story 'Richard Of York Gave Battle In Vain'. We make up songs to remember things because the musical and rhyming pattern makes them stick in our heads, like the childhood songs about the order of the letters in the alphabet or the position of the bones in the body. Today, the concept of mnemonics has come a long way, and we've discovered all sorts of techniques that take advantage of how our minds work. Beyond acronyms and the memory palace, there are even more advanced techniques that make it possible to memorise an entire pack of playing cards, a long list of US presidents or World Cup winners, or a truly astonishing number of the infinite digits of pi.

Memory, like persuasion, is something that works the same for all of us because we all have human brains that work in fundamentally the same way. Both abilities can be improved by understanding a system of patterns, but what memory shows us is something that persuasion struggles to make clear. The differences between our relative powers of persuasion are not always obvious because persuasion is a subtle game. On the other hand, when we meet people who are able to remember an improbable quantity of names, phone numbers or anything else, we can't help but think that they must have been born with a special ability. When we see someone perform a seemingly miraculous feat of memory, most of us are convinced that it's the result of a talent given to them by God, by fate, or by having been dealt a good hand in the genetic lottery of life. When the Greeks noticed that knowing something about patterns makes you appear to have inexplicable and almost magical powers, they became the first to realise that they could shape their own intelligence rather than just accepting it.

In seeing the potential of techniques and patterns, Gorgias and Hippias were able to offer something new and exciting to the sons of the rich Athenian aristocrats who could afford their extravagant fees, but the most important pattern of all was still out of reach. The patterns of mnemonics help us to memorise, and the patterns of rhetorical language help us to sound more stylish and more convincing, but there is another set of patterns that's always at work no matter what we talk or think about. Underlying every conversation, every decision, every theory and every argument is a pattern that no one invented or created, but which no one can ignore: logic.

Sometimes we call it *reasoning* or *inference* or *working out*, but whichever label we start from, we can't deny that the pattern exists. When reasoning fails – when we recognise a pattern of logic that doesn't add up – we use a powerful word to describe it: contradiction. Contradiction doesn't care what any of us believe. When someone points out that what you've just said doesn't make sense – that you've contradicted yourself – what can you say to them? That you don't care? That it doesn't matter?

The patterns of memory and stylish speeches are undoubtedly useful, but they don't underpin the way we think and argue. Gorgias and Hippias promised amazing specific skills, but it was another Sophist called Protagoras who managed to outdo them both (in his attempt to steal their business) by claiming that he could provide the holy grail of general intelligence: critical thinking.

Protagoras' promise was that he could turn his students into experts in 'decision-making' in both their private and public lives. He believed that a crucial part of a good education is 'being able to see when the claims made by poets and songwriters make sense and when they don't'. Today, we could replace 'poets and songwriters' with 'politicians and journalists', among others. Protagoras promised that he could teach anyone to use their powers of reasoning to transform the way they think and argue, no matter who they were talking to or what they were talking about.

When Protagoras offered an all-round transformation of the general mind (rather than just a more stylish way of speaking and a better memory), he managed to attract a lot of pupils and make a lot of money, but he couldn't make good on his promise. His understanding of reasoning was competent enough to make *him* an excellent debater and a subtle mind. But by simply calling this ability by different names – 'making sense' and 'decision-making' – he fell into the trap of being clever, but not clever enough to explain to other people how he was doing it.

⌒

Education began as social education and not much else. The traditional social education that has shaped human societies for tens of thousands of years has always aimed to create community through unity. It is inevitable and essential, but its task is to teach us what to believe, not how to think.

Early man stared up at the heavens and prayed for wisdom or goodness. He was barely aware that he had a mind at all. If some of us were geniuses or idiots, he thought it was because God had blessed some people and cursed others. He had no words to describe what went on inside his own head, so he resigned himself to prayer, or simply hoping that fate or luck would send some brainpower his way. In the same way, traditional social education leaves us powerless because it lacks the one thing that's essential to educate the mind: an understanding of how it works.

The Sophists made a true education of the mind possible by discovering and describing – for the first time in history – something fundamental and universal about its nature. The first step in this journey was to realise that all of our minds are structured in the same basic way. In our responses to the patterns of sounds and ideas, in the effect of techniques based on patterns to transform our memory, and in our use of the patterns of reasoning, there are deep and enduring similarities. What the Sophists realised was that despite the differences between us, those basic similarities are there to be discovered if we look hard enough. Thinking isn't random; it has rules.

This early insight into the nature of the human mind created the tantalising possibility of self-improvement, and the proof was in the results. By showing that mnemonic patterns could give anyone a memory so astonishing that it seems like magic to those who don't know how it works, the Sophists opened up a new world of intellectual possibility. They were the first teachers to understand that amazing powers of persuasion, memory, thought and argument could be produced not just by talent, but by technique too. They wrestled education from the lap of the gods when they encouraged us, for the first time, to see that we didn't have to wait for intelligence to be given to us. Intelligence is something we can give to ourselves.

When the Sophists discovered the patterns that exist in our minds and the fact that we can be taught to recognise them, they changed education forever. They had worked out the patterns of style and memory, and we still teach these today. The patterns of style, for example, are taught in every school: alliteration, assonance, repetition, things in threes. We still like to dress up our thinking in nicer-sounding phrases. Mnemonics is still around, though less common than ever, because today there are so many ways to make yourself a note of things easily forgotten. What's mostly absent, though, is what Protagoras promised but couldn't deliver: being able to think for yourself, to make better decisions and to survive in any conversation, or any argument, on any topic whatsoever.

So, what are the patterns at work in every conversation on any topic? This general intelligence – this holy grail that we call *critical thinking* – only became a possibility once Aristotle had discovered a particular set of patterns. Those patterns do far more than make us sound persuasive or improve our memories: they reveal the fundamental and unavoidable principles that underpin the way we think.

Part II

Thinking

Deduction: How to See Through Arguments

The Power of Deduction

Alexander the Great was not someone you would have wanted to meet on the battlefield. He wasn't the type to organise things from a safe distance, and the history books record him frequently charging into the enemy's frontline as if he were just another ordinary soldier. In the midst of battle, if you're worried that you might shortly be separated from your own head, the sight of your commander being fearless probably helps; but in order for this leadership strategy to have worked as often as it seems to have done, Alexander must have been either exceptionally lucky or exceptionally skilled at decapitating, disembowelling and generally despatching his enemies to the next world.

While his army may have been roused by their leader's ability to defend himself in the face of certain death, though, his former teacher would have been less impressed. In Aristotle's book on how to win arguments, *Rhetoric*, he points out that no one should be ashamed if they can't defend themselves in a physical fight. After all, animals fight, but only humans defend themselves with speech. The way we think and argue is what separates humans from the animals, and in life, knowing how arguments work is often what separates the humans who get what they want from those who don't.

So why not just settle for the Sophists' lessons in practical debating skills: the art of style and the careful deployment of the soundbite? Well, says Aristotle, you could, but what you'd learn would be nothing more than a bunch of cheap tricks. Gorgias' powerful and arresting phrases (artfully packaged into speeches that could be memorised and hence delivered with plenty of emotionally direct eye contact thanks to Hippias' technique) did produce results; but even the Greeks of the time could see the limitations of the Sophists' approach to persuasion. Aristotle mentions courts in Greece that forbade people from making irrelevant emotional appeals – what we today loosely call 'empty rhetoric' – and they recognised that some of what passed for convincing argument was often nothing more than a thick veneer of stylish words, arranged and delivered in a stylish manner.

At school, we are still taught how to make our writing and our speech more polished, emotionally affecting, persuasive and easy to follow. We're shown how to recognise the *pleasing pulses* of poetic language and the *rich rewards* of recreating its alliterative patterns. We learn to convince by organising our material into an introduction, followed by our main points and then our conclusion, 'or any of the other divisions of a speech' (as Aristotle writes in *Rhetoric*), or by stylistically polishing our prose in order to arouse 'pity, anger and similar emotions'. Each of these techniques makes a contribution to the art of persuasion, but they fall short of being central to it for one reason: none of them have anything intrinsically to do with the fundamental ways that arguments work. The tricks of style are useful, but those who teach them only dabble in 'non-essentials' and have nothing to say about 'the substance of rhetorical persuasion'. To find things to say that are of real persuasive force, you have to know how to construct and deconstruct an argument, rather than merely polish one.

But even coming this far still leaves us with a problem. The Sophist who got closest to uncovering the fundamental principles of reasoning and truth that underpin every argument was Protagoras, when he started to teach his pupils how to analyse the claims of other people by encouraging them to think about whether they 'made sense'. Protagoras spent hours trying to demonstrate his principle of 'making sense' by arguing in front of his students, just as Gorgias had furnished his students with model essays and speeches. But an example – whether living or written – only has a limited power when it comes to teaching us to do the same. The problem with Protagoras' method was that it lacked the one thing that would have made it effective: *an exact vocabulary of underlying principles*, rather than just a stream of examples. Aristotle's metaphor is this: if you provide nothing more than examples, it is like dropping a pile of different types of shoes at someone's feet and claiming that you've taught them the art of shoemaking.

Diving straight into a stream of real-life examples is comfortingly concrete, but, as will become apparent, the theoretical and the abstract teach us far more than we think. Over the course of Part II, I've deliberately chosen, just as Aristotle did, slightly simplified versions of real-life scenarios. These imaginary situations, thought experiments and conceptual explanations are life*like*, but they are rarely taken from life itself – and there's a good reason for that. Like the practice ring, the simulator and the training pitch, they allow us to internalise the basics away from the complications of real-life encounters. Of course, we can't do away with examples altogether: there would be no material from which we could teach the principles, and the principles themselves are a distilled, idealised and abstracted version of something that's in every example. Without the concrete examples, there would be no abstract idea: theory and practice are inherently linked. However, as Aristotle knew, what transforms the way we think is the power of consciously understanding and being able to explain overarching ideas.

We all want to be able to see through people's words and to make out the structure of the argument that's behind them, but a systematic way of thinking about that structure was impossible until Aristotle discovered a collection of ideas that today we loosely call 'logic', or 'reasoning'. It was a new idea then, but it's still around today, in almost every thought, conversation and argument, even though we don't always know exactly how it works or how to talk about it. The first step towards thinking about how arguments work and why we say that some things are true and others are false is to be able to identify the *three principles of reasoning*, and the first of those principles is called **deduction**.

⌒

All of us get frustrated with 'unreasonable' people. To purposely ignore someone's train of argument and refuse to engage in some sort of reason-based discussion is considered to be a show of disrespect, and being completely illogical tends to be a bad way to try to convince an audience of your fellow humans that something is true. We all accept that you can't say just *anything* in support of an argument, but why not? Because being logical isn't just polite: it's natural. Someone who refuses to reason, says Aristotle, is 'no better than a mere plant'.

So what does it mean to be logical? What do we really mean when we talk about reason? Here are two facts: London is the capital of England, and my mother's name is Susan. These two facts don't produce any new knowledge if you put them together, but what about these next two? If I tell you that the capital of England is its largest city, and that England's largest city is London, you'll be able to *work out* that London is the capital. When people look confused at something you've concluded, they might say to you 'How do you figure?', 'How so?' or 'Does that really follow?' We describe working-out with words like 'entail', 'imply', and 'infer', among others, and we use them interchangeably to refer to completely different types of reasoning. All of our attempts to pin down exactly what's going on when we reason reveal the vagueness of how we're taught to describe (and therefore understand) the engine of thought. This unfortunate state of mental affairs was common to every human that had ever existed, until Aristotle noticed the first of the three types of reasoning, and called it *deduction*.

Aristotle's definition of a deduction is: 'certain things being stated, something other than what is stated follows, of necessity, from their being so.' Have a look at this classic example:

> All humans are mortal
> Socrates is human
> Therefore ... Socrates is mortal

Simply put, what Aristotle pointed out is that deduction is when two things add up to something entirely new. In this example, the 'certain things being stated' are that *all humans are mortal* and that *Socrates is human*. Given that these two things are true, we can say that the 'something other' than those stated things that must 'of necessity' also be true is that *Socrates is mortal*.

So far, so very obvious. But how does the thinking behind it actually work? It's to do with groups, and it is instantly understandable when you see deduction in the form of a diagram:

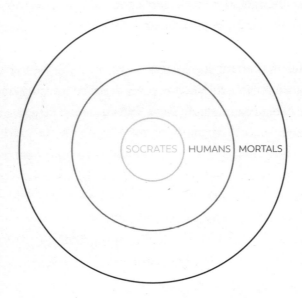

SOCRATES HUMANS MORTALS

Named after the 19th-century logician and philosopher John Venn, the Venn diagram is a clever thing: it is a visual representation of deduction. You can *see* why it works. To be part of a group is to have the properties that make something part of that group. To be a human means having all the properties of a human: say, having a head, warm blood and the ability to reason. The circle that represents humans is *entirely contained* within the circle that represents mortals. It's because *every* human is mortal that we're able to say with 100 per cent certainty that Socrates must be mortal if he's human. Deduction seems so simple. Aristotle would say that it's only so obvious because it's natural; it's just the way we think. That is, until it starts to go wrong.

The everyday meaning of the word 'argument' is what happens when statements and conclusions make us emotional and cause us to shout at each other. In its philosophical sense, though, the ingredients of *an argument* are only *a set of statements* and *a conclusion*. Sometimes, we come across what appears to be a deductive argument because it has all the right ingredients – two statements and a conclusion – but the conclusion contradicts the statements rather than following from them. Some examples of arguments that don't deduce are easy to spot:

> All dogs have four legs
> Fido is a dog
> Therefore Fido has five legs

... and others are slightly more difficult to explain:

> All dogs have four legs
> My table has four legs
> Therefore my table is a dog.

The first has the shape of an argument, but it doesn't deduce anything at all, and the second hopes that we won't notice that being a dog definitely means having four legs, but that having four legs does not definitely mean that you must be a dog. There are many ways to manipulate deductions, but some are more difficult to spot than others.

Aristotle wouldn't have given Alexander the full course in Logic for Philosophers (which he produced when he returned to Athens to set up his own school). That wasn't his aim. What the fourteen-year-old Alexander needed was what we need: to be able to see how an understanding of deduction can teach us to instantly detect the way that people manipulate us. Enter deduction's less reliable cousin: the *dubious deduction*.

The Dubious Deduction: A Likely Story

The bits of knowledge that add up to our conclusions are where the game of argument is won and lost, and they're called *premises*. Premises are to a deduction what foundations are to a house: the strength, solidity and reliability of the entire structure depends on them. Learning to inspect a deductive argument is like being a structural engineer: it's knowing when and why the foundations of an argument are too fragile to support the weight of their conclusion.

Aristotle's definition of a premise, you may have noticed, doesn't mention what's true. He says that premises are 'certain things being *stated*'. His point is that they don't have to be true. We can start with a premise like 'All humans have wings' and because we know that 'Socrates is human', we end up with the conclusion that 'Socrates has wings'. Aristotle's first lesson of deduction is that being logical doesn't make you right.

The secret of a *cast-iron deduction*, which is 100 per cent certain, is that its premises are strong. By strong, I mean that they have to be *universal*: they have to tell us something that's true about an entire group of things. This could be that '*all* men are mortal' or that '*every* child deserves love' or that '*no* fish can ride bicycles'. If we know either what applies to *every* member of a group, or to *none* of the members, we can use that knowledge to work out, without question, what will be true of any individual member of the group. If *no* fish can ride bicycles, and a trout is a fish, then a trout cannot ride a bicycle. If *every* child deserves love, and Alexander is a child, then Alexander deserves love. But what can you deduce from these two premises:

Some humans ride horses
Socrates is a human

Therefore ...? Therefore nothing! As soon as a deduction is forced to work with premises that are not universal – premises that don't tell us that something is true either of *every member* of a group or *none* of a group – it grinds to a halt. When we try to build a deduction on premises that only tell us what is true of *some* of a group or *some* of the time, we're left with a problem: there is no way of saying anything *for certain* about any of the group's members. Universal premises produce *cast-iron deductions*. Premises that aren't universal – even premises that are *usually* or even *mostly* true – can only produce *dubious deductions*.

A deduction built on universal premises has everything that it needs in order to add up to a perfect, undeniable and *certain* whole, while the dubious deduction is only ever, at best, *likely*. But with a little sleight of hand, we can try to pass off the *likelihood* of the dubious deduction as the *certainty* of the cast-iron deduction. This is a strategy that we all use to get ourselves out of trouble, and we do it by swapping a universal premise with one that's only probable, in the hope that no one will notice.

Imagine that one day you hear a knock at the door, and shortly after opening it you find yourself lifted off the ground by two policemen and carried off to court. In the dock, you find that you're accused of having beaten someone up, and you have no alibi. What do you do? In this situation, you should follow the advice of the Sophists, and deploy a barrage of dubious deductions ...

If you're noticeably punier than the person you're accused of beating up, what you do is look incredibly surprised, furrow your brow and ask with an air of confusion, 'How is it possible that someone so scrawny could have overpowered someone so strong? ... Is that really a believable story?'

Alternatively, imagine yourself in a slightly tougher position. Now the opposite is true: this time you're the muscle-bound colossus, and a weakling is cowering in the witness box. What do you have to say for yourself? Your answer should be a variation on our theme of the probable: something along the lines of: 'Really, ladies and gentlemen of the jury, why would I have committed this stupid act knowing that I'd be the obvious suspect?' If this doesn't work, you could try something else from the playbook of *probable arguments*: 'Isn't it ridiculous to suggest that I'd risk imprisonment just to beat up Mr Weakling ... that I'd risk giving up my freedom and all the things I've worked so hard for?' Or perhaps 'Have I ever been seen to beat up anyone else before? So is it really reasonable to suggest that I've suddenly become some sort of a monster?' Top it off with a hard-done-by expression tinged with sadness at the attempts to besmirch your character, and you might just have sown enough doubt into the mind of an audience or jury to get yourself off the hook.

No matter which side of the argument you find yourself on, there's always a probable argument to make, and that's why this particular technique is so popular with lawyers and politicians. Where a situation is uncertain, it always helps to pile some doubt on top of it, and to focus our attention on what was likely. After all, what's likely is more reasonable than what's unlikely, isn't it?

This, Aristotle discovered, is one of the ways that people manipulate those who don't have a clear picture in their mind of what it means to be logical. Deduction, as we have seen, is at its most reliable when it uses universal rules as its premises. If it were true that '*no* weak person can beat up a stronger person', then we'd know that the weak defendant wasn't guilty. If it were true that people with the ability to commit crimes *always* avoid committing them because they'd be the obvious suspects, then the strong man's defence would be a perfectly solid deduction and the jury would be forced to acquit.

The dubious deduction, built with non-universal premises that can only ever tell us what *probably* or *mostly* happens, sees situations of uncertainty – situations in which we don't know for sure what happened – as opportunities. The opportunity is that if everyone has accepted that proving the truth beyond doubt will be almost impossible, it opens the door for a barrage of doubt because all we have to go on is what's probable. What dubious deductions try to do is to use premises that work more often than not, and pass them off as universal ones.

Aristotle is at pains to point out that probable premises, which produce dubious deductions, aren't necessarily wrong: something may indeed have been likely, but that doesn't tell you anything at all about what *actually* happened. If you've been greedy, and eaten the muffin that your partner was saving for their breakfast the following morning, you might try the probable argument: 'Why would I have eaten the muffin when I'd already had four pieces of cake for dessert?' and then look accusingly at the family dog. Wealthy men can claim that they had no motivation to steal money, and powerful men that they would never have risked their positions for a night of socially unacceptable behaviour.

The Weak Man vs. The Strong Man, and The Muffin Argument are two examples of dubious deductions. The first of these reminds us that it's always possible to make some sort of argument that is based on probability. Probable arguments sound convincing because what's likely, usual and probable seems a better choice than what's unlikely, abnormal or improbable. But life is full of unlikely events! The second of these dubious deductions is an everyday example that's intuitive: it helps us to notice that it's not just other people who offer probable arguments to cover their tracks. We don't always make sensible decisions, and whenever we do something stupid we desperately hope that some version of The Muffin Argument will be enough to save us. When we say 'why would anyone do such a stupid and unlikely thing?', we can only hope that other people haven't been shown how to see through what is often nothing more than a desperate plea. If they have, they might curtly reply: 'Because life is full of bad and unusual decisions, and just because something was unlikely doesn't mean it didn't happen.'

What Aristotle teaches us is not to say that someone's argument moves in an illogical way, but to point out the fact that it doesn't work because it started from a place that had no certainty to begin with. *Being logical doesn't make you right.* The key to unravelling dubious deductions is to be able to find the real heart of the argument. When people claim that their argument, or the reasoning that produced it, is *logical*, Aristotle teaches you not to fight them on the grounds of logic. After all, it's not the reasoning itself that makes a dubious deduction seem true: it's the premises on which that reasoning was built.

The Hidden Heart of Argument

The first step in the making of a dubious deduction is to start with premises that are not universal – premises that only work some of the time. Without the important second step that artfully conceals those premises, though, this strategy would rarely work. It's time to get the scalpel out and learn how to find the hidden heart of an argument.

Just like a house built on fragile foundations, a deduction is only as good as the premises that it's built on. So ask yourself this question: if you were trying to sell a house that you knew to be built on foundations that were not absolutely solid – foundations that could only support the house some of the time – what would you do to improve your chances of a sale? In this scenario, you could try to obscure, to conceal and to cover up those fragile foundations – just as a sophist does when they try to hide the premise that dubious deductions rely on. But those who understand the ingredients out of which deductions are built are more likely to notice that premise. Alexander would have been told by Aristotle again and again: find the heart of the argument ... find the *hidden premise*.

For example, when someone says to us: 'Don't trust her; she's a politician', they are only giving us the conclusion of their argument. In a way, this is not really an argument at all; it's just a statement of what someone thinks is true. What's missing is the bit of information that makes it true: the premise, which in this case is hidden. But what is the hidden premise that gives life to this particular argument? What's the universal but concealed 'fact' that's hiding in the background of this deduction? Here, it is: *all politicians are untrustworthy*.

What Aristotle realised is that dubious deductions are seductive not just because their probable premises imply that what's *likely* is the same as what's *true*, but because quite a lot of the time, we don't even notice that they're there. The premises of a deduction are its heart, but the heart is almost always hidden deep in the body of the argument.

While some arguments rely on premises that try to pass off what's likely as what is certain, others try to use premises that claim something is universally true when it isn't. In this case, the casual 'you can't trust her; she's a politician' is built on the claim that *every* politician is *exactly* the same. This simply isn't true, but it is a convenient generalisation that makes all sorts of other statements – once they've been transfused with the blood of a hidden premise – appear to be worth considering. Sometimes, it doesn't matter how your premises misrepresent the truth; what's important is that you minimise the risk of them being recognised and pointed out by making sure not to say them out loud.

When we're clever enough to hide our premises, we get to offer people conclusions without having to show them our working-out. This gives us the possibility of not having to explain whether we really believe that *all* politicians are untrustworthy, for example, or whether we accept that, really, at worst, *many* politicians are untrustworthy. If what we mean is the latter, then that fact doesn't tell us anything about whether the politician we're being advised not to trust is or isn't an untrustworthy one. A *cast-iron deduction* is complete because its premises are universal and because they are all openly and honestly stated. A *dubious deduction* can be incomplete because its premises are only probable, but also because its premises aren't really present to be examined. Whenever an essential part of a deduction is missing – either a whole premise, or just the universal *all* or *none* part of it that gives us certainty – it lacks what it needs to be complete and becomes a dubious deduction.

Being taught to see that premises are the foundation of arguments gives you the opportunity to 'see through' other people's conclusions, and to understand the structure of their reasoning. But it's not just the premises themselves that are frequently concealed; equally well disguised are those key words that make a premise what it is. These are words like 'all', 'every', 'none', 'no', 'some', 'most' and others, and they're called *quantifiers*, because all of them measure the extent to which something is true. To successfully expose a premise like 'politicians are untrustworthy', you have to be alert to the fact that what powers it is the one word that's missing. What is really being asserted is that '*all* politicians are untrustworthy', and the distinction between *all* and *some* that's been intentionally buried is the distinction that would otherwise force exaggerated rhetoric to become reasonable discussion.

The process of revealing other people's premises becomes a technique of argument once we get into the habit of looking 'through' a conclusion and trying to make out the premises that it has been built on. For example, when the old and the young get into the age-old argument about the relative quality of two bands – one from the past pitted against one from the present – the old will typically claim that the latest bands are second-rate by comparison. At this point, the young will defend themselves with something like one of these three subtly different versions of a classic argument:

> But they're more popular ...

> Then how come they're so popular?

> How can they be so popular if they're so bad?

The exact words that we use when we reason can be unimportant. Here, the first is a statement and the second and third are questions – but all three rely on the same hidden premise. The argument is about quality, but all three of these defences are about popularity. Underneath the surface is the hidden premise that is connecting the two: *quality is what makes bands popular*. Can you see how the third version is the one that hides the connection between quality and popularity the least, because it explicitly mentions the words 'bad' and 'popular'? The least subtle version of this defence would be to openly state the hidden premise without turning it into a question: something like 'quality causes popularity'. Stated so openly, the rest of the argument becomes easier to make out: we can add this rule to 'the modern band is popular' and end up with the conclusion 'the modern band is popular because of their quality'. Hearing an argument phrased as a simple statement rather than a question, and with all of its ingredients openly mentioned (in this example, popularity and quality) makes it easier for us to see its structure and to test it.

Or, at least, most of the ingredients are openly mentioned. There is still one that remains concealed. If the hidden premise on which the argument turns is 'quality causes popularity', can you spot the missing element? Can you spot the missing quantifier? It is something like *always*. We should concede that there is a relationship between quality and popularity, but the relationship doesn't merit the hidden quantifier that powers this deduction. *Sometimes*, perhaps even *most of the time*, quality causes popularity; not *always*. What makes it possible to pass off what is sometimes true as what is always true, or to pass off what is uncertain as what is certain is the artful concealment of premises and their ingredients.

Finally, it's important not to be a pedant and get carried away with revealing every premise that hasn't been spoken out loud. Aristotle points out that concealing a premise isn't itself dishonest – just like the probable premises that can be honestly used to help our decision-making as long as we remember that they don't prove anything beyond doubt. Arguments can be made up of chains of premises, and quite often it makes sense to leave some of them out if they're obvious. For example, to prove that an athlete won gold medals in his career, Aristotle says that 'it is enough to say "For he has been victor in the Olympic games"', because the hidden premise – *the prize for Olympic victory is a gold medal* – is 'a fact which everybody knows'. There's nothing wrong with leaving out some of our premises – because otherwise our conversations would be unnecessarily long. But it's one thing to omit a premise, and another to conceal it.

Judo, Not Karate

The Sophists' education aimed to give its students the power to persuade through the force of their own arguments, but Aristotle's education isn't just powerful: it's agile too. We think of debates too often as if they were karate: where the aim is to fight fire with fire. Karate, like the most common approach to argument, involves a little sidestepping and occasional evasion, but it's mostly about attempting to land a more forceful and devastating blow than your opponent. Once you're used to seeing through people's arguments and noticing the premises that they depend on, though, you can start to counter their arguments in a different way. What the spotter of premises can do is to fight not just with karate, but in another style too; one that involves far less effort yet has a far more devastating result: judo.

Judo, in contrast to karate, places the emphasis on using the force of your opponent's attack against them. Instead of attacking them as they run at you, you simply step to the side, leave your leg sticking out and watch them tumble into a confused heap on the other side of the mat. Consider again The Muffin Argument – only this time imagine it with the roles reversed. When your partner asks you, with crumbs scattered at their feet: 'How could I have eaten the cake after already having eaten four portions of dessert?', you reject the urge to fight by offering your own claim or argument: perhaps by shouting at them that they're greedy. That would be karate. Instead, find the premise and force them to water it down. Something like 'Well, that's what you'd normally expect, but let's be honest, eating a fifth portion of cake is hardly impossible is it?' If the crumb-covered villain continues to maintain that the whole accusation is very unlikely (without ever simply saying that they didn't do it), then you should be able to hear the desperation as they search for new ways to point out the same thing: how unlikely it was. Instead of trying to bash other people over the head with the stick of your own arguments, you can sometimes get to the truth just by giving their argument a little poke. Quite often, this will provoke them to puff their argument up into a more exaggerated version of itself in order for it to survive. As they do this, they risk looking increasingly ridiculous as their argument begins to collapse under the weight of their desperate attempts to add more probable premises to the pile.

Karate, as an argumentative approach, can be stressful for those with whom we argue. When someone gives you an argumentative punch in the face, it can be hard for the ego to recover. A directly combative approach tends to push people into a corner. But the way that we interact with other people can be transformed by the ability to see the internal structure of an argument. When we start to clearly make out and focus on what other people believe and we engage with that, we are fighting on their ground with their ideas. To fight by first engaging with someone else's argument rather than your own gives others the satisfaction of a duel on grounds that they decide. Fighting on someone else's terms means that you can politely focus on the merits of other people's arguments instead of only attempting to dominate them by offering your own. One advantage of judo over karate is that it gives us the opportunity to be (or at least, to appear to be) more polite.

Picture the following scenario: one afternoon, as I am staring into space in a corner of the British Library, thinking about how to explain the ideas in this very chapter, I am brought back into the room by a quiet but unmistakeable shrieking sound. I turn to my left to see two faces looking back at me in confusion. The two faces are as puzzled as I am, because the gentleman sitting between the three of us is listening to a female vocalist whose piercing soprano voice is warbling its way straight through his headphones, and everyone can hear it. The gentleman is sitting closer to me than to the two faces, both of which are looking at me with an air of expectation, so I wave my hand gently in the periphery of the man's vision, hoping to attract his attention. He stops the music, and removes his headphones.

'Yes?' he says.

'I'm sorry to disturb you,' I say, 'it's just that I think your music is escaping your headphones.'

He pauses, perhaps for dramatic effect, but I suspect mostly that he's just processing the embarrassment that we all occasionally experience when we realise that we're being an unintentional nuisance to others. I am, however, entirely wrong. The gentleman – bearded, bespectacled and now aggressive – looks at me like I've just insulted his mother. He's pausing to stock up on anger, not to apologise. He looks at the faces to his left and then back at me. And then, in a tone of utter disdain, he finally says:

'Well, you lot came and sat down next to me.'

And replaces his headphones. The two faces and I look at each other with that amazed smile that's fun to share with those who are on the same page as you when you're all in the company of someone who clearly isn't, and it's in this instant that I have to decide what to do. In the past, I would have just come back at him with something aggressive. Perhaps something along the lines of 'Mate, the rules apply to everyone'. Maybe I'd have tried to belittle him with a sarcastic 'I could read the rules to you if you're having trouble seeing them from up there on the moral high ground'. But not these days. These days, thanks to Aristotle, I don't have to punch him in the face.

The foundation of his argument – his hidden premise – is that because he arrived first, his needs and desires trump ours. His argument is balancing precariously on a single idea that he's using as a premise: *priority*. The bare bones of his deduction look something like this:

> He who arrives first makes the rules
> I arrived first
> Therefore ... I make the rules.

So what do I do? Do I tap him on the shoulder and say, 'I'm terribly sorry! My mistake! You seem to be saying that everyone in the library has to follow the same rules, unless they arrived first, in which case they can do anything they like. Is that how it works here?' Of course not: this final part of the conversation happens only in my head. As he puts his headphones back on, he turns the warbling down, and the two faces and I smile at each other before turning back to our computers. In the end, I say nothing.

When we take care to listen to other people's justifications for what they do, we can learn to find the point on which their argument balances. Instead of being distracted by the rhetoric of their words or the anger on their faces, we can learn to instantly see *what they're saying*. Not only is a 'judo' approach, when used in the right spirit, more polite than a 'karate' approach, it simultaneously presents those we argue against with a problem: if their own arguments are dissected and found wanting, they find that there is nothing of ours to attack. This can produce immense frustration on their part as they wind themselves up in preparation to take a swing at our argument before suddenly realising that there is nothing to take a swing at. Angry Headphone Man's attack – 'Well, you lot came and sat down next to me' – only makes sense if the foundation of his argument is about priority. Knowing that every argument is built on a premise that works as its ultimate foundation is what gives us the opportunity to look for and recreate the structure of other people's arguments in our own mind. By having an idea of what we should expect to find, we become far more likely to find it – more likely to successfully dig down towards the heart of the argument and reveal its weakness without having to offer any counterclaim of our own – and to do it gently if we can find the strength to do so. In another situation, priority might have been a very good argument, and in that case we get the opportunity to use what we know to help us realise that we're wrong – to not be *that guy*, and to apologise.

But having silly arguments is one thing. The arguments that really matter to us – the ones that make us most passionate, angry or willing to use violence – rely on premises that are much more tricky to handle. Premises are the foundation not just of trivial arguments, but also of the most important political, spiritual and ethical debates we have – the ones that shape the way we live – and they're not always as easy to uncover as straightforward statements like 'all politicians are untrustworthy'.

Some premises are so seductive that we don't notice them even when they're not hidden at all. Some premises are so good at sneaking under our radar that not only do we not notice them, we even actively embrace them. The tragedy is that these premises – these foundations of so much of what we say and do – are an invitation to think as little as possible. Sometimes, the biggest ideas are the most dangerous.

Kick the Soapbox

> 'When arguments reason to a false conclusion the right solution is to demolish the point on which the falsity depends; for the demolition of any random point is no solution.' (Aristotle, *Topics*: 8.10)

Understanding how we use deduction – how we combine chains of premises to produce a conclusion – shows us the fundamental and unavoidable ingredients that make up every argument, and once we become accustomed to breaking down an argument into a chain of premises, we can start to notice the premise with the most important role: what I call a *soapbox*. A soapbox is not the exact words of a premise but *the rule or principle that those words try to express*. Every deductive argument requires some sort of rule that we claim to be true – whether it's the universal *all politicians are untrustworthy* or the non-universal *most people who've already eaten four desserts don't go for a fifth* – because that's how deduction works: by applying general rules to individual examples. Knowing to look for the rule that supports an argument, as well as knowing that both it and its crucial parts – the quantifiers – are usually hidden, helps us to find and, as Aristotle puts it, 'demolish the point on which the falsity depends'. But there's a problem. The soapbox – the crucial premise on which an argument is built – can be hidden completely out of view, but it can also be hidden in plain sight, in disguise ...

Rules, principles and generalisations are all different ways of expressing that something is generally true or desirable. Very often, the rules, principles or generalisations on which deductions are built are easy to spot, even if both the premise and its quantifier are hidden. For example, in the muffin-eating defence ('Why would I have eaten the muffin when I'd already had four portions of cake for dessert?') we can 'map' the argument as one that is being supported by the hidden premise *most people who've already eaten four desserts don't go for a fifth*. This 'mapping' of an argument is what happens when we're taught to pay less attention to the conclusion of an argument than to the premises that it relies on: it is being able to produce a mental picture of each part of an argument and see how they fit together. To achieve that, we should not only look for premises, but, in particular, premises that are generalisations: rules that say that something is *always* or *usually* the case. This process – of learning to looking past the exact words that come out of someone's mouth so that we can make out the rule that they're implying – can be made more difficult by the fact that some generalisations have become so familiar that they often appear as if they were trustworthy old friends. We call these generalisations 'sayings', 'proverbs', 'maxims' or 'aphorisms', and their function is to lure us in with their seemingly ancient and comforting wisdom.

If someone says to you *it's better to be safe than sorry*, all sorts of applicable situations come to mind. After all, it seems to be eminently sensible advice. But what about the opposite advice: that *fortune favours the bold*? What about the actors who waited tables for decades and risked financial meltdown while their parents and friends told them *it's better to be safe than sorry*, only to hit the big time and realise their dreams? What about the men who risked death to leave our home and set foot on the surface of the moon? As they looked back at our tiny planet and experienced the insignificance of Earth not just as an idea, but with their own eyes, did they think *it's better to be safe than sorry*?

The fact is that life is more complex than the proverbs we sometimes use to justify our decisions; and yet we love the simplicity of a general rule. If only it were always true that *fortune favours the bold*, then we'd always know what to do. If *better safe than sorry* were actually a cast-iron law, we'd know not to waste our time on pursuing anything risky. Proverbs are no different to probable reasoning: they are the blandest general statements of what's sometimes true.

However, unlike the claims we might make for a specific topic, proverbs are easy to apply to almost any situation. Proverbs make the same generalisations as other fundamental premises that support an argument, but they do it with a veneer of poetic and rhetorical flair that makes them less noticeable as generalisations. You don't have to mention a single detail of the balance of risk and reward in a particular example; you can always claim that the best soapbox is *safety first* – or *be bold* – and proceed to build your argument on top of it. The most clichéd proverbs and sayings can be slipped under the radar of thought because very often that's all it takes to convince an audience. As Aristotle explains, it is the very familiarity of these proverbs and sayings that makes them stick: 'Even hackneyed and commonplace maxims are to be used, if they suit one's purpose: just because they are commonplace, everyone seems to agree with them, and therefore they are taken for truth.'

Aristotle cleverly points out that occasionally, a proverb can be sexed up into a whole dramatic performance: the fable. Aesop's story of the tortoise and the hare is merely a more seductive, narrative version of the rather dull-sounding saying 'slow and steady wins the race'. The eventual loser – that hubristic hare – reminds us that it often pays to be more meticulous and more careful with our strategy than we might choose to be, given our talents. The rule that comes out of a fable – the moral – is the same rule that we hear expressed succinctly in a proverb. Since the proverb is an impersonal statement that could apply to anyone, and the fable is a dramatic story that happens to characters to whom we have the possibility of feeling an emotional attachment, the fable makes the same basic point but with an extra layer of emotionally distracting cover. On top of this emotional disguise, which helps to bypass our attempts at an unbiased judgement of the arguments that are offered to us, fables have at least one advantage over real-life examples: as Aristotle points out, you can simply make them up.

But proverbs and fables, despite the advantages that make them excellent soapboxes, are not the most dangerous. The most dangerous soapboxes are the ones we're seduced into thinking that no reasonable person could object to anyone standing on. Some soapboxes, we're convinced, are places to argue from that are protected by some shield of invincibility. It's one thing to say that proverbs and fables are clichés that blindly generalise, but who has anything bad to say about the grand ideas for which people have died, and on which whole civilizations and societies are built? When is it dishonest to argue from a platform of *Big Ideas*? Who could possibly object to the soapbox of *Freedom*?

Not only do we misuse proverbs and Big Ideas, we are completely enthralled by a combination of the two. Benjamin Franklin's 'those who would give up essential liberty, to purchase a little temporary safety, deserve neither liberty nor safety' is much more balanced than the version that's usually quoted – which omits the 'little' and occasionally the 'temporary'. Franklin's proverb claims that liberty is not to be traded for 'a little temporary safety', but it is normally used by those pushing a simplified and one-sided cliché: don't give up your rights in return for security. The real juice of the question of course is in the middle, not at the extremes. What Franklin was asking us to consider was *how much* liberty is the right amount to give up for safety. Franklin wasn't warning us to not to swap rights for security; he was warning us to swap them for *the right amount* of safety. The complexity of life simply doesn't match up to the simplicity of one big idea in the same way that a proverb doesn't help you to decide what to do in a particular situation. Proverbs are general principles for guidance in the same way that the idea of 'freedom' is generally desirable: as one principle balanced against other principles.

A soapbox is more than the exact words we use; it's the idea behind the words. Headphone Guy's 'Well, you lot came and sat down next to me' adds up to the principle of priority. The words amount to the idea that being the first to arrive gives him the right to make the rules. The principle that supports his argument – the soapbox – is priority. Priority, just like freedom, is a perfectly good rule of thumb, but that's all it is: a rule that is only *sometimes* true. All deductive arguments, no matter which type of premise they're built on, rely on some sort of rule or generalisation. These ultimate justifications for what we claim to be true, although they instantly appeal to us because of their familiarity, conceal the complexity that makes every individual situation and decision what it is. When we dig down into the reasons we give for our actions, and the way that we justify them to others, what we find is that very often the foundation of our argument is nothing more than the most simplistic and clichéd saying or idea.

There is no rule that covers every scenario, and though we shouldn't be pedants who go around telling everyone that what's probable is not what's certain, we *should* be the ones who see that proverbs, probable reasoning, fables and Big Ideas are very often used as if they were universal and unbreakable laws rather than guiding principles.

We are all far less neutral in assessing arguments than we believe, and the sometimes lazy, prejudiced and angry part of us latches on to the safety and security of simple and general rules. As Aristotle says, 'people love to hear stated in general terms what they already believe in some particular connection.' When we learn how to make out the structure of an argument, though, it gives us the power to point out the simplistic and seductive reasoning that covers up the true complexity of decision-making in a complicated world, and it allows us to show up those who would prefer to conceal it.

Real-Life Deduction

In order to transform the way we think, we need to be able to consciously recognise and explain the fundamental and ever-present ideas *themselves*. It's the abstract and general concepts of deduction and premises that, once firmly in our minds, make it possible for us to see how they apply to any argument on any topic. Individual examples can quickly fade from memory, and fail to help us to recognise general concepts when we run into them in the course of our real lives. Once examples of *particular* deductions or *particular* premises are what comes to mind most easily, we can find it hard to apply them to the full variety of arguments that life throws at us.

It is the highest and most general level of understanding that truly transforms the way we think, and yet, in spite of the power of the abstract, we don't live lives of theory. Once we have begun to internalise the principles of argument as general ideas, we need to return to the real world and apply them to the constantly changing problems of our actual lives. The Sophists – that group of ancient Greek teachers – are all dead, but *sophists* – those who make use of fallacious arguments – are very much alive and well. Talented rhetoricians with the ability to conceal, distract and equivocate abound, and this unchanging feature of human experience forces us to use the power of our own thought to fight them. Here are some examples of how to do it.

The Hidden Premise

During a radio phone-in show in 2016, Donald Trump was asked what he thought about wind power, and this was part of his reply:

> And it kills all the birds. I don't know if you know that ...
> Thousands of birds are lying on the ground. And the eagle.
> You know, certain parts of California – they've killed so
> many eagles. You know, they put you in jail if you kill an
> eagle. And yet these windmills [kill] them by the hundreds.

If you could break down these 55 words into an argument, it would look something like this:

> Killing birds is bad.
> Windmills kill birds.
> Therefore ... windmills are bad.

But the sophist in Trump cleverly develops this straightforward bit of reasoning into a second deduction. It's still a matter of debate *how* acceptable the death of birds are in the context of the benefits of wind power, so the first premise still doesn't entirely work. Though Mr Trump would like people to accept this deduction, he knows that what we're hearing is something more like this:

> Killing birds is bad (but acceptable)
> Windmills kill birds.
> Therefore ... windmills are bad (but acceptable).

This is the position that balances the cost and the benefit to the environment, but Mr Trump's aim isn't to get you to settle for a balanced view, so he reworks the first premise into something a bit more persuasive. Killing birds is bad, but killing eagles in California is *a crime*. As he says, 'they put you in jail if you kill an eagle'. In just two sentences, we've moved from 'killing birds is bad (but acceptable)' to 'killing eagles is criminal'. So what we've got is a new deduction:

> Killing eagles is a crime in California
> Windmills kill eagles
> Therefore ... windmills are criminal.

The conclusion of this deduction doesn't entirely add up, but that doesn't matter, because Trump isn't making this argument – he's only implying it. Even though Trump hasn't made that final leap of stating his implied conclusion out loud (that if killing eagles is a crime in California, we ought to consider the killing of eagles by windmills a crime too) he has taken the first step by mentioning the two cases side by side. He's leaving us to make the leap so that he can't be accused of pushing us. But that's the genius of rhetoric: it's not philosophy – no one is forcing you, or even asking you to spell out exactly what you mean. This is the difference between rhetoric and philosophy: clarity. As long as you never state your case openly, you can always claim that you weren't implying anything at all.

The truth of the eagle argument is that there is no direct comparison. There's a difference between a government that accepts the death of some animals to save others and an individual who enacts the premeditated killing of an animal without the intent to protect others by doing so. The only similarity between the two situations is that in both cases animals end up dead – but *how* we kill them and *why* we kill them make all the difference. When Trump tries to substitute his first premise of bad-but-acceptable with worthy-of-jail-and-therefore-unquestionably-wrong, he hopes we won't notice, but the more clearly we can see the structure of an argument, the more easily we do.

Quantifiers

So how to fight back? Quantifiers – those little words that make a big difference to the extent to which something is true: words like 'none', 'some', 'most' or 'all' – are where the battle of rhetoric is frequently won and lost. Here, Trump opens with an all-encompassing 'all'. In our attempts to uncover, reveal and make clear the structure of the arguments we want to probe, it pays not to point that structure out ourselves, but to ask questions that force the person we're arguing with to do it for us. That way, we can draw out the premises and quantifiers that matter without being accused of putting words in other people's mouths. When you find a premise that's suspect for any reason – by virtue of its being hidden or being infused with the strength of an exaggerated and unwarranted quantifier – start by asking a question that isolates it, and clearly holds it up for examination. Here, the interviewer could ask:

> President Trump, you said that wind power 'kills all the birds'. Is that true?

If Trump were to answer that he didn't mean it literally, then at this point, you would need to think your strategy through. We don't always speak literally, and it's a challenge to always be precise about what we mean, but if we accept this basic idea – that the words we use don't matter – we open a door that every sophist will walk through if given the choice.

Sophists don't just grab the strongest quantifier that they can – they don't just make a land-grab for 'all' when they're only entitled to 'some' – they try to cover themselves by mentioning most of the options even when they contradict each other, but if you pay attention to the first premise a sophist wants us to accept, you'll notice when it changes. Here, Trump opens with 'it kills *all* the birds', but he soon waters this down to '*thousands* of birds' before going on to talk about '*so many* eagles' and eagles 'by the *hundreds*'. My point is not that this misrepresents the real figures (though it does), but that we fail to notice when we're purposefully being offered a confusing mess of options so that there's nothing concrete for us to question.

When we're offered a steadily weakening argument whose premises slide from the solid ground of 'all' to what is essentially 'some', we need to point out where it started, because the smart rhetorician, the sophist, knows that we can forget piles of nonsense if we're offered a smart-sounding conclusion. Put another way: when we've been given a good ending to an argument, we can forget the beginning and the middle.

The most common response to having your steadily weakening argument publicly pointed out is to try and salvage whatever you can from what is left of it. When one of Trump's misleading opening salvos was pointed out during a press conference shortly after his election – when his argumentative cards were put on the table for all to see – his response was to try and strike a deal. On the subject of his election, he'd claimed: 'I guess it was the biggest electoral college win since Ronald Reagan.' When a reporter pointed out that not only was that not true, but that he had in fact received fewer votes than both George Bush and Barack Obama, he replied 'Well, I was just given that information. I don't know. I was just given ... We had a very big margin.' The thing to look for isn't necessarily the opening lie or exaggeration – it's the offer for us to buy a weaker premise than the one that was first advertised. The deal he offered was this: 'Well, I don't know. I was given that information. Actually, I've seen that information around, but it was a very substantial victory, do you agree with that?'

What's vital is not whether his electoral college win was or wasn't substantial. To accept the offer that this question presents us with is to let Trump off the hook. The deal is designed to make us forget that the claim he originally offered is completely different to the one now on the table. A sophist persuades by hiding a trail of exaggerations or lies behind whatever truth they can finally get us to accept. The reporter's reply to Trump's offer was a deferential, non-confrontational and perhaps ironic: 'You're the President'; but it could have been both more revealing and more excoriating: 'President Trump, you're only offering to water down your original claim because I've pointed out that it wasn't true.'

In the bird example, when faced with a picture of the shifting sands underneath his own argument, Trump would probably say something like: 'I didn't mean it literally, but they do kill a *lot* of birds. A *significant number* of birds.' If you allow yourself to get drawn into the question of exactly how many birds were actually killed without noticing that all the earlier claims are still swimming around in the background of the conversation – blending false premises into a soup of implied arguments that are never forced to be openly and honestly clarified – you allow the rhetoric to hang in the air and work its persuasive magic. But if we start by making it clear where the argument started and how it developed rather than just focusing on the question of whether or not it's true, then even if we don't find the truth, we can at least point out any dishonesty along the way. If we can see the whole argument – and, crucially, if we can make sure that everyone else can too – then we've got a chance to find something concrete to grab hold of and interrogate. If we can't, we're left grasping at the mist of rhetoric.

Find the Soapbox, Kick the Soapbox

So premises, quantifiers and the deduction that brings them together can help us to notice and point out the structure of an argument. This doesn't just give the participants a chance

to notice the argument's journey; it provides the same opportunity to anyone else who's listening in too. But what about
those premises that form the foundation of an argument? In
the last chapter we looked at how fables, sayings and Big Ideas
are used as the ultimate justification for an argument. If we can
work out which soapbox a sophist is standing on, then we can
give it a kick or ask ourselves if they've got any right to argue
from where they're standing. The real problem at the heart of
President Trump's argument about the danger of wind power to
birds isn't that it's illogical. By itself, it's absolutely logical to say
that if something damages the environment, we should think
twice before doing it. But arguments don't exist in a vacuum ...

The soapbox that supports Trump's bird argument is this:
harming the natural world is bad. Trump's argument only makes
sense if he is arguing from the soapbox of environmental protection: it's the concern for the death of birds that he uses to
criticise wind power. But how can you claim that the environment is the soapbox you're standing on, when the alternative
that you're suggesting is coal? It's not that Trump's conclusion doesn't follow from his premise: if killing birds is bad for
the environment, then it follows that wind power *is* bad for
the environment. The soapbox of environmental protection is
entirely reasonable, but what we need to be able to notice is
that *it's not his soapbox.*

You could point out that on this one issue – wind power vs.
coal – you can't excuse the greater and wider environmental
impact of coal on all animals and ecosystems, *and* argue at the
same time against wind power from a soapbox of environmental protection. Months later, Trump would pull out of the Paris
Climate Agreement. If you'd asked him how it's possible that he
could argue against wind power because of the death of a number

of birds in the USA but then withdraw America's commitment to a strategy that would contribute to environmental protection on a global scale, you would be challenging him to rank his soapboxes in order of preference, and to do it in front of you.

One limit of what you can achieve through intelligent analysis of the structure of individual arguments (or even whole systems of belief) is that no one is ever obliged to take up the challenge of arguing openly and honestly. For anyone who has not already made up their mind, though, the turning down of a challenge to explain yourself rarely goes unnoticed. The line between an honest and open philosophical approach to explaining your beliefs, and the rhetorical approach that just confidently states what it believes without ever stopping to explain why is one that we can't force people to cross. But without the ability to draw the line we're not just helpless to force them to be open, we're helpless to notice it ourselves, or to point out to others that they're crossing it. This ability to point out a lack of argument – that assertions are being made without evidence – is particularly important in relation to Trump, for whom the confident repetition of his belief that his policies or people are *great/fantastic/amazing/the best/any other superlative* is a common rhetorical strategy.

When you notice the ideas that people have to stand on in order for their arguments to work, it's easier to keep track of when they contradict themselves – not just within one argument, but across everything they say. If every time you heard your least-favourite sophist speak, you were to make a mental note of the Big Ideas that they constantly return to, then the contradictions both big and small would become apparent. If we look past the individual premises and conclusions that people make and are able to see the principles that are the real foundation of their argument, we can notice not just what they are, but how all of them fit together.

Whatever the balance of principles and justifications, or the inevitable compromise between them, they often exist buried away in the depths of an argument. We know 'roughly what people are getting at', but because we are not in the habit of looking for the ultimate principles that power an argument, we don't recognise all the contradictions we could. Some people are open, and willing to discuss the inherent and unavoidable tensions between the principles that matter to us, but with everyone else, we have to coax them out.

Judo, Not Karate

The greatest advantage of being able to summon up a mental map of both the premises and the ultimate principles of an argument is that it makes it possible to put into action the most effective technique of discussion and debate: the Socratic method. More than 2,000 years after his death, Socrates is still remembered for being incredibly annoying to talk to because he was an expert at revealing the structure of other people's arguments. If we want to learn how to be a fly in the ointment of what other people claim to be true, we can learn to do what Socrates did. He was known for resisting an urge that we all feel: the urge to show other people that they're wrong by offering them our own theories about a subject. Socrates constantly describes himself as lacking knowledge, reminding us that he isn't 'a bag of arguments', and he warns us not to misunderstand the way he thinks when he says:

> you don't realise what is happening. The arguments never come from me; they always come from the person I am talking to.

What Socrates did was to make a mental map of what *other people* claim is true and why – what their premises are and how they fit together – and then present them with it. Without raising a finger, he tripped up his opponents with the weight of their own arguments. What he did was judo, not karate.

We don't always have to point out the implication of an argument; sometimes it's clear for all to see. When one British politician was questioned on national television about the bargaining power of the Prime Minister at the start of the UK's Brexit negotiations, she deployed an ancient bit of political rhetoric: she claimed that asking too many questions is 'unpatriotic'. She said: 'It would be helpful if broadcasters were willing to be a bit patriotic. The country took a decision [to leave the European Union]; this government is determined to deliver on that decision.' The interviewer, Emily Maitlis, was smart enough not to fight this comment, but simply to hold it up for further scrutiny. She responded: 'Are you accusing me of being unpatriotic for questioning how negotiations are going, questioning whether you have the position of strength that she [the Prime Minister] wanted?' The implication of the politician's comment was clear: she wanted us to deduce that you can add her 'patriotism means not asking questions' to 'Emily Maitlis is asking questions' and conclude that 'Emily Maitlis is unpatriotic', but when confronted with this deduction out in the open, she was forced to deny it: to backpedal and try to move on. What makes Maitlis' answer Socratic is the fact that she was able to unsettle her interviewee without disagreeing with her, and without offering any opinion of her own. She was able to expose the argument simply by asking a question. To clear the smoke of opaque political rhetoric, we could all make use of the Socratic skills of a good journalist.

Socrates' famously effective way of thinking depended on his ability to first make the premises of any argument clear, and then to publicly dissect the details of those premises *without offering any of his own*. As we build on top of our foundation of deduction – the first secret of intelligence – we'll be able to see more of the important details of premises and the ways that they fit together, but the level at which we perform this task is less important than the technique itself. The judo approach to argument and debate is the essence of what Socrates contributed to the search for truth, and it's the most important component of the Socratic method. The Socratic method, even though it equips us to succeed in arguments that range from cursory skirmish to all-out combat, amounts to more than just a technique that helps us to debate; it's also a state of mind. Very often, when our opponent is talking, half of us is trying to listen to their argument, but the other half is paying no attention at all. The other half isn't making a map of what the enemy is saying; sometimes, when it appears that we're listening, all that's really happening is that we're waiting for the other person to stop speaking so that we can go back to explaining our own argument. But the irony of the way we approach arguments is that the more desperately we want to win them, the harder we make it to understand them and the people that make them, and the less persuasive we become.

The essence of Socrates' method is to think about clarity first and victory second. The Socratic method is more than just a debating technique: it's a way of approaching both friendly discussion and acrimonious argument. It's the reflex that makes you ask yourself if you understand someone else's argument well enough to be able to publicly outline all of its parts – to make their argument for them – before you openly disagree with it. It's the desire to understand, and to be able to show that you understand what other people say and why they say it. Once we have made it our habit to mentally map an argument – to scan the surface of the words we hear and make out the patterns of ideas that really matter – we make it more likely that we'll be able to demolish that argument, or be surprised by the fact that we actually agree with it.

The Socratic method makes us more understanding, better able to see the holes in our own truths and far more skilful at fighting the tricks of rhetoric. But the ability to map an argument in our heads and share our thinking with others develops out of what we can say about the concrete, practical and unavoidable ideas that describe what an argument is. Socrates wasn't, as he said, a bag of arguments about any one subject; he was a master of powerful ideas about thinking and argument. But while Socrates could walk the walk, there is little evidence to suggest that he could or did explain the ideas that teach us how to do it. What Socrates represents is the desire to question, think, talk and argue with a rare philosophical thirst for the truth, and to do it with an arresting openness and honesty. That desire and that *ideal* is still around today, but what we lack are the concrete *ideas* that reveal the fundamental structure of what both we and other people claim is true. It is only when we are shown the deductions, premises, quantifiers and soapboxes that are the unchanging ingredients of the human mind that we can start learning to understand the premise-detecting, deduction-revealing, argument-mapping hardware that defines the way we think.

Induction: How to Make or Break a Theory

Do You See The Signs?

With great confidence, deduction tells us that if all politicians are untrustworthy then we shouldn't trust the Prime Minister or the President. It tells us that if every member of the cat family must eat meat to survive, then your family's cat is no different. But how do we come to know about the morals of politicians or the diet of cats in the first place? If deduction is working out what's true given what you know already, then you might ask yourself, as Aristotle did, where did 'what you know already' come from?

The things that we know are the foundation from which we work, but we don't come into the world clutching a basic encyclopaedia of truth to get us going. Nobody gifts us a magical starter pack with some of life's answers already filled in. Whatever force or forces brought the world into existence, they failed to label everything. When we go out on a date, we don't find that the person sitting opposite us has a sign that reads COMPATIBLE or INCOMPATIBLE hovering conveniently above their head. When we're on a tour of potential schools for our children, the head teachers don't wear jumpers with the words COMPETENT LEADERSHIP or COMPLETELY CLUELESS helpfully stitched on the front. If only young footballers had FUTURE STAR or NOT GOING TO MAKE IT printed on the backs of their shirts, then managers' lives would be simple. But this is not how the world works, nor how our minds work. So how *does* it work, and how do we work it out?

The process of making theories about everyone and everything is the path that leads each of us to our own understanding of the reality in which we live, but we give it very little conscious thought. At first, it seems so natural; barely worth explaining. In working out the nature of people and things – what they are like – and in working out what causes certain events to happen, we sit back in the armchair of life, and a picture just seems to emerge. We watch the way that people and things behave, and after a while we 'see' how they work.

Theories are what we use to explain the past and predict the future, but have you ever thought about what theories are, how we create them, or why not all of them turn out to be right? The thinking that produces the theories that orient us in the world and supply us with the rules and generalisations we need to survive in it is the mysterious twin of deduction, and it's the second of the three fundamental ways that we reason. If we understand the way it works, it can help us to be less likely to jump to unwarranted conclusions, to be wrong less often, and to understand what went awry when we do. It's called **induction**.

⌐

The reality of trying to find the truth when it's hidden is that we're forced to work it out by scanning the surface for clues.

Imagine that one day you're out for a walk with Aristotle, Alexander and six friends, somewhere in the lush countryside around the school that King Philip built for his son. Lunchtime is fast approaching and, a little bored of hearing Aristotle talk about deduction, your mind and your eyes start to wander. As luck would have it, they land on a colourful patch of succulent-looking mushrooms. The rest of the group notice them too, and before long, all nine of you are gathered in a circle staring at a patch of exactly nine mushrooms.

Standing this close, you notice that three of the mushrooms are red, three are green and three are blue. Everyone gets a mushroom for lunch, but not everyone enjoys it. While six of you swap mushroom-tasting notes about the delicacy and subtle flavour of the green and blue varieties, the three unfortunates who ate the red mushrooms throw up violently. Ten minutes later you come across another identical patch of mushrooms, and someone offers you a succulent-looking red mushroom. Do you eat it?

I would hope that you'd be sceptical about whether eating the mushroom would be a good idea, but Aristotle would have encouraged us to focus not so much on the answer – whether this new patch of red mushrooms is poisonous or not – but on the thinking that gets us there. If our rule is 'red mushrooms are poisonous', what happened that led us to it? How does the thinking behind our theories work?

Theories begin with what we see. If you don't perceive the world, then of course you can't make theories: in order to spot a pattern, you must first be able to see it. But this isn't enough. If you instantly forgot what happened when you ate the mushrooms, you'd have no memories, and without memories, you'd have nothing to organise into a pattern – so we need memory, too. But even this isn't enough. What really makes us see a pattern is what memories *have in common*.

Aristotle explains it like this:

So from perception there comes memory ... and from memory (*when it occurs often in connection with the same thing*), experience.

The italics are mine. What I'm trying to show is that Aristotle saw that it is not just memory that makes the magic happen. The magic only happens when we notice *similarities* between the things that we've seen or heard. When different memories have something in common, they become something more special than just memories. They get grouped together and become experience. When your mind notices that different memories of different situations are connected by 'the same thing', you start to think of the memories not as separate, but as one. What transforms memories, making them into more than just a disorganised pile of sensations, is our ability to see what they have in common.

But what exactly are we seeing? What's the pattern made of? What is the one common thing that we notice? In the mushroom example, what is it that we experienced that connected our three now-sick mushroom eaters? What was the *sign* that we noticed and remembered that was 'the same in all' of the mushrooms that made some of the group sick? It wasn't the convenient label 'POISONOUS' written anywhere on the mushrooms' tasty-looking flesh. They had their own sign: *they were red*.

Induction – the fundamental process by which we work out what people and things are like – is an indirect process. What we want is to be able to recognise the properties or attributes that matter to us. We want to be able to see the untrustworthiness of people, the incompatibility of potential partners or the poison in a mushroom. We want to know whether a mushroom – or a medicine – *caused* sickness or health, because the properties that things have are what make them good or bad, and our knowledge of those properties is what determines the quality of the choices we make. However, the nature of induction is to force us to look for attributes not directly, but through a third party: other 'connected' attributes that we take as *signs* of their existence.

Induction, at its simplest, is the process of *creating universal rules from particular examples of signs*. We notice a connection between one property and another, and we take the second property – the one we can see – to be a sign of the first. If, in the past, we have connected a few examples of sickness to red mushrooms, we will theorise – which is to say, *induce* – that there is a universal connection. 'If there is a connection here and now,' our minds tell us, 'then there might be a connection always and everywhere.'

The connections that exist in all the scenarios that we encounter are tracked by the pattern-mapping software in our heads, and as a result, we experience similarity as a pattern that jumps out at us. Add an explanation for the connection (like 'plants and animals can evolve to protect themselves by making use of the most visible colours to signal to others that they are poisonous') and you have a theory ... but at the heart of all theories (before you get to the difficulties of explanation) is the connection itself. We can't see the poison in the mushroom with the naked eye, but we can see the connections that suggest that the poison is there: a pattern of *signs*. The truths we want to see are hidden, and signs are what we use to find them.

So far, so seemingly obvious; pattern spotting can seem self-explanatory – the most natural thing in the world – until we realise that what seems obvious is the very thing that we don't think about. Signs are what we're stuck with; but just like politicians, not all of them should be trusted.

Backwards Thinking: The Case of The Fallible Sign

To see why what appears to be certain is often nothing of the kind, you have to understand that not all signs are equal. There are two types of sign, and Aristotle wanted Alexander to be able to tell them apart. But what exactly is a sign?

The basic idea is straightforward, and Aristotle explains it crisply: 'when it is, another thing is.' So if *event A* happens, then *event B* happens as a result. Aristotle's example is what happens when it rains. If raining is *event A*, then what happens as a result is B: *the ground gets wet*. A causes B, and therefore B is a *sign* of A. Could anything be simpler?

But consider another example. In the same way that rain causes the ground to get wet, *lightning* causes *thunder*. If lightning is our A, then the resulting thunder is our B. A causes B, and therefore B is, again, a sign of A. So, you might wonder what possible room for confusion there is in the seemingly obvious fact that B follows A: that thunder is a sign of lightning and that the ground being wet is a sign of rain? Well, the answer is plenty.

What Aristotle realised was that these two examples appear on the surface to be both identical and impossible to argue with, but they aren't. The two cases are actually examples of two different types of sign. One is absolutely and always reliable, while the other is not. One sign is fallible, whilst the other is infallible.

The way to understand the difference between the fallible and the infallible sign is to think about how we reason both forwards *and* backwards. When reasoning forwards, from A to B, both examples are identical. Rain always produces wet ground and lightning always produces thunder. When A happens, then B *always* happens. Like clockwork, forward reasoning never lets you down. But what happens when we try to travel not from A to B, but backwards, from B to A?

In the second example, working backwards from B to A presents no problem at all. It's true that lightning causes thunder, and the reverse is also true: if we hear thunder, we know that it was *caused by* lightning. There is simply no other way to produce thunder. But apply the same backwards reasoning to the first example, and you get a different result. While it is always true that rain causes the ground to get wet, it's not *always* or *only* true that wet ground is caused by rain. It's absolutely possible to make the ground wet without a drop of rain. The fallible sign, unlike its wholly reliable partner, doesn't tell you with any certainty what has produced it. Rain does cause the ground to be wet, but so does a burst water pipe, melting snow, the condensation that we call morning dew, someone watering their garden, or even a tsunami. No matter how likely or unlikely the other potential causes of wet ground are, they exist; and because they exist, wet ground doesn't tell us that it has rained.

The difference between fallible and infallible signs, though they can superficially appear to be the same, is that an infallible sign is *uniquely* connected to the event that causes it. When B is *only* caused by A, then whenever we see B, we can be 100 per cent sure that A has happened. That is what it means to be an infallible sign.

The way that we understand, visualise and calculate the relationships between two *properties* or two *events* is ripe for the admission of error. We are good at seeing As causing Bs, but far less conscious of the fact that working backwards from Bs to As is not simple. And yet our first thought – that B must have been caused by A – is often difficult to resist, so persuasive and obvious does it sometimes seem. Think back to the mushroom example. When we look for the signs that 'connect' one situation to another, like the redness of the mushroom's skin, we're often not looking at the sign that really makes the difference. Can you think of alternative explanations for why the red mushrooms caused vomiting? It's possible that a poisonous insect likes living in red mushrooms, in which case it would be the insect, not the mushroom or its colour that makes you sick. Though you were unlucky enough to find three red mushrooms with poisonous insects inside, there may be plenty of red mushrooms that are insect-free and perfectly safe. It's possible that someone spilled something poisonous over the three red mushrooms. In that case, it's the spillage that caused the vomiting, not the red mushrooms. Perhaps the three members of the group who ate the red mushrooms were the only ones who drank from a dirty jug of water earlier that morning, and it's that, rather than the mushrooms, that caused the reaction. Maybe there's only one species of red mushroom that's poisonous – the kind that the three ate – and all the other types of red mushroom are fine.

In the same way that we connect events, we connect properties too. The thought *event B is a sign of event A* and the thought *property B is a sign of property A* are two sides of the same, connected coin. To illustrate how easily we misread the connections between properties by thinking backwards from signs, consider one of Aristotle's more colourful examples. Imagine that you're a private detective of many years' experience and that you've been hired by a woman who's suspicious of her husband's recent behaviour and wants to know whether he's having an affair. Your task is to find out whether there's any truth to her concerns. From your vast experience of similar cases you've noticed two things that go with wandering partners – two clues that always turn out to be signs of the unfaithful: they are *always smartly dressed*, and they *always wander about at night*. You set about following the husband in question, and lo and behold, you discover him not only dressed up to the nines but also prowling about in the hours of darkness. Assuming that your rule is completely reliable and true, is it time to call the client and confirm her suspicions? Something deep in our minds shouts 'YES!' but the answer isn't that simple.

If you were quick to condemn the well-dressed and night-wandering husband because *all adulterers get dressed up and wander about at night*, then heed Aristotle's words: 'There are, however, many people of whom these things are true, while the charge in question is untrue.' This is what Aristotle called 'affirming the consequent', and it is embodied in this example by the observation that just because *all adulterers get dressed up and wander about at night*, it doesn't follow that *those who get dressed up and wander about at night must be adulterers*. Out of all the people who get dressed up and wander about at night, the vast majority are into fashion, or trying to get into a club that opens late and has a strict dress code, or out gambling in casinos or taking part in many other activities that involve dressing up and going out at night. Even if it's true that *every* adulterer *always* shows us *both* of the signs – smart dressing and night wandering – so do a large number of other people. By rounding up all of the smartly dressed night-wanderers, you'd be able to say with certainty that you had all the adulterers in front of you, but you'd also have plenty of other people who like doing a wide range of other things, and no way of telling them apart. It's all very well claiming that all signs provide sure-fire evidence, but this simply isn't true, 'any more than it follows that if a man in a fever is hot, a man who is hot must be in a fever'.

Aristotle tried to warn us that our inductive shortcomings can make us easy to manipulate. One example is his dissection of the classic rhetorical strategy of pointing to any event that happens before another, and claiming that it must be the cause:

> Another line [of argument] consists in representing as
> causes things that are not causes on the ground that they
> happened along with or before the event in question. They
> assume that because B happens after A, it happens because
> of A. Politicians are especially fond of taking this line.

When Aristotle wrote these lines, they were meant as a warning.
But they are a warning that we can only really hear and make
practical use of if we understand the process of thinking that
seduces us with false impressions, overstated evidence and the
promise of a simplistic world whose causative web is easy to
discern.

Our lives are packed with judgements about events and
causes, and the outcomes of these decisions can be a matter of
life and death. I was once asked what I thought of marijuana as
a cure for cancer. When I asked what had provoked the question, the answer came that a friend of the person had smoked
marijuana and subsequently gone into remission. I asked
whether their friend, while they were smoking marijuana, was
also receiving conventional chemotherapy – a treatment whose
efficacy no one doubts. The answer was yes. The inability to
make use of basic ideas about causality or probability – the ideas
which prevent us from fundamentally and even fatally misreading the world – should worry us.

What we cite as 'evidence' is, most of the time, no more
than a fallible sign. I was recently watching a well-known TV
programme about a famous chef who helps the owners of failing restaurants and hotels to return their businesses to their
once-profitable beginnings. At one point, the chef shouted at
the owner of a hotel because he'd found a bowl of a suspicious-
looking substance that had been left behind a cooker for some

time and had started to fester. Holding the bowl of dark goo in his hand and gesticulating wildly, he shouted at her: 'IS THIS A SIGN OF SOMEONE WHO CARES?'

Instead of pointing out that there are many reasons why people make mistakes – being disorganised, having too much to do or simply being overworked (perhaps as a result of caring *too much*) – the owner was unable to find a way of defending herself. The truth, it seemed to me, was actually somewhere in the middle. She didn't come across as particularly organised or experienced and she also didn't seem that bothered about it. But who wants to have a proper conversation about how to fix things when you can create an emotional drama from a single infallible sign that doesn't tell you very much at all?

The desire to convince by pointing out any connection, no matter how tenuous, is one that we are all prey to. But we can develop a reflex – every time we think about the factors that might have caused an event, or might indicate the attributes of a person or thing – to resist the urge to be persuaded by any possible cause or sign. The dangling in front of us of fallible signs is essentially how detective dramas and murder mysteries work. In the same way that an experienced scriptwriter might begin not to accept the first or most obvious explanation in the shows that she watches as a result of her own practised ability to mislead by setting traps made of fallible signs, we can learn to do the same. Just as we can learn to read and watch fictional worlds with a reflex that rejects superficial analysis, we can do the same in the real one.

The reflex of non-acceptance is one that's only made possible by properly understanding *why* we should question what first occurs to us, or what first appears to be true. It's not enough for us to be given gnomic utterances like 'all that glitters is not gold'. There is no deep or novel truth in the fact that our impressions of the world – our theories – are frequently wrong; that much we know already. But without understanding why, we stand little chance of creating opportunities to think again.

Backseat Thinking: Don't Jump to Conclusions

Every day, our inductive minds serve us up a menu of signs to consider, and the connections that we notice give us the opportunity to try to predict the nature of the world around us. The way that the software in our heads tracks the connections between the events, people and things that it observes is essential to our survival. However, this menu of possible signs can also work against us if we succumb to our instinct to pick whatever is right at the top. Our pattern-spotting minds are truly powerful and productive, but the nature of induction makes it an inherently dangerous tool. To be skilful readers of reality rather than naïve swallowers of easy answers, we have to appreciate two things about induction: its automatic nature and its inherent limitations.

To see the inherent limitations of induction, you only have to compare it to its less mysterious twin: deduction. Deduction is solid and dependable because it can start with what we know or believe to be true of an entire group of things. Deduction, when it relies on universal premises like *every*, *all*, *no*, or *none*, is 100 per cent foolproof. It's cast-iron. If we were certain that *every* red mushroom was poisonous, then we'd know that any particular red mushroom that we found in the forest would be poisonous too. Deduction starts from a universal rule, and all we have to do is apply it to any example that we come across.

But think about how induction works. It's not half as solid as a cast-iron deduction. It works backwards! Deduction starts with a rule – what's true of everything – and applies it to each individual example; it starts with the answer and applies it to the question. Induction, however, does exactly the reverse. Induction doesn't know what the rule is. Induction can only see different examples of things that it suspects might have something in common, and that might be part of a group. Induction takes the individual examples it has seen in the past and creates a rule for *everything that it will see in the future*. Deduction starts with what it knows. Induction starts with what it sees.

But you might now wonder: *how reliable is what we see?* How reliable are the signs that convince our minds that we've seen the pattern that reveals the truth? Did we not make a rule that applied to *every* red mushroom, *anywhere, for evermore*, on the basis of just three red mushrooms? We were ready to condemn every red mushroom on the basis of just a handful of them. We were ready to make the leap from individual examples to a general rule as if it were a definite and unambiguous logical step.

Deduction is so reliable a method that we can use it to be certain about things. But when we ask where those universal and dependable rules that describe what's true of *every* example of a thing come from, we find that the answer might not be quite as dependable as it seemed. There is a gap between what we've seen and heard, and what we believe. On the side of experience we can have even fewer than three examples, yet bravely hypothesise our way over the gap and infinitely widen our rule from a handful of examples on one side to *every example* on the other.

Aristotle defines induction as 'a passage from particulars to universals', which distils our definition from earlier (the creation of *universal* rules from *particular examples* of signs) into its essence. What's essential to ask about, though, is the nature of that 'passage'. How do we get from observing particular examples to the all-embracing power of a universal rule? The answer is not so much via a logical step as via a logical *leap*. In 21st-century everyday language we use the same words – 'logic' or 'reasoning' – to refer to both deduction and induction: two distinct processes that are the mirror image of each other. Deduction can be a certain step from universal rules to particular examples, but induction can only ever be an uncertain leap from particular examples to universal rules. The fact that we use the very same word to describe two types of thinking that are not just different but *fundamentally opposed to each other* reveals a great deal about why we struggle to clearly understand and easily explain the reasoning that supports the beliefs that we and others hold to be true.

Aristotle was aware of the shortcomings of basing your universal rules on isolated examples, and tried to stress that it's only when you've got every example in your sights that you can really make reliable conclusions. Long before a detailed theory of probability existed, Aristotle worried about how many particular observations we use to make universal rules. When he says 'induction proceeds through an enumeration of *all* the cases', he's contrasting drawing on only a few examples and drawing on every example. In a perfect world, he seems to suggest, we'd observe *all* of the examples. But can we ever see all of the examples?

Getting to the truth is, in fact, even harder to do through induction than Aristotle suggests. Philosophers like David Hume would later sound the worryingly murky depths of induction by pointing out that no amount of observation of examples ever leads to the certainty of a general rule. The most delightfully chilling illustration of the inherent limitations of induction is Bertrand Russell's. Imagine that you are a turkey who is approached at the same time every morning by a farmer who brings a delicious handful of turkey feed. After 100 consecutive days of the morning feeding ritual, as the farmer approaches, you'd feel more confident of being fed than you did on the first morning, and with every morning that the farmer appears and produces a handful of food for you, you'll become increasingly convinced that food is on the menu. After 364 days of feeding, with more observational data than you've ever had, you would be *more certain than ever* that day 365 will bring the same result. What demonstrates the shortcomings of trying to generalise from a set of examples to a universal rule is Christmas morning, when it transpires that the farmer's visit brings not food but a knife, and it is you, the turkey, that is on the menu.

I tell the story of Russell's turkey to bring us to one of Aristotle's most useful insights into what we should learn from a philosophical understanding of induction: that naïvely failing to question the seductive pattern-spotting of inductive thinking is extremely human. Because of the way we leap so easily from examples to rules, we find that examples are a persuasive form of argument, but we're not particularly good at considering *all* the examples: we don't tend to scrupulously look for counterexamples or think about what percentage of all the available examples we've used to make our conclusions. The extent to which we naturally misread the nature of people, things and events would be left to later scientists to uncover. We'll meet some of them and their recommendations in Part III, but Aristotle knew and was troubled by how easily we make the inductive leap; how persuasive we find it. In *Topics* he says that, compared to deduction, induction is 'more convincing', that 'it is more readily learnt by use of the senses' and that it 'is applicable generally to the mass of men'. Induction, he writes, is 'most useful against the crowd'.

What does he mean when he says that induction persuades a crowd? He means that all of us, thanks to the nature of our minds, are capable of thinking like turkeys. We're presented with examples of a connection, and our minds immediately begin to leap in order to grasp the potential riches of a rule. Like any animal with pattern-spotting software, we are assailed as much by potential connections as we are by doubt. The computational engine of the mind makes suggestions more often and with more vigour than it suggests caution in the interpretation of the data. We talk endlessly about the power of data, but rarely about the techniques and limitations of its interpretation.

The danger of the mind's amazing ability to notice patterns is not just that it's inherently uncertain, but also that there's something passive about it. There's something in pattern-spotting that's less than fully conscious, and there's a sense in which we don't 'think up' theories. Sometimes, patterns leap out *at us*. We *experience* similarity as a pattern. We don't so much 'think about it' as 'notice it'. Patterns almost occur *to* us. This is 'backseat thinking': the coercive power of the mind's ability, sometimes unbidden, to spot patterns and generalise from them without stopping to examine the process or the result. Add to the automatic nature of the pattern-spotting mind the inherently uncertain nature of induction, and you have a way of thinking that is just as mysterious as it is powerful and difficult to wield effectively.

In the great challenge of trying to understand the world, signs are all we have. None of us can see the poison in a mushroom's flesh, the hatred in another human's character or the unlocked potential in an athlete's body. If only life were simpler;

but it isn't. We don't just judge mushrooms by the colour of their skin; that's how we judge people too, because skin colour is one of the things that's most visible – one of the signs we can most easily see – and any similarity can lure us into confident but mistaken beliefs about our fellow humans. It's in the nature of the pattern-spotting mind to automatically leap to conclusions, but by understanding it, we can learn to question whichever explanation first pops into our heads.

Real-Life Induction

Causality bothers us: we want to know what causes health or sickness, economic expansion or recession, intellectual growth or mental stagnation. Attributes bother us, too: we want to know how we can tell the difference between a good school and a bad school, a team player and a sociopath, an interesting book or a dull one. So how can we use what we know about induction to avoid misreading reality? When it comes to working out the nature of events, people and things, all we have is what we observe, but if we understand the leap that we're forced to make over the gap separating what we see from what we believe, we can recognise when we're doing it – and consider the possibilities that we might not have noticed.

One type of question that illustrates our tendency not to think inductively is this: what's the cause of success at school? Why is it that some people do better at school than others? What secret factor might influence our ability to get to the top of the class?

If you scour recent decades of SAT scores, an interesting pattern emerges that shows a connection between the students who outperformed others in tests of reading, writing and mathematics, and those who studied one particular subject. In 2008, the average scores of students taking this class were higher than those of any other in both reading and writing, and when it came to maths, they came second, only behind those who studied physics. There's one subject that seems to offer its students not just better marks in that subject, but in the others too: Latin. But why?

One often-suggested explanation draws our attention back to the unavoidable position of language at the centre of almost everything that we do. The roots of many English words, especially those considered to be part of a higher register – 'excavate' instead of 'dig', 'subterranean' instead of 'underground' or 'vocation' instead of 'job' – come from Latin. The building blocks of so many words in academic, scientific and literary vocabularies are their Latin roots, and if you recognise the ingredients out of which these words are made, you can begin to see words in a completely new light. Students who know that *sub* means 'under' and *terra* means 'ground' aren't just less likely to forget what 'subterranean' means because they see the parts as well as the whole: they will also be able to guess the meaning of words like submarine, subtext, sublet, subconscious, subprime, subhuman, terrestrial, territory or terrarium.

Alongside the idea that Latin can transform our English vocabulary is the suggestion that it reveals things about English grammar too. Learning any second language helps us to see things in the grammar of our native language that we don't notice – but Latin is particularly special. Latin has an unusually rich system of verbs and nouns that English mostly avoids by having a relatively rigid word order. Take English verbs, for example. We say 'I go', but also 'you go', 'we go' and 'they go'. Latin, on the other hand, uses not only pronouns (I, you, we, they) but a rich system of verbs too: what in English is 'go', 'go', 'go', 'go' is, in Latin, '*eo*', '*is*', '*imus*' and '*eunt*'. Every language solves the problems of communication in a different way, but some of them showcase more variety than others. Latin doesn't just make use of a wide range of grammatical structures; it makes its grammar visible. Whether it's the case system, the subjunctive mood or the conjugation of verbs, Latin sentences are puzzles with all the clues on the outside. English is the designer of the language world: it hides the structure beneath the surface and presents a clean exterior. Latin is the architect: it forces us to see the structure because you can't speak Latin without it. The grammatical complexity that Latin forces us to understand hones our appreciation of grammatical structure in general, and, perhaps, it teaches us to see what we might otherwise not have noticed in our mother tongue.

Finally, apart from the linguistic advantages that Latin offers, there's the idea that classical culture is central to Western culture: that reading Roman authors gives Latin students some advantage in the understanding of key ideas that have obsessed the Western world since the time of the Greeks. You might find this final explanation more far-fetched than the first two. It's possible you don't buy any of them or that you can think of other intrinsic reasons why, of all the subjects we could study, the one that connects generally high-achievers is Latin. But there's one explanation that's always worth considering: that no matter how strong the connection between studying Latin and generally good results appears to be, it may not be Latin itself that contributes to better grades at all. While we search for reasons to do with Latin, we miss a deeper explanation revealed by our modern distillation of the problem of induction: the warning that *correlation is not causation*.

Two Simple Rules of Induction to Keep in Mind

A useful idea is a versatile idea, and this idea – that *correlation is not causation* – is endlessly versatile. When Aristotle discovered the difference between a fallible and an infallible sign, he noticed that fallible signs come in two different versions, and that together, they're enough to change the way we think about the nature of events, people, and things. If we could boil down all the concepts we've looked at that explain inductive thinking into two rules to keep in mind, they would be these:

> RULE 1: Just because A *goes with* B, it doesn't mean that A causes B.
>
> RULE 2: Just because A *happened before* B, it doesn't mean that A causes B.

It doesn't matter whether we're talking about how to spot an adulterer or how to work out what causes great test results: our minds have a tendency to connect things that are not always connected in the way that we think. These two rules are important to bear in mind: they remind us of the inherent uncertainty of trying to leap from correlation to causation.

The notion that Latin causes us to become better at other subjects is a perfect example. Imagine two different schools: one in a wealthy part of the country and another in a deprived inner-city community. At the first school, the children's parents earn more money. These parents are more likely to have a college education, to read for pleasure and to have books at home. Their homes are more likely to be quiet, spacious and comfortable. The teachers at this school are paid more, have more experience and enjoy smaller class sizes, the right equipment and better facilities. Given the reputation of Latin – that august language of Roman poets and statesmen, scientists and philosophers – which of the two schools do you think is more likely to offer Latin? I would wager it's the first.

If you were to line up all the students in the country by combined test scores for maths, reading and writing, and then ask them to raise their hand if they study Latin, you'd notice that the closer to the top of the class you get, the more Latin students there are. This is the connection that our minds can't help but notice. There *is* a correlation between studying Latin and doing well in other subjects: they *go together*. But rule 1 – just because A goes with B does not mean that A causes B – reminds us not to believe that this tells us anything about whether Latin *causes* its students to become generally smarter and get better test results.

It's far more likely that those students who outperform the others do so not because they study Latin, but because they go to a school that provides what's truly essential for success. What causes better grades is well-financed schools full of children who have the time, support and equipment they need. The weight of connections that suggests the decisive cause isn't between Latin and good grades; it's between Latin and expensive or selective schools.

Our problem is that our minds see the connections between all sorts of things, and when we can think of reasons that could plausibly explain those connections, we perceive them as being powerful and causative. To see how this works in our Latin example, imagine what would happen if you stood in front of that line of students and asked them to raise their hand if they wore a tie at school. What you'd find would be similar to the connection that exists between Latin and good results (the better the student's grades, the more likely he or she is to wear a tie), but would this mean that wearing a tie makes you smarter?

Wearing a tie is correlated with good performance – it's a sign of generally good grades – but for reasons that have nothing to do with intelligence or the mind: the more expensive or selective the school, the more likely you are to be made to wear a tie. When the example is ties rather than Latin, we notice that connection doesn't always equal causation, but only because we can't think of reasons why wearing a tie would make you smarter.

The concept that underpins both rules is the leap over the inductive gap – the space between the connections we notice and the theories that we make from those connections. Sometimes it's not completely clear whether we are talking about an *event* or a *property*; Latin classes are *events*, but together they add up to a *property* for the students: having a knowledge of Latin. But we don't have to get lost in philosophical musings about the nature of events and properties because the way we theorise about both of them is fundamentally the same and can be captured by the two simple rules mentioned above.

What prompts us to think of powerful abstract ideas like fallible and infallible signs at the right moment is still something of a mystery, but the two simple rules of induction work together to create the possibility of seeing the world in a more sceptical way. By having a small vocabulary of powerful concepts with the potential to connect every example, we get the opportunity to develop an internal alarm bell that makes it possible to snap out of the mind's groove of semi-automatic thinking. Suggestions like 'think again', 'pause for thought' or 'think harder' are too vague to make a difference to our ability to see what we used to miss, but if we can develop a strong understanding of what the ingredients of a concept like induction are – including all of the slightly technical but concrete parts: *fallible* and *infallible signs*, *universal rules* and *particular examples* – there is a far better chance that we'll recognise them no matter which real-life situations of theory-making we find ourselves in. If a clear understanding of the two rules exists somewhere in our minds, then there's a far better chance that any mention of *causes*, *events* and *properties* will trigger a cautionary thought: that induction is always a kind of leap over a gap that we can never bridge for certain.

Backwards Thinking and Superstition

The automatic way that we misread patterns is the root of mindless superstition. It's the reason I've stopped wearing my team's shirt to watch their matches. For the last three big matches that I wore the shirt, my team lost. No matter what I think about induction, connections, patterns or any other abstract idea, when it comes to choosing to wear or not wear the shirt, all I can think about is the disappointment of those games.

Emotion, just as it can be harnessed by rhetoric to cloud our judgment, can itself harness our mind's over-enthusiasm for patterns. The more emotional we get – the more we worry about or care about a particular issue or outcome – the more easily we accept any connection that's thrown our way or that our mind produces for us. There are many athletes who firmly believe in the power of a lucky charm they wore during a past sporting success. If we had a lucky charm the last time around, and we ended up winning, then something tells us we should keep it with us next time too. We believe in the causative power of things even when we admit we have no explanation for them. The connection alone can be enough to give us confidence. Failing to examine things too closely can serve a purpose, but it brings us equal amounts of trouble too. It's only a short step from lucky-charm superstition and football-shirt paranoia to the suspicion and even hatred of entire groups of people.

Depending on the colour of people's skin, country of birth, class, religion and other factors, our minds make suggestions about *what people are like.* The initial judgements we make about the individuals we meet aren't based on that one person; they're a statistical collage of impressions of other people from the past. So when you see a hooded teenager on the train, your impression of what they might be like is built out of the echoes of every other hooded teenager you've experienced, not from anything that has to do with the one sitting in front of you. A friend who's an editor at a publishing house recently told me that he'd approached the desk of an editorial colleague he'd never met before to discuss a book, only to be asked a question completely out of context: about his fellow worker's computer. He soon worked out what had happened. His colleague thought he was from the IT department – because of the colour of his skin.

Let me be clear. I'm not saying that this judgement of probability is either unreasonable or, in the strongest sense of the word, racist. We use the word 'racism' to cover offence that is caused by different degrees of conscious thought – ranging from shamelessly deliberate to thoughtlessly accidental. The *Oxford English Dictionary* defines prejudice as 'preconceived opinion that is not based on reason or actual experience', but while the judgements of probability that we make can be based on both those things, they can also still offend – and we owe it to each other to make the effort to avoid offence. We owe it to each other to be sensitive to the effect of the way that we interact, to put in the mental effort and to learn from experience.

If you were a woman called Jamie who travels a lot on business, though, you wouldn't be surprised, every time you enter the arrivals terminal at an airport, to be met with a confused look on the face of the taxi driver as they expectantly scan the men walking behind you and appear not to have noticed you at all. You'd accept that they were expecting a Jamie, that a Jamie is usually male, and that they made a judgement based on reasonable past experience. Judging people and things based on what we remember of other people and things is just the way our minds work. We've all made these sorts of assumptions for that very reason.

When Aristotle explained that smartly dressed men who wander about at night appear to be prime suspects for the detective looking for adulterers, he foreshadowed a 21st-century warning about the power of similarity to convince us to focus our attention on one factor alone. Whenever we turn on the television and are exposed to one particular feature of the political situation at the beginning of the 21st-century – a confrontation between one interpretation of Islamic belief and the forces that it considers inimical to its way of life – we make a connection between political violence and the Islamic religion as a whole. Every time we see this connection, it's reinforced, but what we don't always notice as we pile up these connections is that we've seen only the tiniest fraction of the whole. Just as with the Latin we could easily believe is directly correlated with success, we see a single factor, not a complex of related causes and effects. We easily make a judgement about the whole from just a part, and overlook the causes that bring all humans closer to political violence: economic stagnation, hunger, poverty, lack of opportunity, injustice and inequality.

We don't need to reverse-engineer our observations into theories about what's true with the precision of a detailed mathematical model. What we need is a basic set of alarm bells to remind us that we misread the world because our minds are suckers for a pattern. Understanding the principle of induction doesn't solve the inherent problems of having to work out general rules from an incomplete set of examples. What it does do, though, is to put the unchanging nature of the way we think front and centre. It trains us to recognise those problems and gives us the tools to deal with them.

We know from experience that appearances deceive and that the assumptions we make about people and things can turn out to be both wrong and embarrassing. We know about the dangers of 'stereotyping' and 'generalising', and we're familiar with the notion of 'jumping to conclusions'. But because we don't see *how* we do it and because we can't *point to* or *talk about* the detail of what's true and why, we're left with good intentions but a deficit of the concrete ideas that help us to carry them out. It's not always possible to convince people that their assumptions about entire groups of people can be founded on nothing more than casual observations. But if we could see *how* we arrived at the theories we stand by, see that this way of thinking is inherent in the human mind, and learn to doubt the connections that our minds make, we can all reap the rewards. We could be less superstitious, slower to accept one factor as 'the' one before searching for others, and far harder to persuade that the connections we make say as much about what's true as we think they do. When we understand how often, how automatically and *why* we misread the world, we get the chance to see it clearly for ourselves.

Analogy: A Sign of Genius

Simple Comparisons, Simple Labels

Seeing the similarity or the difference between one thing and another could save your life. If someone cut the poisonous red mushroom down the middle, you wouldn't believe that one half was dangerous while the other half was safe – after all, the two halves are from the *same* mushroom. What's more, you'd probably feel no safer about eating a red mushroom that you came across a mile further into the forest: a different mushroom, but of exactly the *same type*. But what happens when the similarities start to disappear?

Would you eat a red mushroom that was noticeably smaller than the ones you suspect are poisonous, or a red mushroom of a different shape? What if the mushroom wasn't red all over, but was covered in red spots: still worried? What if your potential lunch wasn't a mushroom at all? If you had to choose between eating a red or a green frog, would you stay away from the red one because of the red mushrooms? It's not even the same type of thing as a mushroom, but it is red, and the last thing you ate that was red made you sick ...

When similarity starts to break down – when the things we try to understand have less in common with the things we already know about – it becomes harder for us to make judgements about them. But even when we're talking about completely different things, just one sliver of similarity can make us think again. There's something about similarity that sticks in our minds.

Similarity is what allows us to connect one situation to another. Though we do it so naturally that we tend not to notice, comparison drives the way we think. We use it to describe things, to understand and explain them, and, crucially, to argue about them too. When you try to justify your conclusions about what's going on in the world, you compare things, and so does everyone else. 'This situation is just like that situation,' people say. 'If that was wrong then this is wrong,' they cry. Without similarity we couldn't apply what we learned in one place to anything else. After all, if the future wasn't like the past, if one set of affairs had no similarity to any another, how could we learn anything from the lives we've lived?

But is the past always a good guide to the future? When is what we know of one thing a good guide to another? And how does similarity tie everything together? As Aristotle told Alexander, both the way we work out what's true and the way that we argue revolve around our ability to compare things. Arguments are, very often, a battle of comparison. Of all the things we can do with our mind, it's the skill that each of us has for seeing what two things have in common that Aristotle tells us is, above all else, 'a sign of genius'.

⌒

How much comparison would you say you get up to during the average day? To put it another way, what do a train network, a washing machine and Usain Bolt have in common? For one thing, they all 'run'. We say, 'What's that noise? Is the washing machine running?' or 'Are the trains running today, despite the weather?' Running, when it usually comes to mind, is something human beings do – it's movement powered by legs. Trains and washing machines are very obviously different from Usain Bolt; they are entirely without legs, but that difference doesn't appear to hold us back. Despite their not having the one thing we usually think of as absolutely necessary for running – legs – we still happily say that that's exactly what trains and washing machines do. Different things power them, but the result is the same: movement. Just one similarity is enough for us to call different things by the same name, and we do it all the time.

Curries don't have hands or feet, but we still sometimes describe a spicy one as having 'a serious kick' or being 'punchy'. When someone tells you a truth you might not have wanted to hear, they don't physically touch you, and yet we say that those words were 'the kick up the backside that we needed' – just as Socrates says that a good argument feels like being 'punched in the face'. What all these things have in common is the effect they produce: shock.

Chillies and human language are very obviously different things, and neither of them has much in common with feet. They're not made from the same stuff, they don't look the same, and they don't cause shock in the same way. But they do have one thing in common, and just one island of common ground in a vast ocean of differences is all we need. Despite the over-whelming differences between two things, the human mind is brilliant at seeing just a single element of similarity and using it to describe them both. There's a subtle and quite brilliant play of echoes just beneath the surface of the way we speak, but Aristotle's aim wasn't to make Alexander into a professor of linguistics or psychology. His aim was to show Alexander how similarity isn't just a way of describing; it can also be the battlefield on which arguments are won and lost.

Where, then, does a lesson in comparison begin? It starts with the simple simile, and the slightly more tricky metaphor – before swiftly moving on to the good stuff: ***analogy***.

Just as an English teacher who's more interested in showing you how to use ideas rather than simply labelling them might do, Aristotle warns us not to worry too much about the difference between a metaphor and a simile. He says that they're 'really the same thing except for the difference mentioned' – the difference often being the word 'like'. Sometimes we say that one thing is 'like' something else, and sometimes we say that it 'is' that thing. We don't just say that someone is 'like' a pig; we can also say that they 'are' a pig. Most of the time, these simple comparisons are more or less straightforward descriptions; they're a code that everyone knows. Depending on the context, to say that someone is a pig, or like a pig is really just a more colourful way of saying that they're messy, dirty, rude, or greedy.

When we use comparisons to describe things, we don't often run into problems because the outstanding feature that we're trying to label someone with – the *essential* feature – is usually agreed on by most people and understood. We might say that Aristotle was 'an Einstein', and everyone knows that this doesn't mean that he was German, Jewish, or the owner of a white bushy moustache. What it means is that he was clever. To be 'an Einstein', you could be from any conceivable country, an adherent of any religion, and you could even be a pig.

These comparisons can be controversial, but only because people object to being used as the archetypal example of something that's often some sort of insult – in the way that pigs might if they were aware we used them as a shorthand for dirty. If you have an occasionally grumpy friend called David, and you say to another friend of yours: 'stop doing a David', David objects because, understandably, he doesn't want to be used as a synonym for occasional grumpiness. On the other hand, this works in reverse too, because our character traits are often – metaphorically – a double-edged sword. When someone brightens your day by producing, as a result of their grumpiness, an acerbic and witty character assassination, you might also say: 'that's so David', and make a comparison while also paying your friend a compliment.

Whenever you make a comparison between something that your audience recognises as a standard example for a particular attribute, there's rarely any confusion. That said, there can also be offence, or even comedy. If one person says: 'well, Matthew's son is quite the Einstein isn't he?', you're missing the point if you reply: 'yeah, what's up with his awful moustache and enormous head?' This sort of mishap of thinking isn't a big deal. Most comparisons are so straightforward that everyone knows what you mean and laughs if you don't. That one feature that everyone recognises shines so brightly in our minds that we may as well have just said 'dirty' or 'clever' instead of 'pig' or 'Einstein'.

Most of the time, the comparisons of simile and metaphor are relatively simple. Every culture has a large repertoire of people or things with an attribute that is mutually understood to be quintessential, and which is used to describe other people or things. This 'code' is usually so well understood that our minds 'translate': from 'lion' to 'brave' or from 'mouse' to 'coward' automatically and instantly. The everyday metaphor and simile require little, if any, conscious or effortful thought.

In so far as everyone understands their culture's metaphorical code, it is a direct and clear way of describing things that causes us few problems. But not all comparisons are so straightforward. When we use similarity not just to describe, but to argue too, things become more complicated, more easily misunderstood and more controversial.

Complex Comparisons: The Argument from Analogy

When we describe by using a code of comparisons, it usually amounts to nothing more than name-calling. Describing someone with a metaphorical comparison is like walking up to them and sticking a big label on their forehead, except that the label says 'lion' or 'mouse' instead of 'brave' or 'cowardly'. What's important about the simple simile and metaphor is that their descriptions offer little or no 'working out'. To say that someone is brave or cowardly isn't an argument: it's just a statement of what someone claims is true. And the problem with statements is that they tend not to convince anyone who doesn't already agree with them.

When we reason, however, we don't just offer an answer but the working out, too. Instead of merely *saying* that two things are similar in one way, like the straightforward simile and metaphor, an analogy *reasons* that two things are similar in one way *because they are similar in another way*.

Imagine that you're out camping with some friends, and that one of the group has been unlucky enough to cut themselves while trying to chop up some wedges of lime to add to the beers that they were thoughtful enough to bring. It transpires that someone has forgotten to bring a first aid kit, but just as your injured friend begins to panic about the risk of infection, you suddenly remember watching a segment from a television programme that explained the marvellous antiseptic properties of the humble lemon. You don't have any lemons; but you do have some limes ...

The question is not so much what you're thinking about suggesting, but why it occurs to you to suggest it. The answer is *similarity*, but instead of simply using similarity to *say* that limes are antibacterial and antiseptic, you're using similarity to *argue* that it is. Their similarity in one or more ways – their bitter taste, their colourful skin with a white pith or the fact that they're both known as 'citrus' fruits – is what make you wonder if they might be similar in another: having antiseptic properties. An analogy makes judgments about one property that two things might share by considering *the other properties* that they do share.

To understand the pitfalls of analogies as well as their potential, though, it helps to consider the nature of something that's harder to be sure of than the seemingly regular physical properties of physical things. To understand the limits of analogical thinking, we need to apply it not to the simplicity of lemons, but to the somewhat messier problem of human psychology. We need to look at the structure of the most depressing, most routinely facile, and sadly, the most common of analogies: the 'Hitler Analogy'.

In politics especially, but in other types of discussion too, the one comparison someone can draw that will label another person as definitively evil is a comparison to Adolf Hitler. In this context, the essential attribute of Hitler as 'bad' or 'evil' is most strongly derived from his belief that some people should be put to death on the grounds of their race. The Hitler label is one that, if you can make it stick, puts someone into a category from which they can't escape. But how does it work?

The Hitler Analogy uses not essential attributes, but non-essential ones to make its case. To *say* that someone is evil isn't an argument: it's merely a statement. But humans are convinced that what happened in the past is a good guide to what will happen in the future, and so Hitler is used as an example not just of evil itself, but of the *signs* of evil. While it is true that Hitler is overwhelmingly thought of as evil for his policy of racially motivated and systematic genocide, and that this is his essential attribute, he has other attributes too. For example, the Nazi regime, under Hitler's direction, made use of uniforms at all levels of social organisation: in the army, the intelligence services, the Hitler Youth and in other groups too. It encouraged large, organised gatherings of people and the use of songs and slogans. Perhaps the most common image of Hitler is of his public speaking; his shouting into the microphone at well-organised and uniformly dressed crowds marching in choreographed unity and chanting songs and slogans together. So, bearing in mind these attributes of Hitler's Germany, how is the Hitler Analogy put into action?

Imagine that the debate you're having is about some world leader who the person you're arguing with absolutely despises. They can't just label the person in question as 'evil': because that would simply be *saying* that something is true rather than trying to offer any *evidence* for it. So instead, they do it indirectly. They argue like this:

> Have you noticed how the leader has set up a national youth movement? Have you seen them marching in the streets, all in the same uniform? Doesn't the propaganda remind you of anyone? The chanting of slogans is really scary, and those long, shouting speeches ... can't you see the similarity? He/She is just like Hitler.

Just like Hitler: a comparison that's no longer a mere statement, but an argument. Think about how it works. The argument rests on just one example: Hitler himself. It says 'in the example of Hitler, the attribute that I suspect might also be true of the leader in question [the potential or desire for racially motivated genocide] went hand-in-hand with other attributes [support for national youth movements, uniforms, propaganda, chanting, slogans, etc.]. So if you look at this leader, you'll see that their support for any of those other attributes shows that they're hiding other similar attributes, and maybe the one attribute that really matters.'

But ask yourself to what extent this is true. Because we accept that some behaviours and beliefs are reliable signs of other behaviours and beliefs, it's hardly ridiculous to suggest that there's a link between particular attributes and the essential attribute. However, if we accept that this is true, are we not then forced to examine some other non-essential attributes too? Are we not then forced to concede that others who like uniforms, group solidarity, songs, slogans and chanting are also candidates for the embodiment of pure evil – like scout leaders or Buddhist monks? Hitler was known to be passionate about art and animal welfare, and there is evidence that he was vegetarian. It's been said that he felt a greater affinity to certain types of mysticism than to Christianity. But to what extent are any of those attributes a sign of an evil that might stretch to racially motivated genocide? If you met a mystical vegetarian artist with a passion for protecting animals, and someone suggested that sharing so many similarities with such an evil man was a dangerous sign of also advocating genocide, how is this argument different from the first version of the Hitler Analogy?

The Hitler Analogy is more complicated than a simple comparison. It doesn't just say 'Person One is like Hitler'; it's more subtle than that. It's a comparison that's reaching out towards other comparisons, and if it can grab any of them and convince you that those other comparisons are just as true as the first one, then it becomes an argument. If we could put the Hitler Analogy under the microscope of reason in order to make out its internal structure, it would look something like this:

> Hitler believed in A, B and C. And he also believed in D.
>
> Person One believes in A, B and C.
>
> Therefore Person One must be like Hitler, and also believe in D.

A diagram often helps to make the inner workings of our reasoning clear, and this diagram represents the different levels of comparison that make up the internal structure of The Hitler Analogy.

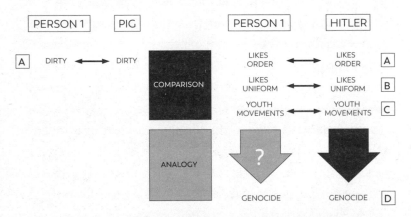

This more detailed comparison – a comparison that says if certain properties or attributes went together in one example, then they also go together in a different example – is an *argument by analogy*. Though we can never be certain that one similarity reveals others, we are always tempted by the analogical consideration that it might do. That's simply how our minds work. This insight into human cognition was put to use by Aristotle when he turned it into a rhetorical strategy: a strategy designed to produce the maximum amount of conviction in your audience. One of the most insightful lines he ever wrote is a golden rule that reveals exactly what gives an analogy its persuasive force: similarity.

> Try to secure admissions by means of likeness; for such admissions are plausible, and the universal involved is less patent.

Any admission that you can extract from the crowd about one or more similarities between two things will get them considering the possibility of other potential similarities. As a general rule, the more likenesses that two people or things share, the more likely they are to share other properties too. It's for that reason that shared properties are taken to be *a sign* of other shared properties.

Just the mention of that word – sign – is no doubt enough to trigger the realisation that analogies work in a similar way to something that you already understand: induction. Fundamentally, analogy is more like induction than deduction because it doesn't start with rules. Both analogy and induction are forced to infer rules from the behaviour and properties of the things that they observe, but while induction tries to draw conclusions from *many or all examples* in order to make a rule, an analogy only tries to make a conclusion from *one example*. Induction moves from many examples to a rule; analogies move from one example to a rule, and then they apply that rule to another example.

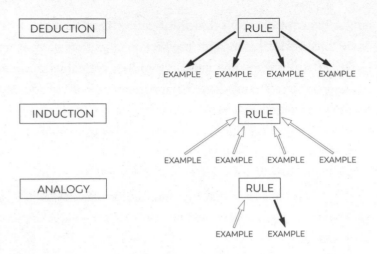

In a perfect world, induction would line up *every* example: it strives to be universal. Analogy, on the other hand, is bolder. Analogy tries to make a rule out of just one example – one that we suppose to be particularly instructive and revelatory. Induction is supported by a number of cases, but analogy rests its substantial weight on a single archetypal example.

When Aristotle said that likenesses – the similarities between two things – make 'the universal less patent', he meant that by presenting just one example that is teeming with detailed similarities, the number of examples that we've drawn on becomes less obvious, and as a result, the comparison seems more persuasive. In order to draw attention away from the fact that analogies don't make use of a great number of examples, it pays to point out as many likenesses as you can.

What differentiates a good analogy from a bad one is often not the number of similarities, though, but whether they are *significant*. A bad analogy tries to make you focus on some element of likeness. It says, 'Look how similar these two situations are!' Aristotle's response is to say, 'I can see you want me to focus on the similarity of the particular example you've given, but what *exactly* is that similarity, and does it mean anything?'

When we decide to support or oppose a decision to go to war, we claim some sort of rule – perhaps that fighting your neighbours ends badly – but these rules are ultimately based on examples that make for better evidence the more similar they are to the situation at hand. If we want to argue that fighting your neighbours ends badly, 'conviction of this is obtained from similar cases, e.g. that the war against the Phoceans was an evil to the Thebans.' In Aristotle's day, they argued about whether past wars could teach them about potential future ones just as we do, but what hasn't changed is that the path (from the examples we cite to the rules we claim to be true) is still just as difficult to navigate. We might well argue that war A was bad and therefore war B is bad, but how comparable are the political, social, economic and historical circumstances? Is it really as simple as listing examples of wars that we think were worth it against the ones that weren't?

A sophist's task is to point out the similarities between two examples so that what's true of the first will appear to reveal a lot about the second. But the weakness of arguing from individual examples lies in the distance that separates them from a general rule. A sophist doesn't want to get into a discussion about whether a love of uniforms is generally or universally a sign of an evil disposition; what they want is for you to stay focused on the one memorable example of when it was. The difference between Aristotle and a sophist is that Aristotle *wants* to discuss the difficult journey from experience to working out what might generally or universally be true, and he wants to discuss the fact that many similarities aren't significant. What Aristotle asks us to do when we compare is to question the weight of evidence and ask whether the similarities we notice are deep and significant, or superficial and misleading.

The likenesses that we notice between one thing and another make all sorts of patterns and theories occur to us, but these patterns very easily deceive. We are so attuned to similarity, and so convinced by it, that it can be hard to see the fact that examples sometimes reveal very little. The detail of the similarities between different examples is what is truly revealing – but our minds love likeness. When the most important of topics makes our blood boil, it's easier to play spot the similarity than it is to make a balanced comparison. Isolated and superficial similarities are easier to find than deep and enduring relationships. When our attention is drawn to one shiny example that appears to offer us insight, it can seduce us into forgetting the wider picture. But just as the alarm bells should go off when we come across the tricks of deduction, we can start to notice the difference in the weight and significance of the comparisons that make for the best and the worst analogies. We can learn to look, instinctively, not just for the reasons why what we already know can tell us things about what we don't, but also why it might not tell us very much at all.

Whether we're thinking our own way to a picture of what's going on in the world, or trying to convince others to agree with us, we often make sense of things by comparing them to other, sometimes incomparable things. This is how we understand the world. This spotting of similarities – and the guessing at the potentially deeper connections they might or might not reveal – is how we think inductively and analogically. It's how we arrive at our own theories about how the world works, and just as we compare when we search for the truth, we compare when we argue for it too.

Aristotle's greatest achievement was not so much to have whispered *The Truth* into history's ear; it was to have conveyed something fundamental and unchanging about the road to truth. Aristotle's unique vision of education isn't a cheat-sheet with *The Answers*; it's an introduction to the eternal structures of human thought. The psychological understanding and insight that his mind managed to carve out of the rock of its own experience made a new type of education possible for all the minds that would follow. Aristotle's philosophy of education promises us an introduction to *the unchanging ways that we think and argue*, and it alone is what reveals the inner workings of the mind that are the foundation of everything that we believe to be true.

Real-Life Analogy

Metaphors, similes and analogies aren't some special way of communicating. Almost every sentence we utter is packed with comparisons, but because comparison is so fundamental and automatic, we're often not even aware that we're doing it. When someone describes a person who is preventing something from happening as 'a roadblock', we don't need even a second's pause to 'see' (which is itself a metaphor) what they mean. Comparison isn't like arithmetic: it requires almost no mental effort. Analogical thinking – the essential process of comparison that unites similes, metaphors and analogies – is one of the default modes of the human mind. It is central to the way we describe and explain the world, the way we understand it, and the way we want other people to understand it.

When we describe one thing in terms of another – a person as a roadblock, a hurdle, a headwind, a bottleneck, a drag, a pain in the neck or a cancer – we're painting our own subtle picture of reality. We choose our comparisons carefully, because while the above examples are all joined by the fact that they are unwanted and that they slow progress, they each have *other connotations*. While both of them impede progress, a bottleneck slows things down while a roadblock brings them to a halt. To compare someone to cancer is to say far more than to call them a pain in the neck.

When Walt Whitman wrote 'whoever walks a furlong without sympathy walks to his own funeral, dressed in his shroud', he pointed out the similarity between the emotional separation of having no sympathy for others with the worst separation of all – death. But is the absence of sympathy quite the same thing as the absence of life itself? Is a lack of feeling for other people an emotional blanket that wraps itself around us and isolates us like a shroud? Perhaps not exactly, but it makes us stop and think. Analogical thinking is how we describe things in new ways – as we do in the metaphors of poetry or song-writing – but we use analogies to do more than find new poetic colour. Analogies are what we use to make out and argue for different philosophical, scientific and political visions of the world. We use comparisons as the basis of strong claims about what is true.

There is no clear dividing line between similes, metaphors and analogies; what sets them apart is the complexity that's in our comparisons of two things, two people or two situations. What's important to have though, is not a fine taxonomy but a functional anatomy. What's important is not the names we give to each comparison, but our ability to make and interrogate those comparisons in the course of our daily lives. As Aristotle puts it, 'The greatest thing by far is to be a master of metaphor.' He could just as easily have used 'analogy' instead of 'metaphor' – what matters is that it is 'a sign of genius, since a good metaphor implies an intuitive perception of the similarities in dissimilars'.

A sharp eye for subtle similarities and crucial differences is how we make sense of the present. It's how what we know and what we have already experienced is brought to bear on the novel, the unfamiliar and the strange. Every echo that comes to us when we try to interpret the situations that life presents us with – the echoes of someone or something that we know, or an event that we have lived through – is an opportunity to see it in a new way. Analogy is the creator of possibilities.

Aristotle saw that thought-provoking comparisons were the product of a sharp mind that considered what seemingly unconnected things have in common. The ability to see subtle differences and similarities is central to intelligence because so much of the way we interrogate, describe, argue and explain is analogical in nature. If we can sharpen our awareness of this fundamental mode of human thinking, we get the chance to see the structures of comparison at the heart of our own understanding of the world, and we get to make up our own minds about whether the analogies we're bombarded with are illuminating visions of reality or manipulative illusions.

⌒

What's often crucial in interrogating the quality of metaphors, similes and analogies is the significance of the similarities that they rely on. Two things can very easily share properties, but not every shared property is significant. Take, for example, an analogy made by the former governor of Alaska, Sarah Palin. The fiscally conservative Palin, speaking at a fundraising event in Iowa, controversially compared foreign debt to slavery.

Referring to the national debt – and, specifically, borrowing from China – she said:

> When that money comes due – and this isn't racist – but it'll be like slavery when that note is due. We are going to be beholden to the foreign master.

When someone makes an analogy between two things, the first step in interrogation is to ask yourself 'in what ways are they the same?' and 'in what ways are they different?'. To start with the former: what comes to mind when you hear the word 'slavery'? At the centre of the concept is, unquestionably, some denial of freedom. You could be a *freed* slave, but not a *free* slave. In so far as you are a slave, you cannot be free.

So what point of similarity can be found between this minimal definition of slavery as the denial of freedom and the concept of debt? One answer is that being in debt presents you with an 'opportunity cost': being obliged to pay back a debt means that you cannot spend that money in another way. In so far as paying back debt is an obligation that must be met, and an obligation to repay a debt means having less freedom to spend, debt does restrict freedom.

Palin, however, didn't compare debt to 'restricting freedom'. She compared it to slavery – and this is where the differences become more apparent than the similarities. Slavery, unlike debt, doesn't restrict your financial freedom. It *wholly denies* rather than *restricts*, and it wholly denies *every aspect* of your freedom.

Exaggerated comparisons like this one can be interrogated in classic Socratic fashion: by assuming that the person is correct and seeing what follows that cannot be true. If slavery is really no different to being in debt, it follows that Palin would be just as unhappy being enslaved as she would be were she in debt. If debt is slavery, then is lending slave-owning? If American banks lend money to foreign companies, does that make them slave masters? If you borrow money from a bank to expand your business, would you describe yourself as 'in slavery'? The weakness of analogies that grab more argumentative ground than they are entitled to is that the ground is often impossible to defend. Far better to attack only the ground you can reasonably hold, and avoid having to make a public retreat.

Very often, the quality of an analogy can depend on a question of language because of the differences in the connotations of words in different forms. If Palin had said 'we don't want to *become a slave to* debt repayment', she would have aroused less controversy. In the same way that someone might point out an imbalance of benefits and obligations in their work – by saying something like 'I think that I've become a slave to the job' – the metaphor 'to be a slave to' doesn't contain all of the connotations of the word 'slavery'. Especially in the American context, 'slavery' brings to mind particular places, particular people and the echoes thereof. There is an art to wording comparisons in a way that removes as many incidental properties from the analogical table as possible. The more options we leave on the table, the greater the risk of misinterpretation. When only the comparisons that we really want to communicate are the ones we bring into view, we make the precision of our thinking more apparent, and open to far fewer opportunities for misunderstanding.

Another way that we use analogy is to try to help us to understand the nature of large and complicated systems or concepts. When it comes to the workings of entities like time, space or society, we constantly resort to comparisons in order to understand. We might speculate that the things we know to be true of electromagnetic force might also be true of other forces, like gravity, or that what's true of population dynamics for an animal like a squirrel might tell us something about population dynamics in humans. Most of us don't have enough specialist knowledge to judge just how deep these sort of analogies are and we don't worry too much about it, but there is one large and unwieldy entity that everyone does care about, and whose workings are a perennial topic of political debate: the economy.

An analogy that explains the nature of debt in a different way to Palin's is one that was made popular by the German Chancellor Angela Merkel, and it is known as the 'Swabian Housewife Analogy'. The Swabians, one of Germany's traditional tribes as well as a modern-day cultural and linguistic group hailing from the country's southwest, have a reputation for thrift. The Swabian housewife is a cultural stereotype of frugality, and the particularly Swabian trait of spending little and saving a lot is perhaps only a more exaggerated incarnation of a general German suspicion of debt (the German word for debt is 'schulden', and the word for guilt/shame is 'schuld'). As Max Weber observed, this suspicion of spending and enthusiasm for saving is born of Germany's Protestant roots, but whatever the origin of this model of how to run a household, it is the centrepiece of Mrs Merkel's analogy about how to run an economy.

In 2008, after the collapse of Lehman Brothers, Mrs Merkel gave a speech in which she explained that 'one should simply have asked the Swabian housewife ... she would have told us that you cannot live beyond your means'. This analogy rests on the likeness between an individual household and a country's economy: it says that in the same way that spending more than you earn spells disaster for an individual household, it spells disaster for an economy too. On the surface of things, this principle is immediately understandable to any child who has ever owned a piggy bank. Even a squirrel that eats more nuts than it collects knows that this strategy is a dangerous one. Or is it?

The problem with the analogy of the Swabian housewife is that her household, while it shares some similarities with the economy as a whole, also has a number of crucial differences. First, the housewife only has to think about her own household, but what works for one household may not work if everyone does it: the strategy of the individual may not produce the best result for the economy as a whole. Second, it is far easier for governments to borrow, and to borrow at lower rates of interest than it is for a household. Lastly (though it isn't the only remaining difference), households don't typically borrow in order to invest and produce more value in the way that governments do. The opportunities for a household to invest in order to produce a net increase in value – say, by adding an extension to your home – are limited in comparison to the opportunities for net growth through investment that are available to a national government. Households simply don't borrow and invest in the same way that national economies do.

The Swabian Housewife Analogy is, in truth, a weak one. The value of any analogy lies in the depth and significance of the similarities between the things it compares. While, in the case of the Swabian Housewife Analogy, the similarity of having more leaving your pockets than entering them certainly holds in part, it ignores the differences between the economy of a country and the economy of a household, Swabian or otherwise. I don't doubt that Mrs Merkel's understanding of economics is more profound than the simplicity of her analogy would have us believe, but convincing voters to understand the world in your way involves getting them to accept your analogies even when they simplify its complexity.

The problem with the Swabian Housewife Analogy is that of all rhetorical analogies: they point out similarities without being too precise about what that similarity is, or indeed, about any differences that might remain. For an analogy to be precise and helpful, it has to highlight which element of likeness is the important one, and to be as clear as it can that it's not reaching out in an attempt to grab any other likenesses or connotations.

Analogies, when precisely crafted, can be powerful tools for making clear what is important in the way that we understand complex systems. While fiscal conservatives bemoan high public spending, those who are fiscally liberal object to low public spending – what has come to be known as 'austerity'. In the course of debates about the merits or the problems of austerity, I've heard an argument put forward that calls out for a precise and clarifying analogy, and which illustrates its value. The argument was this: the fact that the national debt is going up shows that austerity cannot be working.

To make the case in mathematical language leaves us cold – and for those not familiar with it, both cold and none the wiser. To say something like 'the debt is still rising, but rising at a slower rate' asks us to make sense of rates and ratios, but there is a vivid analogy that makes the same comparison without any technical language. In the same way that an ocean liner heading towards the rocks at great speed can fire up its engines and begin to thrust itself away from them, neither an economy nor a ship immediately changes direction. Like an ocean liner, an economy is a large and complicated entity, and the forces that act on it take time to produce an effect. Having engaged reverse thrust and feeling a wave of relief as the ship begins to slow down, we'd be confident that the continued movement towards the rocks was not a sign that engaging reverse thrust was the wrong thing to do. In the same way that the principle of inertia works for ships, it illustrates the nature of economies too.

A good analogy clearly and precisely draws our attention to a likeness that matters between two situations or things: the similarity that gives us real insight into the way things work and the way things are. The problem with analogies is that when we compare two things, it isn't always clear which likeness is being drawn. Very often, when politicians use analogies to persuade, their strategy is to leave as many unpleasant connections on the analogical table as possible. That way, if you generally agree with what the politician believes, you can take your pick from any elements of the comparison that appeal to you and your way of seeing the world. So when a demagogic politician calls immigrants 'rats that sneak through the border', the ability to pass unnoticed is being highlighted in the foreground, but the rats' supposed lack of hygiene and the fear we have of things that scuttle is what's hanging around in the background. The line between metaphorical language and analogical argument is thin, because it's never clear exactly which parallels we're making. When a politician argues that having no border fence is like leaving the front door of your house open, we should be able to point out which parts of the analogy are weak and which are strong. Yes, it is true that a fenced border prevents unwanted visitors in the way that a closed front door protects the inhabitants of a house, but is your front door 2,000 miles wide?

Finally, in order to see that our collective skill in pointing out the structure of comparisons – and especially those that create the most social and political controversy – is not as finely honed as we imagine, I must briefly return to the most common and tiresome analogy of all: the Hitler Analogy. In the same way that we have a *sense* of when we're being presented with an illogical deductive or inductive argument, but not always the precise understanding that allows us to point out the argument's structure and publicly reveal its weak points with a well-placed explanation, so it is with analogies.

In 2016, a former mayor of London made a comparison to Hitler that raised a lot of controversy. He said: 'Let's remember when Hitler won his election in 1932, his policy then was that Jews should be moved to Israel. He was supporting Zionism.' Many claimed that these words – 'He was supporting Zionism' – were offensive, to the extent that the former mayor was suspended from his political party. But few were able to point out why they were offensive. The basis of his defence of his comments was his claim that he was factually correct – that Hitler *had* made early efforts to move the Jews to Israel – but those facts are irrelevant.

To be a Zionist is to believe that the Jews have some sort of right or even a duty to live in Israel. If you are a Zionist, then it follows you'll be in favour of moving the Jews to Israel – but it isn't the desire to move the Jews itself that makes you a Zionist. Imagine that you run a country, and that you dislike an entire group of people to the extent that you want to deport them. You could claim that you're 'supporting' the people themselves, since they too might like to be somewhere else, but while you share the same policy objective – them leaving your country and ending up somewhere else – crucially, you couldn't claim that you're doing it for the same reasons. You couldn't claim in good conscience that you were a 'supporter' of their cause. The truth is that sharing a policy objective – the moving of German

Jews – has nothing intrinsically to do with supporting Zionism. Both Zionists and Hitler may share the property of wanting to move people, but that doesn't mean that they must also share the property of wanting to move them for the same reasons. The politician in question pointed out a superficial similarity that was supposed to prove an intrinsic one, and that is the fuel of weak analogies.

The problem with not being able to succinctly point out how an argument works is that it allows rhetoricians to protect themselves with irrelevant defences. The debate about the former mayor's comments rumbled on for years with little clarity as he continued to try and draw attention away from the analogy itself and towards the factual truth of the similarity it was based on – but in the same way that we can combine two absolutely true statements in an illogical way and end up with nonsense, the truth or falsity of any likeness that analogies are based on can be completely irrelevant.

The depressing ubiquity of comparisons to Hitler – or their variations, which compare things to the Third Reich, the Gestapo or other entities of Nazism – is enshrined in what's known as Godwin's Law, which states that the longer a debate on the internet rages, the more likely it is that a comparison to Hitler will be made. That is just a hyperbolic way of saying that if someone is likely to compare you to anything when they're angry or upset, it's Hitler. It's so common precisely because of that urge, when we want to win an argument that we really care about, to say the most hurtful or extreme thing. It comes to mind when we're backed into a corner and are desperately trying to conjure a daring argument that we believe will win the debate there and then with one fatal blow. The surge of emotion we feel when we're about to lose our grip on a debate causes us to become desperate. That is the emotional energy that fuels Godwin's Law, but the reason why the fires of public debate *continue* to burn is our public lack of understanding – and therefore our lack of ability to point out and explain to each other the parts of an argument that don't add up.

Overcoming our anger is a lofty, perhaps divine goal that's out of reach. What is eminently reachable, though, is a public understanding of one the most basic forms of facile and dishonest argument. Being able to see – in your mind's eye – the structure of the argument that you're offered is what allows you to test the solidity of its construction. A smart inductive thinker asks how many individual examples you used to make a universal rule and looks for exceptions. A smart analogical thinker asks whether the similarities between the examples that analogies connect are really significant – they look for differences. Were we all better at exposing the shallow comparisons that fuel not just political disagreements but other kinds too, how much more incentive would there be to argue with balance and honesty?

Modern politics suffers from a dearth of attention to the nature of comparisons. A stretched comparison – one where the similarities are frayed – always sounds good in the head of the person making it, but it usually amounts to little more than simplistic posturing. In an era of increasingly acrimonious politics there is plenty of incentive to excessively demonise those with whom we disagree. We shouldn't accuse – in a facile manner – those whose politics we dislike of being the archetypal versions of whatever it is that we charge them with. Instead, we should learn to develop a set of alarm bells that detects when someone's argument is beginning to strain under the weight of unwarranted exaggeration or insignificant similarities, so that we can point it out to the neutrals on whose support we depend to make change possible.

We use analogical thinking all the time, both consciously and unconsciously, to describe, understand, argue and explain. Analogy is, as the cognitive scientists Douglas Hofstadter and Emmanuel Sander describe it, 'the core of cognition'. Comparison is a fundamental mode of thought that impinges on the way we think about everything – from the daily arguments of our personal and political lives to the highest flights of philosophical and scientific fancy. Our mental worlds are, on close examination, a bafflingly complex universe of analogies and metaphors. An argument is a 'war' in which we attack positions, reinforce defences, deploy evidence and shoot down barrages of points. An economy can be a 'ship' when it founders on the rocks, faces a headwind or enters choppy waters. Love, when we talk of bewitching, enchanting, or casting a spell over someone, can be 'magic'.

We compare when we describe, we compare when we strive to know the unknown through the knowledge we do have, and we compare when we want to paint a picture of reality that's convenient. In so far as analogical thinking is at the heart of human cognition, we can have our eyes opened by developing our ability to test the weight and depth of comparisons. If we were more familiar with the fundamental thought processes of the human mind – the comparative thinking of similes, metaphors and analogies – we could make out their structure with more caution and skill. We could more easily expose and defuse the worst of them, explain and argue with greater precision, and describe with more colour. If we can't point out the structure of a comparison that offends us or that attempts to manipulate us, all we can do is call the person who made it 'stupid', 'insensitive', 'offensive' or even 'racist', but without being able to say why. If we can't clearly see the workings of the fundamental process that we call analogy, we run the risk of being misled by superficial similarities, and finding ourselves and our societies at the rhetorical mercy of those who can.

Reality, Evidence and Meaning: How to Think Like a Philosopher

Get Real: Ideas are Not Things

> 'Nothing that you will learn in the course of your studies will be of the slightest possible use to you in after life – save only this – if you work hard and diligently you should be able to detect when a man is talking rot, and that, in my view, is the main, if not the sole, purpose of education.'
> (J.A. Smith)

There aren't many promises more seductive than The Big Promise: the ability to win *any* argument about *any* subject. It seems like a no-brainer. Why bother to specialise? Why waste your time learning different subjects when you could learn just one? As the anonymous author of a popular sophists' textbook claimed, 'the man acquainted with the skills involved in argument will also know how to speak correctly on every topic' because 'arguments are about everything that is'. But is it that easy? Can we win any debate just by studying how arguments work *in general*, or do we need something more?

Aristotle's principles of reasoning are fundamental to the way we argue, but alone, these ideas aren't enough. The people we admire for their general intelligence – for their ability to master a range of topics – aren't just debaters; they're philosophers too.

117

But what does a philosopher see that a debater doesn't? And isn't philosophy just an academic thing – a pointless exercise in beard-stroking that never goes anywhere and never seems to have anything to do with real life and real arguments? An answer to the second question – which forms the epigraph to this chapter – was given by the professor of philosophy J.A. Smith as the opening of a lecture series he gave in 1914. Despite Smith's deep learning, his knowledge of Greek, of philosophical theories and the history of philosophical thought, *philosophy* was not the point. The reason we should learn to think like philosophers is that it teaches us to notice 'when a man is talking rot'. Philosophy, at its most useful, is the art of detecting bullshit.

There is no magic education that can tell us everything we want to know, but there is a way to make sense of who's right and who's wrong, no matter which part of our world is up for discussion. Philosophy's job is to show us questions that can change the way we think about what is true and how we prove that we're right. Philosophy, when it's at its educational best, doesn't stuff our heads with knowledge: it shows us new and different ways of thinking.

When it comes to arguing about who's right, who's wrong, what the truth is or isn't, and what it really takes to 'prove' that you're right, the simplest ideas are the best ones. If you ask the right questions, you don't have to absorb whole sections of the library to learn how to think differently – and philosophy teaches us to ask just three basic questions: *what's real?*, *what do you mean?* and *what counts as evidence?*

So, let's dig in to what's really 'scientific', what really counts as 'evidence' and why some explanations sound plausible but don't explain anything. It starts with the first question of philosophy: **what's real?**

⌐

Imagine that every human on the face of planet Earth has just disappeared, while the rest of life continues as if nothing has happened. Imagine that the animals are still here, along with everything we made, but that there are no humans around to enjoy it. Picture that world and ask yourself this: where are the ideas?

Our books would still be here, but what about the ideas they contain? Libraries wouldn't be collections of ideas anymore because there would be no one to understand them; they'd just be piles of paper and ink. Our war memorials wouldn't be reminders of important ideas either; they'd just be lumps of stone. The world we live in and the physical things we've made could go on existing without us, but our ideas could not. If there are no humans, there are no ideas. Ideas don't exist in the world; they only exist in our heads.

But why should this matter and what has it got to do with arguing about what's real? The answer is that it demonstrates a simple idea that's the first step to thinking in new ways and being able to pick out the 'explanations' that don't explain anything: *ideas are not things*.

Philosophers throughout history have spent many hours asking themselves questions like 'if a philosopher combs his beard in a forest and there's no one around to see him, can he be sure that his beard exists?' Aristotle realised that they were missing the point. The first victim of Aristotle's attack on the way we think about what's real was his own teacher, Plato. The first conversation that helped us to look more closely at what's real went, I imagine, something like this:

> PLATO: Aristotle, shouldn't we spend our time trying to work out what justice and goodness are? Wouldn't that makes our lives better?
>
> ARISTOTLE: Maybe you're on to something there, Plato. Go on ...
>
> PLATO: Well, you know how the geometry teachers study triangles? Their thinking is just so wonderfully *logical*! It's amazing what they've discovered, and their calculations produce such perfect and neat answers. I think we need to do the same sort of thing, but instead of explaining what triangles are and how they work, we could explain what justice and goodness are.
>
> ARISTOTLE: Plato, I think you need to calm down.
>
> PLATO: Why? What do you mean?
>
> ARISTOTLE: Well, can you *show* me a triangle?
>
> PLATO: Of course; there's a triangular lump of cheese over there, and here's a triangle ... [*Plato fumbles around*] ... made of three sticks.
>
> ARISTOTLE: I don't see it that way. As I see it, those aren't triangles. Those are things arranged in the shape of a triangle. You can make a triangle *of cheese* or *of sticks*, but not a 'triangle' by itself. You see, triangles aren't made of anything. Triangles aren't things. A triangle is just an idea. A piece of wood is a thing. You and I are both things. A frog is a thing. But triangles aren't, and neither is justice.
>
> PLATO: Well, what do you mean? We talk about justice and goodness all the time? We have knowledge of them!

ARISTOTLE: I'm not saying that they don't exist *at all*. They exist in the way that ideas exist – we know roughly what we mean when we talk about them, but they're not like the things we can see, taste and touch. Talking about ideas is completely different from talking about things: the word 'exist' has many senses. When we talk about completely different things and ideas, we sometimes talk as if they were all the same, and the result is a lot of meaningless drivel. As much as you want to believe it, there is simply no love or justice in the physical world. That doesn't mean that they're not the most important of things or that they don't exist, though. Of course ideas *exist*! Just not in the same way that physical things do: *ideas* are not *things*.

When Aristotle first disagreed with Plato by saying that ideas aren't things, he drew a line down the middle of reality that's difficult to forget once you've seen it. The point of the line is to make us see that we talk about things that exist in completely different ways as if they were the same, and we often don't notice that we're doing it. Think about the difference between these three sentences:

> Frogs eat flies.
> Unicorns have one horn.
> Freedom is a good thing.

First of all, ask yourself which of the three statements you agree with. Which of them are true? Would you say they were equally true? Aristotle didn't think so. He would have said, 'It's all very well you saying what unicorns are like, but tell me this ... what even *is* a unicorn anyway?'

When we say that frogs eat flies, we're describing physical stuff. The frog is an object that eats flies, and flies are also objects. But what are we really talking about when we say things about unicorns? Aristotle's example of a creature that's just an idea is something he calls a 'goat-stag', but for ease of understanding, let's replace it with unicorn. He says that 'no one knows the nature of what does not exist – one can know the meaning of the name or phrase "unicorn" but not what the essential nature of a unicorn is.'

Asking the basic question *what's real?* doesn't have to push us down a philosophical rabbit hole. The question *what's real?* is Aristotle's way of saying that when it comes to investigating the world, we first have to ask what kind of things we are talking about. We can shout until we're blue in the face about what freedom *actually* is or what unicorns are *really* like, but what would we point to in order to prove that we're right? 'Freedom' is not a thing out there in the world that we can compare with the idea of freedom that exists in our heads. There is no *physical thing* called freedom anywhere in the world, just as there are no unicorns. Both of them only exist in our minds.

Philosophy isn't just an abstract conversation about reality – it allows us to understand and point out the first step in the manipulation of words like 'truth', 'evidence' and 'scientific', and it changes what it occurs to us to say when other people claim that they've 'proved' that they're right. It takes just one question – *what's real?* – to make us aware of the fact that *all of the things we argue about do not exist in the same way.* Once you see the difference between ideas and things, it becomes easier to understand why so many explanations about how the world works are nothing more than facile and seductive drivel.

Made-Up and Meaningless: How to Spot Pseudoscience

Just as we can divide the world into two categories – physical things and non-physical ideas – we can also use them to explain it in two different ways. When a magnet attracts another magnet, we explain this phenomenon by talking about the physical world. We say that magnets are made of a thing called metal, and that metals can attract and repel each other because they contain positively or negatively charged things called particles. Magnets are things, metals are things and particles are things. The explanation requires no unicorns, no freedom and no justice. A scientific explanation explains how the physical world works in only one way: by explaining the physical things that are in it.

But consider another way of explaining how magnets work: we could do it with ideas instead. We could say that magnets attract each other with love and repel each other because of hate. But what exactly could that mean? The forces of love and hate aren't physical things. They don't physically exist in a magnet in the way that the charged particles do. But if love doesn't physically exist in the magnet or anywhere else, then what sort of explanation is it to say that love is what brings magnets together?

The answer is *a pseudoscientific one*. Though this sort of explanation may seem like the kind that no one in their right mind would offer, pseudoscientists of different kinds succeed in persuading people by doing exactly that. Pseudoscience never explains how the physical world works by describing the physical objects and forces that cause things to bump into each other, interact and physically cause everything to happen. Instead, it explains the physical world with ideas.

⌐

There's a modern pseudoscientific explanation that would have fascinated Aristotle and it neatly illustrates why non-physical explanations of the physical world sound good but don't explain anything. To see how ideas divorced from the physical can lure us into believing all sorts of nonsense, consider this thought experiment: it's late in the afternoon, you're feeling tired, and you decide to perk yourself up with a cup of strong coffee. You have a choice between drinking a shot of espresso, or pouring that same shot of espresso into an Olympic-size swimming pool, stirring the water with an enormous spoon, and then dipping your espresso cup into the pool at random to produce a cup of what is more than 99.999 per cent water, and drinking that instead. Which option do you choose?

I imagine that, working on the principle that the more coffee you drink, the more alert you become, you would go for the original shot of espresso rather than the heavily diluted glass of what is now, overwhelmingly, water. A homeopath, however, would recommend that you choose the water. What's important isn't whether this is right or wrong; what's important is the type of explanation that they'd give you: a pseudoscientific one.

Homeopaths believe that when a tiny amount of a substance (for example, coffee) is heavily diluted by adding a large amount of water and is then stirred vigorously, then any of the coffee that comes into contact with the water through the stirring will be (as they put it) 'remembered' by the water. This means that even though the cup you dip in the imaginary pool of water into which the single shot of espresso has been poured may not contain any coffee at all, the water in the cup still retains the 'memory' of the coffee. It is this 'remembered' coffee which supposedly remains in the water that is supposed to have an effect comparable to – or even greater than – the pure espresso. Homeopathy explains the physical behaviour of water by saying that it has 'a memory'.

Notice, however, that this explanation refers to nothing that's physical. It 'explains' the process by pointing to another process – human memory – but without claiming that what's physically going on in the water is the same as what physically goes on in our heads. Water 'memory', since it draws no parallel between the physical process of human memory, is not a physical explanation. Without actually describing any physical process, the idea of 'memory' doesn't illuminate what's going on. If the question is 'how could water retain traces of substances that have previously been stirred through it?' and the answer comes back 'because water retains', what has been explained? To say water 'remembers' other substances is no different to saying water 'retains' other substances. The idea of memory doesn't explain anything about the properties of water, it only pretends to describe them.

Pseudoscientific explanations are those which point to nothing that we can physically understand. They describe no physical object or force and refer to nothing that has been objectively measured, detected, photographed or scanned. The vague intuition that one physical process might work in the same way as another can be the tentative *beginning* of a search to describe what's going on physically, but it is not an explanation itself. For pseudoscience, however, speculative ideas are not something to be explored: they are themselves the finished 'explanation'.

From a scientific perspective, the problem with non-physical explanations is that what isn't physical cannot be measured physically. A concept like 'love' can't explain the physical workings of the world, because love doesn't exist physically. The power of non-physical explanations to illuminate our understanding of the physical world is, by their very nature, limited. As science sees it, what isn't physical shines no light on what is physical. To say that there are objects with no measurable physical reality but which explain physical reality is not science.

It might very well be the case that earthquakes are caused by angry gods, or that water really does have the power to retain some trace of other substances, and that some future insight into its structure will prove this to be true – but what's essential to being able to see through pseudoscientific ideas is that even when they turn out to be close to the truth, the explanations they offer are still scientifically meaningless. In Aristotle's time, a fellow ancient Greek might have argued that Aristotle was wrong to say (as he did) that the Earth is at the centre of the solar system because the dragon who made the universe placed the Sun at its centre. They would, on the question of the positions of the Sun and Earth, happen to be right. But since it is not possible to see the dragon and there is no physical evidence of its existence, the ancient Greek would not have physically explained anything.

Scientific explanations for the physical world have to be rooted in the physical world itself. Pseudoscientific explanations, however, only *appear* to describe physical processes and objects. If you understand that a physical *thing* (like a baseball that hits you on the head) is real in a way that a thought (like an *idea* that 'hits' you) is not, then you are something of a scientist. Some ways of speaking sound as if they describe what's going on in physical reality, but they do not. The 'memory' of water is one of them.

Science restricts itself to the hard currency of the physical world, while pseudoscience makes up ideas and tries to avoid the tricky question of whether they have any physical reality at all. Concepts like water memory, auras, chakras, gods, fate, destiny and other similar ideas make no attempt to explain the physical world in terms of the physical world. Explaining the physical world scientifically is a grand and ambitious endeavour, and that's why science has always been a slave to technology. Science is dependent on the machines we've invented to look at, measure, scan and record the world because scientific investigation relies in large part on what can be independently and physically measured. As science itself gave us the telescope, the microscope and then the electron microscope, we've been able to move away from having to speculate with ideas alone. What we can see and measure makes all the difference. We can't boil down everything to what physically exists, but if we want to describe and explain the world in a meaningful way that produces results (that is, in a scientific way) we have to explain the physical world – as closely as possible – by means of the physical.

Explanations made out of ideas alone can sound extremely persuasive because, since they describe nothing physical, we can easily modify them to 'solve' any particular problem. Not being weighed down by the necessity of having to relate the details of our explanatory ideas to some measurable physical object or force affords us a certain amount of freedom. This freedom makes it easy to add to or change our ideas so that they appear to 'work', but it also brings with it a problem: consistency. To give one example that throws up obvious questions for homeopathy, consider the fact that the principle of dilution, as understood by mainstream science, explains more than one situation. If you want to float in water, you add *more salt*, not less. If you want to get more drunk, you add *more whisky*, not more water. And if you want to wake up, you add *more coffee* to your cup, too. Whether it's caffeine, salt or alcohol, dilution produces *weaker* solutions and *weaker* effects of those substances. So why should the rule of dilution work everywhere except in a homeopath's clinic?

When another philosopher claimed that we see by shooting light out from our eyes, Aristotle asked wittily why we can't then see in the dark. Apply the idea of consistency to water memory and you get awkward questions like 'if water remembers substances that have passed through it, then why is every drop of water not *full of stuff*?' Water circulates endlessly around the planet, touching countless billions of molecules as it goes. If water remembers, then every drop of water should have a long and rich history, and be packed with substances. If the theory of water memory is true, then every drop of water should be a powerful medicine packed with homeopathic power.

The ad hoc nature of pseudoscientific explanations means that they not only fail to illuminate our understanding of a single phenomenon, but that they do so while incurring the cost of not being able to explain any related phenomena. Simply put, the theory of water memory contradicts too many of the laws that explain the fundamental ways that matter works. If the theory of water memory were true, we would have an explanation for homeopathic medicine, but no explanation for everything else. The sort of science that produces explanations that work in 1 per cent of cases while making the other 99 per cent impossible to explain is no science at all. Pseudoscience appears to explain the world but, unwittingly, it creates more problems than it solves.

Aristotle's idea of consistency is like a village of explanations in which all the buildings have similar foundations. Homeopathy can't just make up its own rules while ignoring chemistry and physics, because they do explain a whole host of phenomena throughout the natural world. A biologist who studies the lives of animals must ultimately have some fundamental explanations about the *stuff* – the physical matter – that animals are made of, and how that stuff works; and at that point, the biologist becomes a chemist and a physicist too. When you can explain a wide variety of phenomena with the same set of principles instead of being forced to invent a new principle for every phenomenon, you can feel more confident that what you're building on is truly fundamental. Pseudoscience builds its house in the hope that no one will closely inspect its ad hoc foundations.

Sometimes, pseudoscience is obviously vapid. Most of us would laugh if a mechanic told us that our car has a bad aura. We'd realise that the mechanic is either joking, speaking metaphorically, or making up a story to avoid having to say anything concrete about what's going on. Sometimes, though, pseudoscience appears to us to be deep and explanatory. This can be because what is simple is more easily understood, and what we do not understand is unlikely to persuade us. Very often, pseudoscientific approaches are also a last medical resort for conditions that bring us such emotional and physical pain that we become more open to any explanation, no matter how frivolous. Even without an incentive to believe, we often prefer to have *any* explanation that makes sense of the complexities of the physical world rather than face the alternative: having no explanation at all. Pseudoscience capitalises on the fact that we're uncomfortable staring at the bare walls of the mind's empty rooms. As Northrop Frye put it, we sometimes prefer 'a waste space to an empty one'.

If, when investigating the physical world, we ask *what's real?*, we become more likely to find the explanations that show us how it works, rather than made-up and meaningless ideas that only sound like they do. The plausible explanations that can be invented, twisted and changed on a whim eventually fade from history's memory. Fewer and fewer people remember the pseudoscience of the past, and today's pseudoscience will fade in turn. The reason why fewer people want to buy what pseudoscience is selling is that Aristotle created something that gave birth to far more impressive results: science itself. Science was born when Aristotle asked the question *what's real?* and decided that scientific thinking begins with a common-sense answer: ideas are not things.

Politics: How to Fight a War of Words

So, we started with a simple question – *what's real?* – and chose one of the possible answers: things. We sketched the outline of a way of thinking that explains the physical world in a meaningful way and rewards us handsomely for it. But not everything *is* physical. The human world is largely made up of ideas – ideas like justice, equality, racism, freedom or democracy – and scientific thinking has nothing to say about them. There is no machine that can, or could, measure fairness.

While most of us are not natural scientists, we *are* all scientists of a different kind. Few of us care much about working out the truth of the matter and forces that constitute the physical world, but we do care a great deal about our human world and the ideas that make it what it is. Philosophy teaches us different types of thinking, and arguing about politics means thinking in a different way to science because politics isn't just about things; politics is about ideas. But if ideas only exist in our heads, then how can we 'prove' that we're right? What sort of thinking helps us to have conversations about some of the fuzziest but most important ideas? To find the answers, we need to ask the second of philosophy's simple questions: **what do you mean?**

Blank words

Everyone knows that some conversations can be harder than others. We find it more difficult to paint a picture of our emotional experiences than to describe what we ate for breakfast. Counting the number of eggs on your plate is just a matter of arithmetic, but when someone asks you how many 'good friends' you have, the question involves more than just counting. It's this sort of philosophical question that illustrates what's important about the nature of all political debate. Politics is a war of words.

In politics, we use words to explain ideas like *what's right* and *what's best*. In short, politics is arguing about what's *good*. So what happens when you apply philosophy's second simple question to the word 'good'? What happens when you ask '*what do you mean* when you say the word *good*?' Aristotle brings us a puzzling answer: the word 'good' means almost nothing at all:

> Things are said to be good in as many ways as they are said to be.

This sentence is one of the simplest and most effective bits of advice that Aristotle ever wrote. It's no understatement to say that once you've considered what this means, you can never think about words in the same way again.

When we call something 'good', we mean something completely different almost *every time we use it*. We say that a particular thing is good in itself, but we also say that something is good if we think there's the right amount of it, if it's the right quality, or if it happens at the right time or in the right place. We say that things are good *for entirely different reasons.*

If you asked me to buy you a good pizza, I could claim – no matter which pizza I chose – that I'd done exactly that. For some, an expensive pizza is good; for others, a cheap one. I could bring you any pizza and claim that it's good because it's the organic one, because it was on special offer or because the ingredients that were used to make it were fair trade certified. Sometimes, even when we're talking about food, what's good isn't the pizza with the most taste or the best value: it's the one with the most justice.

Whatever it is that we're after, what's good here can be bad there, and what's good today can be bad tomorrow. When we say that something is good, what we usually mean is that there's a reason behind it that we believe *makes it good.* But how carefully do we make clear *what it is* that makes something 'good'? How carefully *can* we make it clear? When Aristotle says 'things are said to be good in as many ways as they are said to be', he means that things can be 'good' in completely different ways and for completely different reasons. Some words are particularly blank: they tell us very little about what the person using them actually means.

In politics, words like 'good', 'bad', 'better', 'brighter', 'stronger' and all their fuzzy friends have two main uses: to cover something up or to cover up nothing. If you have an opinion but aren't sure that it's what voters want to hear, then you can talk about how your plan is 'effective', 'decisive' and 'robust', and hope they won't notice you've said nothing. Alternatively, if you're not sure what the party line is on an issue, but want to avoid being seen to disagree with your colleagues, you can hide in the blankness of these nice-sounding but frequently meaningless platitudes. Hopefully, that will have bought you enough time to check what your leader, your party or the voters want you to say on the issue.

Blank words are, most often, a smokescreen that politicians use to buy time. Blank words are like a blank cheque: they give you total freedom, because if you don't say anything now, then you can't contradict yourself later. It doesn't matter whether a politician deliberately wants to say nothing or genuinely has nothing to say, the way to get away with either is to use the blankest, fuzziest words they can think of and hope that no one asks them to explain what they really mean. Aristotle's advice is to 'avoid ambiguities; unless, indeed, you definitely desire to be ambiguous, as those do who have nothing to say but are pretending to mean something.'

In politics, the misty atmosphere of pleasant-sounding phrases like 'better results', 'real change', 'brighter future', 'yes we can' or 'make us great again' can make it hard to see that we're being promised great things without the slightest mention of what those things are, why they should happen and how they should happen. Saying that we want 'what's best', 'what's right' and 'what's good' is easy. Spelling out what exactly those things mean is not.

The highly coloured picture

We all have a sense of what we loosely call 'empty rhetoric' and most of us are already on the lookout for classic political phrases like 'brighter future', but there's more to worry about than just pleasant-sounding platitudes. Asking *what do you mean?* doesn't just lead us to notice the blank words that politicians use to hide either their ideas or their lack of ideas; it also shows us something that's even more sinister.

Many adjectives – words like 'disgusting', 'world-class', 'terrible', 'awful', or 'spectacular' – basically mean one of two things: good or bad. But you can still achieve the same effect, or one that's even more compelling, without having to use any adjectives at all. In the same way that adjectives have a *good* or *bad* meaning hiding inside them, so do nouns. 'Criminals' are bad and 'victims' are good. 'Heroes' are good and 'villains' are bad. There's a way we can say that something or someone is good or bad without mentioning any of those adjectives that set our alarm bells ringing, and Aristotle calls it the 'highly coloured picture':

> Another commonplace is the use of indignant language ...
> We do this when we paint a highly coloured picture of the
> situation without having proved the facts of it ... the hearer
> infers guilt or innocence, but no proof is given.

What Aristotle means by a 'commonplace' is a popular technique for arguing, and this particularly popular technique – using indignant language to create a highly coloured picture – is simple. Instead of *arguing* that something is true, you just *say* that it is. So how do you go about painting a highly coloured picture so that 'no proof is given'? How do you make strong claims without having to offer any evidence or argument?

Quite simply, you indulge in name-calling. One example is when someone calls a person who's committed an act of violence a 'terrorist'. To get into a discussion about when and how using force is acceptable and when it isn't makes a detailed (but meaningful) discussion inevitable. We know that if someone is a 'freedom fighter' they're on the right side of the argument and if someone is a 'terrorist', they're not. In the end, the label doesn't tell you who's right; it only tells a spectator which side of the argument you're on.

The way that the highly coloured picture works is by taking a side, rather than arguing for one. It's when you paint your own picture of reality, having made all the decisions yourself behind the scenes. Instead of showing your audience the process you went through in painting your picture of reality – including all the difficulties of having to explain how you arrived at your conclusion – you just show them the finished picture. To paint a highly coloured picture is to describe something in language that has already made the audience's mind up for them. To paint a highly coloured picture isn't to *argue* that the world is a certain way; it's to *tell* people that it is.

An argument has its own rational force – its strength comes from the logic we use to make it – but the highly coloured picture gets its power from another source: our emotions. What powers the highly coloured picture is what Aristotle calls 'indignant language'. To be indignant means to be angry at injustice; outraged at something you think isn't right.

The goal of indignant language – words of outrage and anger – is to quickly short-circuit our minds: to arouse our emotions before we have a chance to think about the words. The purpose of those words is to arouse our anger, because then we're a little easier to persuade. It's when we're at our most emotional that we're most easily provoked into outrage, and some words provoke us more easily than others. If the job's well done, our emotions fire but our brains don't. The language of outrage is designed to sweep us off our feet before we notice that we're listening not to an argument, but to a statement.

It's easy to say that you don't get carried away by the emotional appeal of words, but all of us do. The Sophist Gorgias was right when he said that words are like drugs: they can stop us from thinking clearly, and they do it most often in the conversations that are the most controversial and important of all. It's easy to score cheap points by claiming that others are 'unpatriotic', but it's hard to say what patriotism is. That's why you hear so many people accusing others of being 'un-American' or not living in accordance with 'British values'. But how many of them could put into words what that patriotism really requires of us, or what exactly those values are? The highly coloured picture isn't an argument; it's simply name-calling. If we learn to look for the most important words and ask what they mean, we give ourselves a chance to notice those that ask us only to feel but not to think.

Don't Get Carried Away

Politics is a war of words – and it's fought with a weapon called ambiguity. As Aristotle says: 'words of ambiguous meaning are chiefly used to enable the sophist to mislead his hearers.' Ambiguity is what gives politicians a chance to say nothing at all, or to appear to have proved, explained or argued for something even though they've done nothing more than say that it's true. Both blank words and highly coloured language make use of the fuzziness of ideas and the words we use to capture them.

But before we get too carried away, there's something important to keep in mind. We should, without doubt, be precise, but it's easy to get overexcited and accuse people of 'saying nothing' and 'being vague', especially when we happen not to like or agree with them. It's important not to get carried away, and think, for example, that any use of the word 'good' is dishonest, intellectual laziness or a sign of stupidity. 'Good' is a shorthand: a word we can use to refer back to an idea that we've already described in some detail. It's not the use of buzzwords like 'great' or 'good' that's lazy: it's the way that they are used. To give a speech explaining exactly what greatness means, and perhaps also how you would make a country great again, and then end your speech with the word 'great' is fine. After all, it's difficult to always be precise about ideas, and we shouldn't assume that other people's ideas are vague before giving them a chance to explain them. We shouldn't strive for absolute clarity absolutely everywhere – that would be pedantic and fruitless – but we do need to recognise just how much clarity each situation needs. Sometimes, we underestimate how much space we need to spell things out, and the result is confusion and misunderstanding. Asking *what do you mean?* isn't something we have to do all the time, but there are times when we don't recognise that the situation demands that we should.

In 2016, the United Kingdom debated a complex political question – the nature of its relationship with the European Union – and yet the question that decided the matter was not complex. The question was 'Should the United Kingdom remain a member of the European Union?' But how could an imprecise and fuzzy heap of definitions, opinions and distinctions be captured by the choice between 'Yes' and 'No'? The way we make our thinking known is limited not just by the way we make decisions – our political process – but by the intrinsic problems of the way we think and talk about ideas.

To say 'Brexit means Brexit' (as the British Prime Minister later did, after the 'leave' voters prevailed and 'Brexit' became accepted shorthand for the intended separation) is not far from claiming that 'a unicorn is a unicorn'. Brexit is not a thing, and one person's idea of the type and degree of separation that Brexit amounts to differs wildly from the next. Some people want a 'soft' Brexit, others a 'hard' Brexit, but what almost no one stops to ask politicians is what either term means to the people who use them. Sometimes an issue is too big to be captured by a single question or a one-word answer. That might be forgivable: an intrinsic problem that has to do with the nature of voting. But even now, years later, are there any widely used terms that we use to describe positions that are more subtle than a yes or a no? There are not. Despite the importance and complexity of this political decision it is still talked about as if it were as binary a decision as the flipping of a coin.

As Aristotle warns us, 'It is possible for it to be true to say "Yes" or "No" without qualification to countless different questions; but still one should not answer them with a single answer; for that is the death of argument.' We should agree what we mean when we use the words that decide the fate of nations.

If Only Truth Were Simple: The Three Questions You Can't Ignore

We're forced to use deduction, induction and analogy no matter what we want to prove and no matter what we argue about, but the fact that reasoning works in the same way regardless of the topic of an argument reveals that it has a weakness. Reasoning sees no depth or subtlety in the ingredients that it adds together. We can reason with premises like 'Socrates invented the iPad' or 'the iPad invented Socrates' and come up with false or meaningless conclusions, because reasoning's job is to work with what it's been given, not to think about it. When a deduction starts from premises that aren't true, the result is something that isn't true *even when the logic is flawless*. Reasoning is a process that's blind to meaning, assumptions and even truth itself; being logical doesn't make you right.

This inability of what we call 'logic' or 'reason' to say anything about the ingredients with which it cooks its dishes explains why the sophists produced more clever-sounding debaters than they did intelligent thinkers. To separate subtle from simplistic truth and to be able to think in different ways about completely different subjects, we need more than the principles of reasoning: we need principles of truth.

But what leads to truth? What proves that we're right? The answer is evidence. Evidence is what we look for to point us in the direction of truth and it's what wins arguments. There is no truth without evidence, and that's why **what counts as evidence?** is the third question of philosophy. But how do we decide what counts as evidence? What Aristotle noticed was that this question can't be answered until we've decided on an answer to the first question of philosophy: *what's real?*

The fact that the things we investigate are fundamentally different in nature – the fact that they exist in completely different ways – presents us with a problem. When we first start to study something, whether it's God, justice, racism, the mind or the Sun, we have to make some sort of tentative decision about *what it is*, and as Aristotle warns us, 'our answer to this question is of the greatest importance'.

The reason why *what counts as evidence?* is determined by *what's real?* is that our evidence has to be appropriate for whatever it is that we investigate. Take, for example, theology: the study of god(s). The nature of many things is mysterious, but none perhaps more so than God. What exactly God *is* and in what way God exists are perplexing questions, but one thing can be said for certain: God does not exist in the same way that a lump of coal exists.

We can't see, measure or in any way track God's movements. In so far as a lump of coal is a physical object, we can describe its appearance and test its properties by subjecting it to physical experiments. We can physically play around with coal and use what we find as evidence to tell us what's true about it. But consider what the non-physical nature of God means for the way we investigate and what evidence we can gather. How can something that does not physically exist be physically measured, investigated, explained or understood? We can't physically understand what is not physical. If God isn't physical, then physical evidence of God will be meaningless.

Once we've decided that God isn't a physical thing in the same way as a lump of coal or a glass of water, we have to set about finding other kinds of evidence that will be meaningful. In theology, this means coming up with a set of principles about what God is that aren't a result of any physical observations. You might call them 'pure ideas'. For example, we might say that God is the thing that created the universe, that God is immortal and that God is all-powerful. These are the essential properties that we might assume of a god. They are the properties that God must have, because without them, God wouldn't be much of a god. So, having assumed these properties, we can start reasoning about what else might be true of God. If God is all-powerful, then it follows that he doesn't share power with anyone or anything else. If there is only one being with complete power, then God must be it, and therefore there must only be one God.

Now, that is a chain of reasoning that started from premises like 'God is all powerful' and 'all-powerful means that you don't share power'. If those two premises are true, then the conclusion – that there must be only one God – is also true. But as anyone who can see the structure of a deductive argument knows, the truth of a conclusion is only as good as the premises it was built on – and these premises are ones that we were forced to assume because we can't know God in a physical way.

The difference between science and theology is in the fundamental reality of what they study, and different types of reality can be fairly distinct when the things they investigate are as different as God and a lump of coal. Where things begin to get interesting is on the border between the hard and soft sciences. Hard sciences like chemistry involve the study of physical things like the stress hormone, cortisol. When three chemists talk about cortisol, they are all thinking of the same physical thing. Measuring cortisol provides very little opportunity for confusion, since the question of what exactly cortisol *is* is not a matter of debate. When three social scientists talk about prejudice, racism or discrimination, though, they aren't describing anything physical. Chemists can argue about what cortisol does and how it works, but not what it is. What racism *is*, on the other hand, is not so obvious.

Humanity's first step towards understanding different ways of thinking, investigating and proving that are appropriate and meaningful for the things they study was Aristotle's monumental observation that 'exist has many senses'. Thousands of years before we were able to say that theology investigates a non-physical god, that the hard sciences investigate the physical world, and the soft sciences investigate a world of non-physical ideas like discrimination or communication, Aristotle understood that the starting point of truth is 'reality'. When you make a decision about reality, you end up being forced to accept certain types of evidence and rejecting others.

What defines each and every way of thinking, first and foremost, is its answer to the question *what's real?* The challenge of saying anything for certain about the physical reality of anything presents us with all sorts of difficulties. Science says that the only reliable reality is found in physical things, and sets about finding physical and empirical evidence. Mystics say that the physical world is an illusion and that ancient books and ancient teachings are the solid ground on which to investigate the truth of the world. Who can prove either of them wrong?

Whatever it is that we argue about, we can't start from nowhere. To have a conversation about anything at all – the physical world, God, unicorns or anything else – we have to first make some sort of decision, no matter how tentative, about *what it is.* What Aristotle realised was that every way of thinking makes its own decisions about *what's real,* and once that decision has been made, it then goes about finding the evidence that it sees fit. What Aristotle realised was that *every way of thinking makes up its own rules.*

This can be an arresting idea: that when we're fighting over the words that win arguments – words like 'evidence', 'proof' and 'truth' – *there is no one type of evidence or proof or truth.* Our truths are only as good as the assumptions we build them on. One way of thinking is no more *true* than any other in some universal sense. Every way of thinking is a different way of producing different kinds of truths. Every way of thinking describes whatever it studies with its own assumptions, its own specialist language and with its own particular evidence. There is no other way.

The idea that each way of thinking starts from what can't be proved leads to a startling conclusion: that different ways of thinking, when they fail to share fundamental assumptions, are incompatible. When people pitch natural science against religion, they fail to see that the two approaches have nothing to say to each other. What could science say about God? It can't measure what's not physical. God, conceived scientifically, isn't a wrong or a false concept: it's a meaningless one. Science cannot say that God doesn't exist: it can only ask philosophy to say this on its behalf. God is not a physical thing, and science only studies what's physical. Every type of thinking has to start with fundamental assumptions, but when those fundamental assumptions differ, it becomes impossible for different disciplines to have a meaningful conversation. As Aristotle puts it, 'the facts which form the starting points in different subjects must be different.' Science and theology don't just have separate conclusions; they have mutually exclusive and incompatible beginnings too.

We frequently talk about what's true while ignoring tricky questions of reality, evidence and meaning. If two people disagree on whether and how something exists, they cannot agree what counts as evidence, and so they cannot convince each other of anything. Without pinning down even a tentative foundation for reality, it becomes impossible to talk meaningfully about anything else. That's why asking *what's real?* is the first question of philosophy.

⌐

What defines a way of thinking is not *what* it investigates; it's *what it assumes* about what it investigates, and, therefore, what evidence it can never accept. Truth is never a single, neat and isolated claim. There are as many ways of thinking as there are attitudes to reality and evidence, but every one of them is forced to answer the same three questions. There's no way to get around it: *what* we argue about and *the assumptions we make about it* make all the difference to how we prove that we're 'right'.

The real power of philosophical thinking is that it's unavoidable. There's no way to have a meaningful discussion if you ignore the questions *what's real?*, *what do you mean?* and *what counts as evidence?* If we want to sound more erudite, we can jazz them up with their 'proper' philosophical names – ontology, semantics and epistemology – but no matter what we call the questions that matter, we can't ignore them.

Ontology is asking yourself whether all the things that we talk about are equally real: love, atoms, triangles, justice or God. Semantics is asking what exactly you mean when you use a particular word or idea. Epistemology is asking yourself what would be a fair way of arguing about a thing or group of things, given what you assume them to be. We rarely consider all the details of the assumptions and methods that we use to find different types of truth; but philosophical thinking is what leads to the ability to make out the structure of every argument as if it were a building. Philosophical thinking shows us how to scan the surface of every argument so that we can see not only the premises that are stacked above ground like the floors of a building, but all the way down to the hidden foundations of fundamental assumptions upon which every argument and every truth is built.

Philosophy isn't a subject; it's *the subject of subjects*. All knowledge exists within a particular perspective – and it is philosophy that creates that perspective. Philosophy is what makes us aware *that* subjects differ by showing us *how* they differ.

When other people want to rubbish the truth you've offered them, they often do it by attacking your way of thinking. Have you ever been accused of being 'too black and white' or 'too wishy-washy'? Have you ever thrown that accusation at someone else? When we play this game of 'whose method makes the most sense for the conversation we're in', we're trying to put an important idea into words: precision. If I had to pick just one line out of everything that Aristotle wrote, it would be this:

> It is the mark of the educated man to look for precision in each class of things just so far as the nature of the subject permits.

In Aristotle's book about ethics – in which he tries to find out the truth about ideas like justice, virtue and *doing what's best* – he opens by pointing out that these ideas aren't like concrete physical reality. He says: 'they may be thought to exist only by convention, and not by nature.' Unlike the unchanging laws of nature, which work the same regardless of our attitude towards them, the laws of ethics are both variable and a matter of opinion. Showing that a substance is radioactive requires a completely different way of thinking than showing that an action is unethical. We can't always be equally precise in every search for truth because we face natural and unavoidable limits. Aristotle wasn't a naïve realist – he didn't believe that what we can see, touch and measure is all there is, but he also didn't accept just any idea about what's real and what counts as evidence.

'A philosophy' is a book of answers, but *philosophical thinking* is a set of questions. Philosophical thinking is what prepares us to embark on the full range of human endeavours that aim at knowledge, understanding or truth. From the hard physical sciences to the soft social sciences, and from the mysteries of theology to the inexact but vital role of poetry, it is philosophy and its unmatched ability to put the whole of knowledge into perspective that teaches us to think in more ways than one. There is no single method for finding truth, and truth is never a single, neat and isolated claim. Every way of thinking has its own principles. If we want to be able to judge every part of our complex world in a meaningful way and to see through simplistic and superficial truths, then we have to know how to ask the questions that define every way of thinking.

Real-Life Philosophical Thinking

Lines of Reality

It is a truth seldom acknowledged that what we call *reality* – a word that sounds like it points at an objective foundation that we can all agree on – is very often something that we create by making our own personal and subjective choices. Were the whole world to gather round a table on top of which sat two small, tall-sided glass containers – one full of flowers and a little water, and another filled with water but no flowers – some would say they were looking at a vase and a glass of water, and others that both were glasses or both were vases. Some might insist that once the flowers are removed from the vase it becomes a glass, and vice versa. But what is it that makes it one or the other – the material? the size? its current use? – and who gets to decide? Even when we can agree that we're all looking at the same physical thing in the same physical reality, we don't always notice that we interpret it differently. We all get to make up our own mind about where we draw the line between calling something by one name or another, and sometimes there can be many lines – but we all have to draw them somewhere.

The question of what a glass 'really is' or what counts as 'a real glass' is something that only troubles students of philosophy and linguistics. But replace 'glass' with 'woman', 'man', 'Christian', 'Muslim', 'Hindu', 'Jew', 'American', 'European', 'Briton' or other labels, and you no longer have a navel-gazing discussion about philosophical subtleties: instead, you have a maelstrom of controversial and divisive issues that whirl through history, scattering peace and unity to the winds.

In 2015, a man was overheard shouting 'This is for Syria' as he carried out a knife attack at an East London tube station, but for the British media, it was neither the victim nor the attacker that framed the event. Rather, it was the judgement made by a bystander about the attacker's identity: 'You ain't no Muslim, bruv'. As the bystander saw it, it was the use of violence to achieve political ends that marked the attacker out as *not* a Muslim. But if you had asked the attacker to explain *his* understanding of what a Muslim is, he might have said exactly the opposite – that the use of violence to achieve political ends is the very thing that defines it. What in one person's eyes makes someone a 'true' Muslim can be exactly what makes another person say that they aren't.

At the bottom of every judgement about what makes something 'a real x' or 'a true x', we're always forced to point to some ultimate foundation for reality. But the problem with the picture of identity that's painted in holy books is that it's built on no 'hard reality': religious identity has no physical foundation.

There is no physical test you can perform that measures any kind of religious identity. There is no machine that distinguishes 'real' Muslims or Christians from those that are 'not real' because religious identity is purely conceptual – but that isn't the case for every debate about identity. One example is gender.

Unlike the conventions of national or religious identity, the perception of gender is complicated by being based in two different realities. On the one hand, gender can be understood biologically – as a description of what is and isn't possible in the physical world. So, for example, put two male rabbits in a room, or two female rabbits, and you can be sure that no matter how long you wait for more rabbits, none will be forthcoming. The reality of being unable to reproduce within gender groups is one instance of a biological definition of gender, but it isn't the only reality that defines gender. The brick walls of hard reality are insurmountable, but the walls of soft reality are not. A person who is born into one biological gender may identify themselves as not being of that gender without entailing any contradiction at all. There is no choice to be made between biological and psychological or social gender: they are different things. It may please someone born a man who prefers the company of women to be called 'one of the girls' by their friends (or vice versa), and the way that it suits them to speak, dress or be – in any way – is independent of any biological physical reality.

The hard reality of mountains, seas and weather shapes our world by forcing us to live here and seek water there, but the soft reality of democracy, law and respect shapes our world through feelings, concepts and ideals. Our attitudes towards hard physical reality don't change it: we can't walk through a brick wall by deciding it isn't real, but we *can* decide to accept someone into our religion, nationality or other conceptual identities.

We live *in* the world of physical hard reality, but we live together *through* the soft reality that shapes our lives. Justice doesn't need to exist physically to keep societies working, but its lack of physical reality doesn't make it any less important. 'Soft' and 'hard', incidentally, are not terms of preference. One is not better for being softer or harder, and the soft reality matters just as much as the hard one. Wars emerge from physical realities like famine as much as they are born of a clash of ideas.

We argue most of all about the lines of soft reality. We argue about whether an athlete is 'really' of a particular nationality by juggling a handful of mutually competing lines of reality like where their parents were born, where they were born, the nature of their accent or how long they've lived in a country. In the same way, we argue about whether you can be a 'real' football fan if the team you support is based 200 miles from where you live, in a city you've never been to. Whether we are dealing with inconsequential philosophising about the definition of vases and glasses, light-hearted arguments about whether someone is a 'true supporter' of a football team as opposed to the fabled 'glory-hunter', or the most important and divisive debates about religion, gender and nationality, what is real is often defined not by one line, but by many. What's more, those lines are mostly not fixed: they often don't describe some incontrovertible reality, but rather our attitudes towards it.

The ultimate foundations of our definitions don't all exist on the same level of reality – but that fact at least gives us something to agree on. We can agree that there is a biological definition of gender while also agreeing to social conventions that have nothing to do with biology. But while there is no inherent contradiction in seeing two different definitions based on two different realities, when it comes to making policy decisions – the laws that spell out what we can and can't do – we are often forced to make a practical choice between them. The debates we have about gender differ in how far physical reality imposes itself as something we can't replace with convention. When a female athlete's testosterone levels give them an advantage that other female competitors claim is unfair, the fact that the difference is rooted in physical reality might be deemed more relevant because the physical difference can't be made irrelevant by changing any social convention. By contrast, it's hard to argue that biological reality is equally relevant to the way we would like other people to address us. Physical differences largely determine our athletic ability, but they have no impact on what we're able to call ourselves.

The challenge that arguments about identity face is to avoid a simplistic understanding of reality – one that argues that there is some single and absolute sense in which things are real or not real. The challenge of arguments about identity is not to 'prove' that someone is or isn't a man or a woman in one absolute sense, but to argue that certain aspects of gender are relevant or not to a practical case – like the question of whether to institute gender-neutral bathrooms or female infantry soldiers. Once we see that debates about *what's real* have no simple and absolute answers, we can argue with greater precision and even make out the lines of interpretation that we draw on top of reality that we might not have noticed.

Standards of Evidence

Every argument we make is built on 'evidence', but as is true of many of the concepts on which whole arguments depend, that single word struggles to explain the vast differences between all of the things we call 'evidence'. Just like 'logic', which refers to deduction, induction and analogy, the apparent simplicity of the words we use to talk about important ideas can conceal the differences between them. In recent decades, a fight has been going on between advocates of science and those of 'creation science'. Advocates of creation science argue that American public schools should teach the theory of 'intelligent design' alongside the teaching of the theory of evolution. As they put it, publicly funded schools should be 'teaching all of the evidence'. The sophistry starts with the use of that word 'evidence'.

While science tries to find explanations by observing physical reality, religion observes only the claims made by ancient books. The difference between these two ways of knowing is the same as the gap that separates a video recording of a mugging and a written eyewitness account of it. Having a video doesn't solve every problem because while it's possible to agree on what's physically happening, multiple interpretations are still possible. A video wouldn't show whether the 'victim' had mugged the 'mugger' previously or if the mugger was being forced into the act by someone standing just out of shot, but despite the lack of definitive answers that physical evidence gives us, we can't fail to notice that it's of a completely different kind to that of an ancient book. A written account of the mugging from a person who is no longer alive would certainly constitute a type of evidence to consider alongside CCTV footage, but to say that it is the *same sort* of evidence is sophistry. When creation scientists say that schools should be 'teaching all the evidence', they're trying to create a new category of evidence where every claim – no matter what it's based on – is judged as equally valid.

Problematically for creation scientists though, when they tried to widen the goalposts of what they claim counts as evidence, what they created was a two-pronged epistemological nightmare. It began when someone noticed that the goalposts had been made so wide that it was incredibly easy to score. If the evidence of creation science can be a deduction based on unprovable claims about an invisible and undetectable being, then what makes one set of claims about an invisible and undetectable being a better explanation than another? Enter the 'Flying Spaghetti Monster'.

Where science has used carbon-dating to contradict claims made in the Bible about the course of history, 'creation science' offers unprovable claims – that there is a being called God who purposefully places objects that contradict the portrayal of historical events in the Bible in order to 'test our faith'. But consider another claim which relies on exactly the same type of evidence – that there is a being called the Flying Spaghetti Monster who does exactly the same thing. Put aside the comic overtones and ask yourself, if there is not only a complete absence of physical evidence of either of these beings but also the impossibility of ever finding any, then what is the difference between them? The answer is nothing. If what counts as evidence is a claim that can't be tested and relies on the existence of an unprovable, invisible and undetectable force, then any unprovable, invisible and undetectable force is just as good an explanation as any other. Notions of divine beings are the ultimate evidence-creating device, as divine beings have the power to do anything we can imagine. Anyone can say that any being exists, attribute to that being any unprovable powers they like, and use those claims as 'evidence'. But the problem of claims that can be invented without limit is that anyone can do it. When the bar of evidence is set low, there's nothing to stop anyone jumping over it.

The first problem of creation science (brought about by its attempt to pass off its notion of scientific evidence as being no different to that of science itself) is that it is forced to accept that this makes any unprovable hearsay just as reliable as its own claims. The second is that our actions sometimes reveal that what we loudly and publicly claim to be a perfectly acceptable and credible standard of evidence is, in fact, the very same standard that we privately reject.

Nowhere is this double-standard of evidence more apparent than in court. Were a creation scientist to be mugged while walking home from church one evening, but be lucky enough to have the incident recorded on CCTV, would they be persuaded by the testimony of a passer-by that, despite the fact the mugger can clearly be identified on the recording, that individual was in fact in another country at the time? But why should physical evidence be preferred in court, yet subordinated to unprovable claims in church? When the religious are told in a temple that a man rose from the dead, very little scepticism is aroused ... and yet if that very same claim were made as part of a court case, it would arouse overwhelming scepticism by those very same temple-goers. But what difference should the building we're standing in make to the type of evidence that we'll accept?

The claims of religion rely on the cognitive dissonance of maintaining two completely separate and contradictory standards of evidence for the very same physical reality. Whether a creation scientist lowers the bar of evidence and unwittingly makes any unprovable claim indistinguishable from his own, or reveals the double-standards of his own judgements of evidence by picking and choosing the situations in which they apply, he shows his disregard for the principles of truth.

What is sometimes referred to as the 'evidence' of faith is

philosophically dishonest in so far as it tries to conceal differences between mutually exclusive and incompatible types of evidence. The line between physical evidence and unprovable claims is so obvious as to not be worth mentioning in the drug testing of sport or the battles of civil courtrooms; and it was in a courtroom that the legal defining lines of what counts as science were drawn. In order to understand the differences between different ways of thinking and proving, we have to be aware that they exist, and be able to explain what makes them different. In Arkansas, in 1982, one judge did exactly that. As he put it, 'The court concluded that creation science is "simply not science" because it depends on "supernatural intervention", which cannot be explained by natural causes or be proven through empirical investigation, and is therefore neither testable nor falsifiable.' Five years after this judgement, the same conclusion was reached by the US Supreme Court, enshrining the gap that separates the evidence of creation science from science itself in law.

Neither the philosophical shortcomings of creation science that I have outlined, nor those of religious thinking in general are meant to offend. As the founder of the Church of the Flying Spaghetti monster put it: 'I don't have a problem with religion. What I have a problem with is religion posing as science.' If we want to go on picking the rich fruit of science and enjoying its benefits, we need a vocabulary of ideas that's capable of revealing different types of thinking about evidence, not one that strives to conceal them.

Russian Dolls: On the Meaning of Words

Blank words – the politician's seductive vocabulary of general concepts like 'good', 'bad', 'effective' or 'robust' – are like empty boxes. Instead of offering us a detailed picture of a particular instance of something good, we're handed an empty box with the word 'good' written on the outside. This game of empty and unexamined concepts is one that is played in politics all the time, and because concepts like good and bad are so general – because they can be applied to an infinity of situations from an infinity of perspectives – they're the ones that slip most easily under our radar.

But politicians aren't the only ones to blame. Everyone uses concepts to paint a picture of the world, and we don't always give much thought to how vague we can be when we use them. We're familiar with the idea that one person's terrorist is another person's freedom fighter – that categorising things depends on our own personal beliefs and perspectives – but we often fail to be able to say very much about the detail of what we put into our own boxes. On the surface, calling someone a terrorist means that they've used violence to achieve political goals that you don't agree with, but the way the word is used reveals more complexity. It includes the assumption that the violence has to be purposefully and mainly directed at civilians, and that the violence is directed and sanctioned by an organisation that is not the government of a state, which is why most people don't call the actions of armies in war 'terrorism'. The box labelled 'terrorism', then, appears to contain the ideas of not just 'violence' and 'politics I don't agree with', but 'violence towards civilians' and 'non-state violence'. Going one step further, notice that the British and American press very often report on non-state-sanctioned individuals who commit racially motivated murder targeting non-whites. These murders certainly count as violence, the overwhelming majority of people don't agree with the murderers' politics of race, and the victims are civilians. So what's missing that causes the British and American press to habitually refer to these murderers not as terrorists, but as 'lone wolves' or 'extremists'? The answer is terror itself. The terrorist label seems to depend not just on whether the attackers kill soldiers or civilians, or even whether you agree or disagree with the politics of the attacker, but on unspoken factors like whether you share the political or racial identity of the victim. If it's your racial or political group being attacked, you become terrified, and you call it terrorism. If it's someone else's, then there is violence but less or no terror, and so it doesn't count as terrorism.

The content of our 'box of terrorism' – the reasons why we might call one person a terrorist but another an extremist – can be incredibly opaque, even when that concept is our own. The problems of meaning – the inherent fuzziness of language and our lack of a set of alarm bells that rings at the point where concepts appear and are used as an argument's foundation – become greater the more abstract the concepts become. The room for confusion grows as we move from discussing what counts as a 'wolf' to discussing what counts as a 'lone wolf'. As we approach the most foundational concepts of them all, we can start to notice the increase in complexity. One example is a concept that's used to justify all kinds of things, from how to eat to how to act. It's 'nature'.

In his excoriating book *God is Not Great*, Christopher Hitchens quotes an argument put forward by the auxiliary bishop of Rio de Janeiro, Rafael Llano Cifuentes, about the church's view of condoms. The bishop's view was that 'the church is against condom use. Sexual relations between a man and a woman have to be natural. I have never seen a little dog using a condom during sexual intercourse with another dog.'

One component of the word 'natural' – one part of its meaning – is a component that everyone agrees on. To say that something is 'natural' means that it occurs naturally – or, simply, that it occurs. What happens is natural, and what doesn't happen is unnatural. When we say things like 'humans being able to levitate is unnatural', what we mean is that human levitation never happens. Sometimes we can water this down from 'what always happens' (i.e. no levitation) to 'what usually happens' – like when we say it's natural to avoid unnecessary physical pain. Most people are not masochists, and so we say that avoiding pain is 'more natural'. Natural, most of the time, is just an observation about what's common.

Bishop Cifuentes' concept of nature, however, relies on more than just the idea of nature being what's most common or what happens. For Bishop Cifuentes, the box marked 'nature' contains a similar definition to the one above – 'things that happen most or all of the time' – but this definition is also entirely contained by another box, and that box is called God. Concepts like 'nature' can be like a series of Russian dolls, where one definition exists only inside another.

For Bishop Cifuentes, there is no notion of nature as 'whatever happens'. Only non-believers think of nature in this way: when there is no God in your mental world, what happens in the world is simply what happens.

But consider what happens if you believe that God created everything that exists and that he did it intentionally – that everything that exists was designed in a particular way for a particular reason. When you add the concept of God to the concept of nature, you add the properties of God to it: i.e. the concept of purposeful design and the implication that what happens must be good and what doesn't happen bad. By putting the concept of nature inside the more fundamental concept of God, it ends up being a completely different concept to the one that non-believers have in their head when they use the very same word. Without God, nature is just *what is*. With God, nature is *what God designed, what pleases him* and *what he wills*.

We've seen how premises can be both hidden and unmentioned while also being the foundation stone of an argument. But the complexity of abstract notions teaches us that even a single word (like 'nature') can act as a premise, or even a series of premises. The definitions that we give to the most important concepts are heavily interrelated: we all build our conceptual worlds as a cascade of mutually reinforcing definitions. When we fail to see just one step in that cascade – the definition of a single word – the possibilities for misunderstanding become almost endless. Cifuentes' mini-argument makes no mention of the concept of God, but it is there all the same.

There are ways to probe the consistency of other people's conceptual world, but without seeing their structure, it's impossible. Through his definition of what counts as natural, Cifuentes is trying to set up an analogy whose basic form is 'what dogs do is a sign of what God wants, and therefore humans should do the same', but this provokes a whole raft of questions like 'why should what's good for dogs be good for humans?' Does this imply that we should give up democracy and live like the other animals – where the strong do what they can and the weak suffer what they must? If we should do what dogs do, why not ignore Christian mercy and charity and live in a dog-eat-dog world? Why should animal behaviour be something to copy when it comes to condoms but not for systems of government? If what's natural for dogs is a guide for humans, might we ask: what conclusion should one draw from the fact that dogs don't pray?

The six secrets – the ingredients of every argument on any topic – help us to see the structure of what other people believe from their own perspective. By starting to think of words not just as simple boxes but as a complicated chain of Russian dolls, we can start to notice the key definitions and assumptions that are packed into them – but this 'unpackaging' of ideas only becomes possible when we notice that a single word can be full of assumptions. We're familiar with the idea that the words we use are a product of our own vision of the world; that we define everything from our own perspective – but we don't learn how to map the depth of that perspective. Every level of argument that we fail to recognise and interrogate – from words to premises to the methods, evidence and assumptions on which entire systems of thought are built – is another opportunity that we miss to understand the complex ideas that shape the way we live.

Part III

Thinking about Thinking

The Modern School of Thought

The Data Delusion: Frequently Wrong and Naturally Oblivious

If we could work out what caused everything, life would be great. We'd know things like how to prevent cancer, which economic policies lead to growth and which medicines restore us to health; and we'd be able to map the inner workings of the natural world. But this, as we know, is far from easy. Aristotle was the first to explain how we use signs to work out what things are like and what causes certain events to happen – which mushrooms are poisonous, which people are not to be trusted or why some people learn to notice more than others – but humanity then had to wait more than 2,000 years for an equally brilliant flash of insight into the way that our pattern-spotting minds work.

Aristotle spent his life, both as a psychologist and a teacher, sketching a blueprint of the human mind. He wanted to understand how it worked, not just to sate his own philosophical curiosity, but also to show others that understanding fundamental ideas about thinking is the key to seeing and avoiding the mistakes that we make in the everyday decisions that shape our lives. Aristotle's education didn't revolve around the knowledge that thinking produces; it revolved around universal and fundamental ideas about reasoning and truth. We use the phrase 'a school of thought' to describe a particular and fixed set of beliefs, but Aristotle's attitude to intelligence and education produced a school of thought in another sense: an educational experience that strives to teach us how to think, not just what to believe.

Fortunately, this endeavour continues in the modern age. There is now a group of like-minded scientists and academics who are exploring avenues of ideas that Aristotle was the first to discover and to investigate. Like Aristotle before them, what fires their curiosity is the relationship between psychology and education: how the human mind works and how its nature affects the success of our attempts at learning to make intelligent decisions. What unites them is their belief in the potential of fundamental concepts of reasoning to change the way we think, and a conviction that the way that we learn them is all-important. In an imaginary staffroom full of history's great teachers, you would find them together, working on a blueprint of the mind that would make it possible to teach new and transformative lessons in the architecture of thinking. I call them *The Modern School of Thought*.

This group of psychologists has deepened our understanding of how our minds work and shown us why the theories we make about the world so often turn out to be wrong. They have revealed why some people notice what others don't and how we can learn to do the same. It turns out that not only are we stuck with inductive thinking – which we have no choice but to use when we work out what's true – but that we're naturally terrible at it, and what's more ... we hardly ever notice.

⌒

Imagine that you are in a great hall, watching pairs of people playing what appears to be a complicated board game, and that your task is to work out – that is, to *induce* – the rules of the game only by watching. You observe countless examples of individual plays, and attempt to infer the rules that govern how each piece moves. Some pieces go forwards, while others are seemingly played in any direction. Some pieces can move diagonally, but one of them only in certain situations. Sometimes one piece appears to be able to transform into another. How difficult a task would this be – to extract a pattern from this sea of data? It seems a tall order; a feat that only the most gifted of us might have the mental power to achieve – and yet every single one of us triumphantly performs a miracle far more wondrous than this without any effort at all.

We are born into a sea of unfamiliar data: a cacophonic chaos of syllables, nouns, verbs, clauses, inflections and conjugations; a bewildering syntax, semantics and morphology waiting to be decoded as only human beings know how. Language itself is our most common means of instruction – it is how we teach. But how can you teach a human to speak if they can't understand what you're saying? Unlike in the case of chess, even those who know how to play the game can't really explain the rules. We speak in intricately ordered sentences that comply with the rules of grammar but, until we're taught how, we can't explain them. A native speaker of standard British English would never say 'me love education' or ask 'did you went to the party?' but they would be hard-pressed to tell you why. They might offer you a grammatically correct version of the sentence, but that isn't an explanation of the general rule or principle, it's simply the answer.

Despite the overwhelmingly complex nature of the task – to grammatically categorise every class of word and work out where it can be positioned in a sentence, to infer the rules by which the system operates, the exceptions that might confound us and even the patterns within those exceptions (and to do it without any help from those from whom we 'learn') – we all do exactly that. This is one of the miracles of the human mind. Only a handful of animals spend more time in their mother's womb, and then at their parents' side, before they are ready to take care of themselves. Our apprenticeship is a long one. And yet before children can easily tie their shoelaces, do basic arithmetic or fend for themselves, they speak in complex, fully formed grammatical sentences.

What stops humans from being able to fly is the absence of the wings that would make it possible, but it isn't a lack of physical machinery that prevents birds from wielding language as we do. More than one species of bird is able to reproduce any sound that a human can make (and many more besides). It is not that birds are physically incapable of speaking. What they lack is a human mind: an automatic syntactic machine with the computational architecture and power to extract, from that bewildering sea of data, the rules that define the language or languages that we speak. Just as birds leap from high-up nests and flight comes to them like something they always knew but can't explain, so our gift comes to us. Language is human flight.

Over the course of the second half of the 20th century, it became increasingly apparent that the theory of learning-by-repeated-exposure favoured by behaviourists like B.F. Skinner couldn't account for the way we learn language so automatically, so accurately and on the basis of so little evidence, as well as Noam Chomsky's theory of universal grammar did. Chomsky postulated that the outline of every language – the parameters that determine how they all work – are already 'in' our brains at birth. But no sooner had this idea of the innate and automatic pattern-spotting genius of our language-acquiring minds reached a point of orthodoxy as a scientific theory than the tide begin to turn. After linguists and psychologists had spent decades investigating and establishing our extraordinary ability to automatically and correctly perceive a pattern in a set of linguistic data, two men began to realise that our ability to do the same with a different type of information was not so brilliant. Although it seems we have a gift for the patterns of language, our inductive thinking – our ability to work out the causes of events and the nature of things through observation and generalisation – leaves a great deal to be desired.

The psychologists Daniel Kahneman and Amos Tversky began to reveal the shortcomings of our natural statistical intuition in their 1974 paper 'Judgement Under Uncertainty: Heuristics and Biases', in which they presented 95 graduate students with a question. They had asked the students to imagine that a town has two hospitals: a large and a small one. In the larger hospital, around 45 babies are born each day, and in the smaller hospital around fifteen babies are born each day. As you would expect, on most days, around 50 per cent of all babies born are boys. The students were further asked to imagine that, over the course of a year, both hospitals made a note of the number of days on which there was a particularly unusual distribution of births. The question the undergraduates were asked was this: which hospital did they expect to record more days on which 60 per cent of the babies born were boys – the larger hospital, the smaller hospital, or about the same as each other?

Take a moment to think through your own answer. If, as 74 of the 95 participants did, you think that the answer is either the large hospital or that both hospitals would be about the same, then you can take comfort in the fact that you are in the majority. To see why those answers are wrong, consider the similarity between the 50 per cent boy–girl split you would generally expect, and an event with almost identical odds: coin-flipping.

Imagine that I hand you a coin and offer you the following bet: if you can flip the coin and it lands heads-up every time you flip it, I will give you a cash prize. All you have to decide is the number of times you are going to flip the coin. Would you try to win the bet by flipping the coin twice, or ten times? Which is more likely; that you will flip two heads in a row, or ten heads in a row?

Both of these examples show the same thing: that, in order to give a false impression of the odds of an event, it helps to have *as little data as possible*. When you flip the coin only a few times, it's easy to get a false impression – that maybe the coin is unfairly weighted to fall heads-up – but the more you flip the coin, the more you will notice that the first two heads you threw gave you a completely misleading picture of the real odds.

The world is full of processes and events with completely different odds, but one thing never changes: the more we can observe, the more sure we can be of what those odds really are. If we want to see the truest picture of the odds of having a boy or a girl, we should count *large* groups of babies, not small ones. If we want to know how a coin is weighted, we should flip it *many* times, not just a few. When we observe only tiny slices of reality – just fifteen babies here or two coin-flips there – we leave ourselves exposed to being fooled by chance. When it comes to statistics, bigger is better. *The greater the number of things that we count, the closer to the true picture of their nature we come.* This is the rule that helps us to avoid being tricked by chance, and it has come to be known as *the law of large numbers*.

One thing that we human beings find difficult to accept is the role of chance in life. We like to believe that there is an explanation for most things: in particular those having to do with human affairs. We perceive that the winds of chance blow strongly to influence the outcome of coins and dice, but human affairs, we believe, are overwhelmingly the product of the choices we make, the actions we take and the factors we can see. When we roll three sixes in a row, we have few problems noticing luck. But when an unlikely team wins the league, we see none of the luck, and instead spend our energy thinking up 'reasons that explain'. When that team fields an almost identical side the following year but finds itself near the bottom of the league rather than the top, instead of saying 'their luck has run out', we start a new search for more 'reasons that explain'. We like to believe that the underdog won the match not because chance dictates that occasionally this outcome will happen, but because of some concrete explanation – the inspirational manager, the motivation of the players, or an ingenious formation. But none of these factors explain why, despite today's impressive victory, most of the time they lose; that's what makes them the underdogs.

Let me be clear. I am not saying that tactics, the motivation and performance of the players or the support of the fans does not play a large part in sporting success. What I am saying is that neither a run of success nor a spell of failure necessarily signals an inherently good or bad strategy. It is only possible to see how effective a strategy is once you've accounted for chance. Those who don't think statistically end up being the faddish followers of whatever strategy won last week's game or last year's title – chasing whichever choices appear, on the surface of things, to produce success.

The sea of data in which we are lost is life itself. In our assessment of the effectiveness of a medical treatment, the track record of a politician, the performance of a company or the risk of a terrorist threat, we think inductively. But unlike the automatic and bafflingly precise analysis that our minds apply to the patterns of language, our attempts to understand the patterns of events around which our lives revolve have been found to exhibit strikingly consistent mistakes.

The human mind is a hungry pattern-spotting machine, but it forgets that the patterns it notices exist only in small slices of reality. Every generalisation that we make – every induction from examples to a rule – is an uncertain leap over a gap that we can never entirely bridge. Induction is a kind of guesswork littered with problems, but the human mind accelerates when it starts to see any kind of pattern, and doesn't easily engage the brakes of doubt. Unlike our linguistic pattern-spotting ability, which is automatic yet accurate, the natural state of our general inductive ability is to automatically overreach and arrive at conclusions that are wrong. As Kahneman puts it:

> statistics produce many observations that appear to beg for causal explanations but do not lend themselves to such explanations. Many facts of the world are due to chance, including accidents of sampling. Causal explanations of chance events are inevitably wrong.

When we hear that a town's hospital produces noticeably more boys than girls (or noticeably more girls than boys), our first instinct is not to remember to invoke the law of large numbers and ask about the size of the sample. Our instinct is to suppose that there's something in the water or that there's some other physical explanation. The same is true of a mother who's given birth to four boys or four girls. A voice deep in our minds tells us that it can't be coincidence; that there must be something biological going on. And yet four coin-flips that all land heads-up seem to us to be nothing more than completely normal chance. Chance is always at work, making odd things happen in small pockets of reality, and we humans are born with a special talent for ignoring their size.

Worryingly, the natural shortcomings of the human inductive mind are not just limited to the way that we ignore the law of large numbers. We not only fail to notice when we're looking at the broad horizon of reality through binoculars that show us only a part of it, but we also point those binoculars in the wrong places. When we wonder about a group of immigrants from a particular country, we might read newspapers from each side of the political spectrum in the hope of developing a balanced view. But while you begin to form a picture of reality based on the number of articles you find about a disproportionate connection between that group and the crime of pickpocketing, you're unlikely to stop and ask this question: how often do newspapers publish stories about the uneventful lives of people quietly contributing to society through tax-paying and charity work? When the window you look through *can* only show you one part of the complete picture, sometimes it doesn't matter how big the window is.

It is alarming to consider the prospect that, in the fundamental way in which we work out how the world works, we are naturally ill-equipped and frequently wrong. The default position for human beings is to overgeneralise – to make inductive mistakes – but even that isn't the end of the story. We don't just suffer from a natural inductive ineptitude; despite a lifetime of opportunity to notice either *the fact that* we do it or *why* we do it, almost none of us do. In Kahneman's words:

> What is perhaps surprising is the failure of people to infer from lifelong experience such fundamental statistical rules ... Although everyone is exposed, in the normal course of life, to numerous examples from which these rules could have been induced, very few people discover the principles ... on their own.

What is ironic about our judgements of probability, correlation, causality and chance is how little we manage to learn from life itself. Our minds' natural tendency to misread reality is one that we rarely pick out from the data. We never systematically write down all of our predictions to see which of them come true. Rather, more often than not, we remember the good predictions while the bad ones fade from memory. The result is that we're left with the impression of a few impressive 'successes' and the feeling that we're better able to judge reality and predict the future than in fact we are. No matter how many times we are wrong, we rarely, if ever, notice why.

Against the background of claims made by teachers both ancient and modern, it simply isn't true that we discover the basic concepts of human thinking on our own. If anything, it's the opposite that's true. We stumble through life failing to notice very much about its patterns because what seems to be true on the surface is what our minds suggest to us is most convincing. In our analysis of politics, medicine, economics, business, sport, people and a hundred other things besides, we make decisions about what's true using induction, and we do it with a predictable and consistent irrationality that we fail to notice. But all is not lost. Even if we aren't born with an aware-ness of the shortcomings of our pattern-spotting mind, it turns out that we are able to learn how to see them.

The Power of Abstract Ideas

So, we have a tendency to misread the world and not to notice why. This is our natural state. But can we overcome it, and if so, how? In 2002, Daniel Kahneman received the Nobel Prize for pointing out that our inductive intuition is subject to inherent biases, and in his 2011 book, *Thinking Fast and Slow*, he not only pointed out the problem but also offered a solution. What we're missing, according to Kahneman, is a common language of the fundamental concepts that we don't notice for ourselves. In those everyday discussions where we get together to make judgements about the world and decisions about how to act based on those judgements (what Kahneman calls 'watercooler conversations'), we need new ideas and we need them to be well explained:

> A deeper understanding of judgements and choices also requires a richer vocabulary than is available in everyday language ... So this is my aim for watercooler conversa-tions: improve the ability to identify and understand errors of judgement and choice, in others and eventually in ourselves, *by providing a richer and more precise language to discuss them* [my emphasis].

But can a new set of ideas – and a new vocabulary to describe them – make us see the hidden angles that it doesn't always occur to us to consider? Can fundamental concepts make a dif-ference to what we notice?

The psychologists Geoffrey Fong, David Krantz and Richard Nisbett wanted to find out, in a study called 'The Effects of Statistical Training on Thinking About Everyday Problems' (1986). They wondered if they could get people to see one aspect of the difficulty of generalising from what they observe by teaching them about the law of large numbers. To that end, they recruited several hundred subjects and posed a range of questions about different types of decisions, like estimating the talent of potential new employees, judging the fairness of a lottery, assessing the effectiveness of new technology, or evaluating the performance of athletes. To explore whether the way that ideas are presented and taught to us affects our ability to put them into practice when solving everyday problems, the researchers split their subjects into four groups. They gave each of the groups a different kind of training to see which – of the four kinds below – might change the way they think.

Group 1 – No training at all
Group 2 – Training in a *statistical concept* and a *demonstration*
Group 3 – Training in three *example problems*
Group 4 – Training in a *statistical concept*, a *demonstration* and three *example problems*.

The 'statistical concept' in question was the law of large numbers, and it was explained in a four-page booklet that broke it down into sub-concepts like 'sample', 'sample size' and 'population distribution'. The 'demonstration' given to Groups 2 and 4 involved a practical demonstration that illustrated these concepts by using a large opaque urn full of red and blue gumballs. By drawing different-sized samples from the urn (either a set of one, four, or 25 gumballs), the experimenters illustrated the principle that the larger the size of the sample you draw, the more reliable a picture you get of the actual ratio of all the red and blue gumballs in the urn (the 'population distribution'). For those in group 3, the booklet of example problems gave almost no *general* explanation of the problems that are inherent in drawing conclusions from small samples, but instead illustrated the concept with three concrete examples.

So which of the groups did best, and why? Unsurprisingly, the first group did worst of all; it only occurred to them to offer a statistical explanation (a reason why what we observe often tells us very little, or even misleads us completely) for fewer than half of the questions for which it would have revealed a good answer. The second and third groups did at least 10 per cent better than the first group, but the final group showed the most improvement, scoring yet another 10 per cent higher than groups 2 and 3. So what does this tell us?

The obvious conclusion is that more training equals better results, but a follow-up experiment carried out five years later by Fong and Nisbett (1991) revealed what actually makes the difference. Fong and Nisbett wanted to find out which part of the training process was producing the ability to see new statistical angles, so they devised a subtly different version of the experiment – one that made their subjects wait for two weeks after they'd received their training – and *then* they tested them. As well as being asked to solve problems, the subjects were also tested to see which part of the training programme had stuck with them, and therefore which ideas they might be using to solve the problems. What the researchers discovered was that the subjects who performed best in the delayed test were far more likely to have remembered not the example problems (which they had mostly forgotten) but the law of large numbers *expressed as a general principle.* What they discovered was that 'performance was not related to memory for example problems, but it was related to *the ability to state the abstract rule*' (my italics).

What the researchers mean by 'abstract rule' is the concept of the law of large numbers when it has been separated from any particular example. Unlike an explanation that's specifically about the problems of judging, for example, the fairness of coins or the potential of an athlete, the *general* or *abstract* concept is one that we can explain and understand independently of examples, with ideas alone. An *example* of the law of large numbers might be something like 'when you want to test how a coin is weighted, it pays to flip the coin as many times as possible in order to get as accurate an answer as possible'. The *abstract definition* of the law of large numbers that the researchers chose was this: 'as the size of a random sample increases, the sample distribution is more likely to get closer and closer to the population distribution. In other words, the larger the sample, the better it is as an estimate of the population.' Whether we use the label 'abstract', 'theoretical ', 'general', 'concept', 'principle' or 'rule', what all these words try to express is the difference between understanding the individual details of individual examples and ideas that are general enough to apply to every example.

So what does an abstract and general rule teach us that particular examples don't? The key is that when you understand the rule itself, you can apply it not just to the examples you know, but to *every new situation where it applies.* If we memorise and recognise only specific examples, then we have to hope that any new problems we come across are similar enough to trigger the realisation that the law of large numbers is relevant in those instances too. When we talk about coin flips, we learn about coin flips. When we talk about 'a random sample', it could be three flips of a coin, three gumballs pulled out of an urn or fifteen babies born in a hospital. Particular examples are just that: *particular*. They are isolated, keeping themselves to themselves. Examples struggle to shine a light beyond their own individual limits, but abstract ideas reach out to every example.

The potential of abstract ideas to help us *to notice that* we misread the world and *understand how* we misread it is the beginning of a recipe for intellectual growth. But there is one final experiment we should consider – one that shows us not just a potential intellectual future, but also the path of our actual intellectual past: how each of us ended up with the minds we've got.

Rather than asking how we can add more strings to our intellectual bow, Darrin Lehman, Richard Lempert and Richard Nisbett (1988) wondered whether the way that we interpret the world is a result of the subjects we have studied (or haven't studied). To find out, they pitted students of different subjects – medicine, psychology, chemistry and law – against each other in a battle of brains. The questions they asked the students, rather than being suited to those studying a particular subject, were deliberately general. They tested the students' ability to reason about everyday problems like analysing the performance of a police chief or athlete, or deciding which of two schools to attend. The results show us the difference between the types of questions that the students of each subject were able to answer at the beginning and at the end of their three year graduate courses, revealing the ways that their subjects had taught them to think. So who came out on top?

It turns out that medical students, after three years of study, not only significantly improved their ability to see the statistical angle in questions of medicine; they also outperformed the law-yers in statistical analysis everywhere else too. Like the first two experiments – where abstract concepts like the law of large numbers helped people to correctly answer questions about *completely different things* rather than just those that prompt us to think about statistics, like cards, dice and lotteries – the future doctors showed, through their test results, that they had learned to see statistical angles everywhere.

To illustrate the way that doctors are trained to think about the world in a different way to the rest of us, compare what would happen in your mind and that of a doctor if you both received a positive test result for a deadly and extremely rare disease (say, one that affects only two in every 1,000 people). You would undoubtedly begin to panic, while the doctor would appear inexplicably calm. Why?

The cause of the doctor's seeming lack of concern for what you see as a likely death sentence is twofold. The first is that rare diseases, by definition, only affect a tiny percentage of the population. The second is that some medical tests are not 100 per cent accurate. This is not uncommon, and the occasional result of a less-than-perfect test is known as a 'false positive', which is when you don't have the disease, but the test says that you do. If 1,000 people are tested for the disease and 95 per cent of them get the right result (i.e. they don't have the disease and the test says that they don't) then what about the remaining 5 per cent? Five per cent of those original 1,000 people tested – that is, 50 anxious human beings – will get a positive result. But how many people out of every 1,000 are expected to actually have the disease? Only two. The result is that out of every 1,000 people who are tested for this rare disease, 50 will receive a posi-tive result that says they have it, but it's still overwhelmingly likely that only two of those 50 will have the disease, while 48 of them are completely normal and healthy. Putting aside the slight complication of false negatives, that's a 96 per cent chance of being fine. That's why the doctor doesn't seem so worried.

The error rate of medical tests is a fact of medicine, and it's a factor in the decision-making process made by doctors and other medical professionals every day. The uncertainty of relying on tests or observations that are imperfect means that doctors have to be trained to think inductively – but what's crucial is that their pattern-spotting minds become attuned to the truth of far more than medicine.

If two in a thousand people are terrorists, and you develop a test that's 95 per cent accurate at spotting them, you'll get the same result as the test for a rare disease. You might catch the two people who are guilty, but they'd be standing in a line of 48 other people who are not. In the 1988 experiment, the doctors outperformed the lawyers in their ability to see the statistical angles of problems that were not just about medicine, but about economics, politics, sport and education too. The ideas that save the doctor from naïvely accepting what's on the observational surface of reality don't have anything to do, intrinsically, with medicine. The doctor sees what we don't, not because of what they know about medicine, but because of what they know about the abstract (and fundamental) concepts that change what we notice – no matter what it is that we want to know the truth of.

So if the doctors are masters of any question about statistics, uncertainty and the skilful untangling of causes, what did three years of studying the law teach the lawyers? Just as was true for the doctors, the researchers found that studying law does more for your mind than merely filling it with the particular facts of the subject. What the lawyers were able to do after three years of studying the law was to develop a mastery of a different medium: not the inductive thinking of observation and generalisation for which the doctors had developed a keen eye, but the deductive logic of legal contracts. The lawyers could also transfer their ability to see through logical problems that had nothing to do with the law itself, but which involved the same type of reasoning. The lawyers showed that, when presented with deductive reasoning problems that work in the same way as legal contracts, they could see what most of us fail to notice. Problems of deductive reasoning – knowing exactly how the ambiguous and fallacious logic that sophists use works – are what a lawyer notices even in conversations that have nothing to do with the law.

So why is it that training in different academic subjects produces different kinds of minds, at home with different principles of logic? Why is it that the way we think is shaped by what we study? The answer lies in the content of each subject: *what* it studies. The world of the law exists at the opposite end of the certainty spectrum to the uncertainties of medicine. The law tries to pin down and clarify everything it can. In the law there is no 'well, it could be factor X, Y or Z that makes the difference'. A good legal contract clearly states exactly what must happen before something else happens. A contract says things like 'Mrs A will pay Mrs B *only* when Mrs A has complied *fully* with requirements X, Y *and* Z.' In the strict deductive logic of legal contracts (unlike the inherent inductive uncertainty of generalising from what we observe), there is no complex collection of possible factors; something is either permitted or it is not permitted.

A good lawyer spots ambiguity and knows how to point it out. One of the key concepts of legal reasoning is affirming the consequent: spotting that just because A *can* cause B, it doesn't mean that it did. 'If the glove don't fit, you must acquit' – but if the glove does fit, remember that it also fits a million other people ... so it proves nothing! A lawyer can come up with probable excuses when they need to, but they can also point out when other people are using that very same method to try to win an argument. And lawyers don't just do it in court when talking about contracts. It's a style of thinking that works in debates about anything at all, from political wrangling in parliament to family arguments over the dinner table.

The chemists in the experiment were completely left behind; they made no progress on either front – inductive or deductive – and the researchers attribute this to the kind of thinking that chemistry involves. Despite the fact that chemists study the physical world, 'the luxury of not being confronted with messy problems containing substantial uncertainty and a tangled web of causes means that chemistry does not teach some rules that are relevant to everyday life'. In psychology, it's exactly the reverse. The social world that social psychologists study is a chaotic one, and the nature of their objects of study equipped the psychology students to perform strongly in tests of their statistical skill. Each of us has many traits – we come in many different colours, have different cultures, different heights and weights, different tastes and dispositions, different assumptions and different histories. So when a social psychologist wants to measure the relationship between two things, they understand that without a way to measure and account for all of those factors separately, it can be extremely difficult to tell what causes what, and that this is just as true for a million other questions about how the world works. The full extent of the angles we miss in everyday life because of the subjects we did or didn't study has not yet been fully explored, but this series of experiments teaches us that the way that we think – what we notice – depends both on *what we study* and *the way that we study it.*

⌐⟋

The Modern School of Thought teaches us that our minds are a double-edged sword. On the one hand, we're born with a pattern-spotting mind that automatically and effortlessly works out the staggering complexities of human language with exceptional accuracy. And yet on the other, when we consciously try to work out the patterns in the behaviour of other people or the physical world we live in, we have an inborn capacity for misreading those people and misreading that physical world. Our mind's natural talent for language is matched only by its ineptitude for induction.

There is, though, a way to make these two unchanging properties of the human mind work together: we can use the first to overcome the second. One aspect of our special linguistic talent – a talent that no animal can match – is that we're capable of talking about more than just the physical world. Animals communicate just as we do when they make noises that refer to things that happen in the physical world, but there is something that animals never talk about: thinking. There is no animal that examines what's going on inside its own head and is able to share it with other animals through language. As if we were special computers that can understand and discuss their own software, and then point out the lines of code that produce better results than the others so that all the other computers can upgrade their software too, our ability to step back and see our own thought through language is unique.

In order to absorb and make use of the principles of reasoning – deduction, induction and analogy – we must, in a sense, rise above them. We must do things 'meta'. We use the word meta in a slightly different way to the Greeks, but the core of our modern idea of 'meta' is something that exists at a higher level. Meta is what you see when you step back after having your nose pressed to a painting and notice that it exists in a frame. Humans don't just think: we step back and think *about our own thinking*. Add this remarkable ability to our powers of language and you have not just thinking about thinking, but *talking about thinking* too. When a vocabulary *about* thinking helps us to become aware of the way we think, we begin to harness the ability to consider even our *own* thought as if from above, or from another's point of view. When we find the right words to *talk about* our own thought – a 'metalanguage' – it changes the way that we *think about* it: 'metacognition'.

The experimental work of the Modern School of Thought shows that a deliberate education in abstract concepts gives us the ability to make judgements in more subtle ways than we're capable of when we are left to discover and work things out by ourselves. Once we learn these abstract concepts, it changes the way we think about intelligence and education. What gives us the ability to see the statistical angles of any type of problem isn't the facts that any subject might teach us about what it studies; it's the mastery of the different concepts that are essential for studying it.

When we're trained to see and understand the abstract and general concept of induction, we develop the ability to see it everywhere: not just in the specific examples that we've already come across. What makes the academic subjects that define our education what they are – the way that they teach us to think

– is not the facts they teach, but the group of fundamental concepts they use to analyse them. Every subject tunes our minds to a different wavelength, but what defines the differences in the way we think and what we notice are not the facts and subject matter themselves, but the set of abstract concepts that we master *through* each subject's facts and subject matter. The doctor knows many facts about the body, just as the lawyer knows many facts about the law, but none of those facts are what teaches the doctor to see particular angles of the decisions that shape our everyday lives. What reveals the angles that others don't see isn't what you know; it's how you think.

If intelligence is knowing what to do once you've left the library – being able to apply what you know in new and uncertain situations – then abstract concepts are what allow us to make use of our studies and apply them in the real world. When we use our natural ability to *talk about thinking* in order to turn our minds in on themselves and *think about thinking*, we're harnessing a natural strength to overcome a natural weakness. The power of language to create a mirror of the mind – one that reflects back to us the unavoidable and unchanging workings of the concepts that we use to make sense of everything – is the most natural thing in the world.

Contrary to the belief that has powered education in the Western world for around half a century – the belief that abstract ideas only confuse us, rather than revealing the fundamental building blocks of the ways that human beings think – the Modern School of Thought shows that Aristotle was right all along. We almost never discover the most fundamental principles that would save us from misreading the world by ourselves. We simply do not work out the 'rules' of our psychological reality by stumbling around alone in the long grass of individual examples and personal experience. The 'school of life' teaches us far less than we think.

Aristotle discovered the fundamental concepts of human thought, and set about describing them in what Kahneman would later call a 'rich and precise language'. Like Aristotle, Kahneman and his fellow psychologists at the Modern School of Thought see a true education of the mind as one that offers no vague 'communication skills', no platitudes about 'analysis' or 'critical thinking' and no waffle about 'creativity'. The intelligence that makes a difference to our lives is neither the product of a vague mist of useless words nor any pile of specific facts. Intelligence is the product of how well we understand a family of abstract yet unavoidable ideas that reveal why some people notice what others miss, no matter what they think about.

Part IV

Thinking about Education

Closed Minds and Fragile Egos:
Where Did We Go Wrong?

What We Believe about Intelligence is Wrong:
Why Misunderstanding our Minds is Intellectually
Disempowering

The classical attitude to intelligence and education can be summed up in two words: *know thyself*. Before the Greeks, human beings were driven – by both curiosity and necessity – to wonder about and attempt to explain the world they lived in. Early man was puzzled by the properties of plants, the motions of the planets and the desires of the gods; but the Greeks changed the way that we see and understand everything by drawing our attention to the thing through which we do it: the human mind.

Almost 200 years before Aristotle was born, a philosopher called Xenophanes made a remarkable observation that changed the way that human beings understood themselves. What he noticed was that wherever you go, if you ask people to tell you what their gods looks like, they will simply describe themselves. He wrote that 'Ethiopians say that their gods are black with small noses, and the Thracians say that they are pale and red-haired.' That led to a more dangerous thought: that 'if oxen and horses ... had hands or could draw with hands and create works of art like those made by men, horses would draw pictures of gods like horses, and oxen of gods like oxen.' What occurred to Xenophanes was this: perhaps it was not God who created man, but man who created God. Before Nietzsche could claim that God was dead, or Freud that God was dad, the Greeks first had to wonder whether God was man.

But what does this have to do with intelligence? The answer is control. When man was powerless to explain something, he brought in God. To explain our minds, our laws, our physical appearance, the weather, the outcome of battles, the workings of the physical world, our own stupidity and countless other things besides, there was only one answer: God. Before Xenophanes, God was used as a metaphor to cover almost everything that human beings didn't understand. In the early days of mankind, God wasn't just an object of worship; he was a way of saying 'we don't really know how this works'. What Xenophanes planted in our minds was a disquieting idea, but one with infinite potential. If man created God, then God cannot be the cause of everything that we can't explain. And what is left when you no longer have an infinite and wondrous carpet under which to brush life's mysteries? An imperative to think about them. By casting doubt on the existence of the gods, Xenophanes encouraged us to shine the light of our curiosity upon something else: ourselves. When Greek thinkers finally began to wonder about, study and explain the nature of the human mind, we entered a new age.

The professor of cognitive science Douglas Hofstadter, puts it like this: 'The Ancient Greeks knew that reasoning is a patterned process, and is at least partially governed by statable laws.' The Sophists, who each contributed a piece of the early puzzle of the mind, looked past specific sets of facts or areas of knowledge and began to describe general abilities like memory and persuasion. The Sophists were the first to teach techniques that reflected the patterned nature of our minds, and the abilities that this gave their pupils drew attention to the principle behind those techniques: *that the way we think has a fundamental and fixed structure, and it is one that we can understand.*

The search for the mind's patterns began with the Sophists' interest in memory and persuasion, but it was Aristotle's attempt to find and explain the truly fundamental elements of human thinking – the principles of reasoning and truth – that made it possible for human beings to see right through to the centre of their own minds for the first time. The collection of six books known as *The Organon* – widely thought to be notes for the lectures that Aristotle delivered to his students – is humanity's first attempt to record the recurring patterns that define the way we think, and to explain them as 'statable laws' that we can make sense of. It is the earliest attempt at a blueprint of the human mind. It is a snapshot of what goes on in the black box of our heads every time we combine statements to produce a deductive conclusion; every time we make an inductive theory based on what we observe; every time we argue analogically that new and puzzling things work in the same way as similar things that we already understand; and every time that we produce truths from a set of assumptions about reality, meaning and evidence.

Organon was the title that later scholars gave to this special collection of books, because it means 'tool'. No matter what type of truth or knowledge we desire to chisel out of the raw stone of experience, they are, and will forever be, shaped by the same tools: the principles of reasoning and truth that are inherent in our minds. Aristotle's *Organon* is the mirror that first showed us the structure of our own thought in the form of those recurring patterns, and no matter what we've added to this staggering insight into our minds, we have never fundamentally changed it. When Francis Bacon tried to improve on it in the 17th century, he called his book *The New Organon*. The 19th-century mathematician George Boole opened his book on logic by explaining its contents, then immediately went on to point out that all the work done since Aristotle was only that of 'remoter influencers'. The medieval scholars of Christendom paid Aristotle the ultimate respect of calling him simply 'the Philosopher', as if the others were but insignificant footnotes scrawled in the margins of history.

The reason why the influence of *The Organon* is so enduring, and the reason why Aristotle's picture of the patterns of reasoning and truth is, inescapably, the foundation of human education and intelligence, is that those patterns are innate and universal. We all recognise reasoning as if it were a person that we've met before, and it's the very *universality* of our reasoning – the fact that we all have at least a loose but instinctive sense of what 'adds up' – that reveals its unavoidable and innate nature. There are deep and enduring similarities in the way that our minds work, and they are there waiting to be discovered. Thinking isn't random; it has rules. That's why neither the distance in time nor the differences in dress or ethical standards between us and the Greeks matters. The shape of the human mind – *the way we think* – isn't a choice we make; it's simply what we've got.

Aristotle didn't invent reason; he discovered it. No human being imposed the limits of our minds on the rest of us. Reasoning isn't a story written by the rich, the powerful or the victors of history, and the ways that we think are not the creation of Greek civilization or any other. They're a product of one thing: the fact that we're human.

The rational nature of the human mind – the fact that we think in patterns – is not, however, its most profound nor its most important feature. The foundation of human intelligence isn't the patterns themselves; it's the fact that we *think about the patterns*. We don't just reason with more complexity than the other animals; we are the only animals *that are aware that we are reasoning*. In the grand scheme of the animal kingdom, humans are weak, slow and less hardy than many of our competitors, but not a single one of those competitors uses language to explain the inner workings of their own minds to the other members of their species. What's truly remarkable and unique is not our communication or our thinking – it's the combination of the two with our awareness: the way we *think about thinking* and *talk about thinking*. Our metalinguistic and metacognitive ability – our natural capacity to describe our mental world in words and to use those words to build an observation deck from which we can study our own minds – is powerful, staggering and unique. Human beings are computers that can upgrade their own software.

The full story of the human mind, however, is one that contains contrasting ironies of genius and stupidity. On the one hand, we all have a deep and innate sense of what reasoning is without anyone ever having explicitly explained either deduction, induction or analogy to us. And yet, despite our innate feel for reasoning, one upshot of the branch of modern psychology known as behavioural economics is that we are far from being infallible machines of logic. When it comes to induction in particular, it turns out that we make surprisingly consistent mistakes; but Daniel Kahneman did not just point out a flaw: he also suggested a solution: *a richer and more precise language*. If you read Kahneman describing the pitfalls that he discovered in his own thinking, you will hear echoes of Aristotle's attempts to show other minds what he had realised about the nature of his own. The reason I call the work of psychologists like Kahneman, Richard Nisbett and James Flynn 'the Modern School of Thought' is that their picture of intelligence and education shares essential features with Aristotle's. After 2,000 years, we are now returning to the classical view. The fact that we can step back, observe, describe and understand the mind is transformative. A significant part of human intelligence and the education that develops it is defined by the unavoidable and inherent patterns that underpin the way we work out what is true – and by how we are taught to understand and use them in our day-to-day lives. The patterned, linguistic, self-aware nature of the mind is what defines – biologically, cognitively and practically – the way that we make sense of reality. In Aristotle's words, 'intellect more than anything else *is* man.'

Both Aristotle and the Modern School of Thought teach us to have faith in our ability to learn to think in new and different ways by trying to master abstract but powerful concepts like *deduction*, *induction*, *analogy*, *reality*, *meaning* and *evidence*. Today, though, that faith is a rare thing. In the modern age, we face a choice between two competing notions of how we should develop our minds: one that embraces the *universal* patterns, structures and concepts that define every human mind, and one that does not – a highly individual and personalised view of education that sells us a story about our own uniqueness and our own inborn talent. The modern Western world has chosen the latter, and in doing so, it has marched us backwards, out through the door of the School of Thought and into the arms of a comforting, seductive and intellectually limiting philosophy of intelligence and education.

When the Sophists began to produce pupils with astonishing memories and impressive powers of persuasion, they undermined a belief of which the aristocrats of ancient Athens had been rather fond: that they were in charge because they were smarter, and that they were smarter because they had been born that way. When the Sophists showed that the ability to stun others with the power of your memory could be learned with the help of techniques that worked the same for everyone, they fractured the myth of inborn genius and unique talent. Today, we've both returned to and reinforced the myth of talent: the belief that ability is, first and foremost, something we are born with.

When we witness someone showing off astonishing powers of memory, our first and strongest instinct is to see talent instead of technique. A few brief lessons on the techniques of memory can make you seem, to those who don't know that such techniques exist, like some sort of wizard born with incredible powers; yet we still fail to notice the power of those techniques. Our obsession with talent is so great that it fills our minds, leaving little space for other explanations. We still believe that if we're not much good at seeing the structure of an argument, noticing the manipulations of statistics or spotting the contradictions of a theory, it must be because we were born that way. We still believe that those who are able to see what others miss in any conversation, on any topic, have that ability not because they learned to see the universal and fundamental principles of reasoning and truth but principally because they are innately and irrevocably different from us. Fewer and fewer people believe that God hands out different abilities, but God's role as the source of individual talents has been replaced by fate, destiny or genes. The mechanism has changed, but we still think in terms of intellectual aristocracy.

Perhaps the most intuitive example of the mistaken strength of our faith in talent is what we believe about artistic abilities like music, drawing or poetry – that they are the paradigm of innate skill. This is a mistake. The power of technique to transform what we're able to achieve isn't limited to the patterns of reasoning and truth; it's true of 'creative' endeavours too. When we experience Churchill's speeches, Mozart's symphonies or Leonardo's art, we can't wait to talk about their innate genius, but if they could return to the here and now, they'd talk about the concepts and structures that define their respective arts. We forget their countless hours of practice, their repetition of technical exercises and their slow and effortful mastery of the vocabulary of ideas that reveals the structures and patterns of each of those arts. No matter how many books are written about the fundamental ideas and the thousands of hours spent practising technical exercises that made Churchill an orator, Mozart a composer and Leonardo an artist, we still want to believe that geniuses are born rather than made. We feel the urge to say that the more you boil the arts down to structures and principles, the more you take away their magic – but the fact is that artistic magic has never appeared from nowhere: *it grows out of principles, patterns and structure.* We forget that creativity is our reward for mastering patterns. That's what turns the painfully thoughtful, methodical and deliberate learning of rules into a magical mind. Eventually, the rules can be summoned with almost no mental effort and they can be broken, twisted and turned upside-down just to see what happens. Structure, technique and patterns are not the enemy of creativity: they are its wellspring and its foundation.

With any type of thinking, there are sets of fundamental ideas that can transform the way we see things. With an hour of technical instruction about the proportions of the face and the rules of perspective, people can draw faces that are no longer childish circles but impressive likenesses. All of a sudden they see that they have more 'talent' for art than they thought. We are too quick to box ourselves into particular abilities and disabilities before we've been made aware of the ideas and structures that lead to ability, and even mastery. We don't know that we have no talent for a particular activity, skill or type of thinking until we've been shown the fundamental ideas that define it, and only during that process can we really tell what talents we have; not before.

To be clear, I make no claim that the notion of talent is baseless. To the extent that our brains aren't all absolutely identical at birth, it is very likely the case that we have different dispositions for different types of abilities, but how do we decide what they are? The way we work this out is simply to observe how well we perform at different types of thinking or activity. In doing so, though, we fall back into our natural inability to see complex factors at work. Children whose teachers are unable to explain the fundamental concepts, patterns and techniques that make particular abilities possible (and those who are unlucky enough not to come across them by some other means) simply assume that those abilities are beyond them, and suffer the fate of resignation. As if we were all blessed with the potential to grow to six feet tall but spent our childhoods being consistently undernourished – and so grew to only five feet – we assume that whatever we are not, we never could have been.

The talent myth narrows our possibilities by encouraging us to believe that our abilities are fixed, and its effect is profoundly disempowering. The consequence of this mistaken faith in talent is to narrow our own view of ourselves until we are just a sliver of the full range of human abilities. But what powers this narrowing of the self has very little that's intrinsically to do with the mind.

In the modern world, talent doesn't function as a psychological or scientific theory; it works as a myth of identity. Many myths have a basis in reality, just as the myth of talent does, but the purpose of the myth of talent is the same as other myths: to shape our view of ourselves or the world in a way that makes life understandable, and thus easier to bear. Many of the most popular myths of cultural history – like the belief that some individuals or religious groups have been chosen by God to receive some special talent or purpose – share the same goal: to give those people confidence and self-belief. Whether it's belief in the unique and special nature of your religion, country, people or intelligence, the thought of being exceptional has always made human beings happy and motivated – and the allure of this belief is no less powerful today.

What we understand about our own minds and what we believe about our own potential is suffused with a powerful strain of individualism that's deeply ingrained in Western culture. We live in an individualist age that teaches us – through its motto, 'be yourself' – to focus on, take pride in and develop what we believe makes us different from other people. We are taught not just to think in a narrow way about our own abilities and potential, but even to take pride in that narrowness. Today, believing yourself incapable is encouraged, because even incapability can be branded as something unique. Incapability is a good thing because it's bespoke – it's *our* incapability. It is unusual to talk proudly about physical, aesthetic or moral shortcomings. People rarely regale us with speeches about how short, ugly or selfish they are – and if they do, they are upset about it – but we proudly say that we're terrible with numbers, have a bad memory, or no talent for music or art. The strength of the expectation that we each have a special talent leads us to believe that talents are opposed to each other. If we're good at numbers, we assume that we probably won't be good with words. We assume that being good at one implies being bad at the other, so we don't bother investigating it and end up gravitating towards whatever single ability we happened to have decided is 'our talent'.

This narrowing of our view of our own ability produces exactly the opposite effect to the one it is intended to produce. The confidence and self-belief that is supposedly instilled by having our talent praised and emphasised does not endure. As the psychologist Carol Dweck, whose work examines the effect of what we believe (and are taught to believe) about intelligence puts it:

> Parents think they can hand children permanent confidence – like a gift – by praising their brains and talent. It doesn't work, and in fact has the opposite effect. It makes children doubt themselves as soon as anything is hard or anything goes wrong.

Exactly the same can be said of adults. The 'myth' of talent is exactly that: a story told to us by our parents and our society, and which we then tell ourselves. It places us in the world. It's a story of definition and of self-definition, but it's one that doesn't help us.

We live in an age that encourages us to believe that the fruitless closing-off of possibilities that we call 'being yourself' constitutes the fulfilment of our intellectual destiny. It claims that the highest form of self-expression is to find, develop and revel in what makes us different from other people, but what produces genuine self-belief – rather than a sham confidence

– is the process of being staggered: staggered by our own ability to achieve things that we previously thought impossible.

When we stop telling ourselves that we're not cut out to do what others can do, and instead immerse ourselves in a little technique, we find that we can be the ones who seem magical to others. Just one experience of producing wonder in others or in ourselves – in any endeavour, artistic, intellectual or sporting – can instil a genuine self-belief that profoundly changes us for the better. The road to both confidence and ability is paved not with talent and praise, but with technique, patterns and practice.

The individualism that charms us into a counterproductive understanding of intelligence with the sweet fruit of stories about our uniqueness and our difference, however, grows out of a noble and righteous cause. For hundreds of thousands of years, human beings have feared the desire of some of our number to force everyone else to live like they do, and so we've grown wary of the idea that there is one objective way to live. The power of our familial, tribal, religious and other social groups has, more often than not, prevailed over the expression of individual desires and differences. Most of history has been characterised by a lack of individual political choice. From a modern perspective, the waning of this trend is a good thing: a re-balancing of the *me* as well as the *we*. But just as we've grown to dislike people who tell us that there's one way of living that works for all of us, we've also come to distrust people who tell us that when it comes to thinking, and therefore education, *there is a great deal that is objectively the case for all of us.* Our desire to individualise and subjectivise intelligence and education is well intentioned but misguided. It relies on a misunderstanding of what is universal and innate in the human mind, and on a bad analogy with our desire for greater individualism in politics. There is no single way of living that is 'true' or 'right' for all of us: the life of children and family is no better, no more noble and no more valid than a life of riches, beauty, fame, or meditative contemplation. But the same is not true of the fundamental outline of the way we reason, nor of the education that reveals it.

We live in an age struggling to work out the proper boundaries of another idea that was birthed and explored by the ancient Greeks: relativism. We love the subjectivity and the freedom of individuality. We hate the idea that some things just are, and that we can't make of them whatever we like. In the same way that we want to say that there is no one way of living that's absolute, we want to say that there is no one collection of ideas that's equally valid for everyone. There is a postmodern urge to say that one way of thinking is no more true than any other. Our lives differ far more than our minds ever will, and yet we've confused the individual nature of political freedom with the universal nature of intelligence and education. We want education to be like politics, where there is no 'right' answer. But the way we think isn't a choice we make, it's simply what we've got.

In the Western world, we are beset by a psychologically naïve and ultimately disempowering understanding of intelligence and education. Education used to be an introduction to something universal and fundamental. The Greeks' passion for self-knowledge led to the first blueprint of the mental landscape within all of us, and it transformed our conception not just of the mind and the universe it sees, but also of our very place in that universe. All of a sudden, human beings lived in a world where the way we think was no longer an impenetrable mystery controlled by gods or spirits, or predetermined by the class of one's birth, but something we could actively understand

and shape for ourselves. What the Greeks achieved when they started to ask questions about man and his mind was to put the power back into our hands.

Every step we take towards a seductive and ultimately dis-empowering philosophy of individual talent is one that takes us further away from the universal, unchanging and fundamental ideas that we'll never be able to avoid, and which we are built to understand by virtue of one thing: the fact that we're human. There are impenetrable enigmas at the heart of human experience, but thinking is not one of them. Our minds work in a particular way, and we can learn to understand them.

Taking Turns to Shout at Each Other: Why an Understanding, Freethinking Society is Impossible without Philosophical Thinking

When Shakespeare wrote that man is 'noble in reason' and 'in apprehension how like a god', he was adding stylistic polish to a melody that Aristotle had been the first to hear. Man is a symphony of experience and Aristotle is our amanuensis. Because of Aristotle, humanity became increasingly aware of the extent to which reasoning defines us. But what else defines us, besides our reason and the self-awareness that allows us to see it? The human condition – the intrinsic and unchanging elements of human experience – is a complex harmony of the mental and the physical that encompasses everything from the philosophical awareness of our own consciousness and mortality to the biological facts of having to eat and sleep to stay alive and healthy. Aristotle's writings explore many facets of the human condition – perhaps none more so than the nature of our rational and linguistic mental world; and the fact that 'man alone of the animals possesses speech' is inexorably linked with another inescapable reality of existence: having to live with other people.

When Aristotle wrote that man is 'a political animal', he expanded thus: 'he who is unable to live in society, or who has no need because he is sufficient for himself, must be either a beast or a god ... A social instinct is implanted in all men by nature.' There is an undeniable and unavoidable connection between our political and intellectual experience: *we live together through the mutual understanding that is made possible by the way we think and talk.* No philosopher so tightly connects the rules of the political game with the rules of the intellectual one as Aristotle did. We have the intellectual condition that we have, and we live in the political condition that we do. This is the lot of man.

So, stepping back from the realisation that we live in a game whose rules we did not decide but to which we are still forced to conform, ask yourself how successfully humankind is getting on with the task of peaceful coexistence through mutual understanding. The psychologist Steven Pinker, in his book *The Better Angels of Our Nature*, argues that throughout history, humanity has become progressively less violent, and he evidences this conclusion with a wide and convincing array of data. But if we have chosen to do less killing and more talking, understanding, negotiating and agreeing, how have we done it? What has given rise to increasingly peaceful and stable societies of understanding, freethinking citizens?

A large part of the answer is a certain kind of education, but before we come to the recipe for understanding, we must do as humanity has done and arrive there by way of its opposite: misunderstanding. To illustrate, allow me to analogise ...

Imagine that you've arranged to spend an afternoon playing football with a group of eleven friends. You meet in the local park and the game gets underway, but very soon you notice that there's a problem. What has happened is that four of you have turned up ready to play Gaelic football, four are dressed up and ready for American football, and the remaining four thought that they were signing up for a game of soccer. Since you've all made the effort to turn up, you decide to play together, but of course, this doesn't work. As one of the soccer players tries to kick the ball, a Gaelic footballer picks it up and starts running with it. Then the American footballers flatten the person with the ball, and everyone really starts to get angry when it comes to deciding what counts as a goal. Some of the players argue that you can score points only by kicking the ball into the goal, to which others respond by saying that kicking it over the goal counts as well, and the rest claim that you have to pick the ball up and run with it into the area behind the goal. Here's my question: who's right?

The answer is that unless you'd all agreed *which type* of 'football' you were playing, the match is pointless. But while none of us would fail to notice if the people we were competing against were playing with a different set of sporting rules, it happens all the time in conversation and debate, and we don't always notice. The result is that each of us tries to score conversational or argumentative goals – to prove that we're right – in a completely different way, but without agreeing where the goal is, how points are awarded or what sort of play is to be considered outright cheating. Over the course of our lives, we take part in thousands of conversations that play out just like that chaotic game of football. We all turn up to the conversation believing that we're playing by the same rules, but we're not. Unaccustomed as we are to thinking of every statement of truth as being built on particular definitions of reality, particular standards of evidence, and particular concepts – all piled up in rafts of crucial but *unmentioned* hidden assumptions – this is exactly the position we find ourselves in.

The conversations of everyday life are different to those that take place at a scientific or philosophical conference. In an academic setting, specialists go to great lengths to lay out the shared boundaries of the assumptions, definitions and methods that lie behind and support what they claim is true. In day-to-day life, every one of us gets to make up our own way of proving and explaining; but unlike the specialists, we don't take the trouble to first agree on a set of rules – and we don't often recognise that we don't. Everyone plays their own game, convinced that they are right and that everyone else is wrong, and though it appears as if a conversation is taking place, what is really happening is that two people are just taking turns to shout at each other.

The literary critic Northrop Frye recognised that if we want to communicate things that are clearly understood by other people, rather than just say things that sound good to us, we have to make the assumptions of our thinking clear. He recommended – even in the case of novels and poetry – that we be more like the 'researchers' who see the importance of sharing key principles and concepts than the 'commentators' who make pleasant-sounding but often meaningless judgements:

> The commentators have little sense, unlike the research-
> ers, of being contained within some sort of scientific
> discipline: they are chiefly engaged, in the words of the
> gospel hymn, in brightening the corner where they are ...

the principles by which one can distinguish a significant from a meaningless statement in criticism are not clearly defined.

What Frye describes – the unsystematic, vague and sometimes contradictory platitudes of some of those who professionally offer truths in the arts – produces much talking but very little understanding on the part of those listening; but it is only the thin end of the wedge. That overly dressed, airy and facile pronouncements occasionally float around galleries, catwalks and literary salons creates few serious problems. But the inability to understand other people's ideas about art (and the inability to notice the depth of that misunderstanding) should be recognised for what it is: a siren calling out a warning that we must not do the same in the conversations that really matter. Today, we struggle to define and mutually understand each other's conceptions of the most important principles of human political life. What damages our prospects of peace, prosperity and progress is our inability to see how easily we get lost in the abstract ideas of politics.

Today, we struggle to define all sorts of political ideas: 'Brexit', 'economic migrant', 'terrorist', 'tolerance' ... and as George Orwell pointed out, we may as well each be speaking a different language. What Orwell wrote about the fundamental misunderstanding that clouds and undermines every debate about the ideals on which societies are built, is, if anything, more true today than it was in 1946 when he put it to paper:

> The word *Fascism* has now no meaning except in so far as it signifies 'something not desirable'. The words *democracy, socialism, freedom, patriotic, realistic, justice,* have each

of them several different meanings which cannot be reconciled with one another. In the case of a word like *democracy*, not only is there no agreed definition, but the attempt to make one is resisted from all sides ... Other words used in variable meanings, in most cases more or less dishonestly, are: *class, totalitarian, science, progressive, reactionary, bourgeois, equality.*

Aristotle's observation that 'things are said to be good in as many ways as they are said to be' is echoed here in Orwell's. People, as he points out, call each other not just fascists, but a thousand other labels too, with the depth and sophistication of children. In the same way that politicians use 'robust', 'effective' and 'decisive' to tell us about their plans, but fail to say what makes them robust, effective or decisive, the word 'fascist' is widely used today to mean little more than 'bad' or 'something not desirable'. The emptiness of political name-calling might make us and our supporters feel better, but it fails to make clear to the objects of our disapproval why they deserve it. What's more, it also fails to persuade the neutrals, even though it is their support that must be secured if we are really interested in consensus, action and change.

It's my contention that much of what we perceive as disagreement can sometimes be mere misunderstanding: the depth of our discord is often less profound than we think. There are, without question, great differences of opinion about almost every subject that matters to us – but the nature of listening to other people is to be frequently forced to guess what they mean. We think that what arises in our minds when we use a particular word will be the same as what arises in the minds of others, but we are wrong. Until we've worked out the detail of *other people's definitions* of a demagogue, a fascist, a racist, a democrat, a man, a woman, a child, freedom, democracy, tolerance or any other concept used in political argument, we are forced to make do with our own. As we piece together the web of other people's concepts and how they fit together, we're forced to use our own as placeholders. As we saw in an earlier example in which the concept of 'God' was hiding inside Cardinal Cifuentes' notion of 'nature', with every additional concept that we add to the self-reinforcing whole, the potential for misunderstanding grows. When we finally understand what was missing in our understanding of just one part of other people's conceptual universe, we can begin to understand why they think differently about the other parts too.

Most of the time, when we call each other 'illogical' or 'irrational', it reveals more about us than it does about the person we are accusing. Most of the time, our complaints about reasoning are our own fault. When we fail to see that other people started their chain of reasoning from premises that we don't see, or concepts that we don't understand, it only *appears to us* to be illogical. Many misunderstandings in conversation don't come from bad reasoning: they arise because we each start our chains of reasoning from different assumptions or definitions that we're never taught to share and which we rarely make clear.

Every conversation carries with it the danger of deep misunderstanding, and that misunderstanding is usually at it is deepest when its object is abstract: when we talk about freedom, equality, justice and what's right. We justify our personal and political lives with complex systems of interrelated concepts; and ethics and politics are imprecise subjects. In our efforts to understand and to communicate our understanding, we run around like butterfly catchers trying to bag Big Ideas and label them with words, but the words we use are often too small to express the full complexity of what we mean by them. That is the nature of ideas.

⌒

The fact that a failure to understand another person's way of thinking means that we don't really understand their truths leads to a troubling thought. Once particular ways of thinking have become established and codified – shared by large groups of human beings – we can end up failing to understand not just other individuals, but entire bodies of knowledge. When this codifying happens, it turns our individual and hidden black box of assumptions into a mutually understood set of rules. Academics may not all agree on one way of thinking, but the difference between them and us is that they're aware that *without understanding each other's way of thinking, they cannot understand each other's truths.* Apply that idea to ourselves – 'non-academic' individuals who don't instinctively recognise that truths are only truly understood in the context of the thinking that created them – and you arrive at that troubling thought: when it comes to codified bodies of knowledge, we all 'know' a bunch of facts that we don't really understand.

The most obvious example of misunderstanding a way of thinking, and therefore the facts that that way of thinking produces, is science. The scientific way of thinking, proving and explaining (what is known as 'the scientific method') is multifaceted. We've already covered some of what defines it by comparing the scientific and the pseudoscientific concepts of reality and evidence, but what we've covered in the greatest detail is how science, having settled on physical experiment as a consequence of its focus on physical reality, uses induction to analyse the results of those experiments. In its attempts to work out whether medicine X causes improvements in health, whether educational programme Y causes improvements in intelligence or if man-made greenhouse gases cause global warming, science developed a range of statistical techniques and ideas that transformed its ability to correctly read the nature of reality. Induction might be a precarious leap from examples to a general rule, but scientists are armed to the teeth with ideas that minimise its inherent problems. The law of large numbers is one example – it warns us to consider the number of examples that we've used as a springboard before leaping to a general rule. But it is not the only one.

Imagine that you're considering an acting career and are trying to convince your parents to lend you the money to go to a prestigious acting school. You might try pointing out all the famous actors who went to the school as evidence of the fact that graduating from it gives you a very good chance of success. What you would have to hope is that neither of your parents thinks scientifically. Yes, they would reply, it is true that there are a hundred examples of famous actors who attended the school, but they aren't the whole story. It's easy to spot the hundred noticeable faces that we constantly see on television, in the cinema, in magazines and newspapers, but what about the many thousands of aspiring actors who attended the school but never made it? This is the idea of 'dead evidence': the examples that we should include in our calculations but which are much harder to notice, often ignored, and therefore lead us to a mis-leading view of reality.

We are entranced and obsessed with data in the modern age. We talk about 'what the numbers say' as if 'the numbers' were some absolute picture of reality. What we don't see is that every set of numbers – every set of examples that we use to leap to a generalisation – are examples chosen by a human being who made decisions about what was worth including and how it should be measured. The pictures we paint with numbers are no different from any other vision of reality: they are highly selective. But if scientists notice pitfalls in the way we think about what's true, and they do it using ideas that we're not truly familiar with, then on what basis can we disagree with them? When other people see what we don't see, we end up in the difficult position of hearing their conclusions but not having any real understanding of them – because the working out, from our perspective, was totally opaque.

After decades of accumulating a disjointed collection of scientific facts, few of us can define the one thing that created them: the scientific method or the scientific way of thinking. Each of us (having studied science at school) keeps a selection of scientific facts in some dusty corner of our mind – facts like 'water is made up of two molecules of hydrogen and one molecule of oxygen' – but we don't think of science as its productive principles: we think of it more as the dazzling facts and theories that other people created *from* those principles. How many of us understand the pillars of scientific thinking: empiricism, experiment, statistical analysis of factors, falsifiability, reproducibility, control groups, double-blind trials or the placebo effect? To be unaware of scientific assumptions, scientific standards of evidence, scientific language and scientific techniques – everything that makes science what it is – is to have a pile of facts without understanding how they came to be. It is to 'know' things without being able to fully make sense of them: to memorise facts that we don't really understand. Many of us do not, in a meaningful way, disagree with scientific thinking; we disagree with *what we think scientific thinking is.* When we object to ideas that we have only seen through a lens of our own misconceptions, we end up criticising what we don't understand. This has been the fate of modern science: to be often disagreed with and mistrusted, yet not widely understood.

If we do not share the assumptions of the people we talk to, or we don't understand why they accept some forms of evidence but not others; or if we have our own meanings for particular words rather than the meanings that the person explaining has given them, then we only understand them in a limited way. This same idea applies not just to individual people, but to entire ways of thinking, proving and explaining. When those with faith in pseudoscience listen to a scientist casting aspersions on the claims of their heroes, to whatever extent they fail to understand the scientist's method they also fail to understand what he or she is saying. When we believe we are listening to those with alternative views, we might be taking the sound of their voice into our ears, but we do not truly hear a new conception of the world. As Goethe put it, 'we only hear what we understand.'

⌒

So we misunderstand people, and we misunderstand methods. Not only are we faced with continuous interpersonal misunderstanding in politics – how to live together – but on top of that, we fail to think precisely and with understanding when it comes to established methods like science. The solution, however, is neither science nor politics, nor any other method itself. There is only one subject that teaches us to understand the method of other subjects, and that is philosophy. Philosophy teaches us to reverse-engineer any claim about what is true by understanding the way of thinking – the assumptions, the type of evidence and the specialist vocabulary – that produced it; and when we become familiar with just a handful of different ways of thinking, we develop the ability to do something special: *to compare them.*

Just one new and completely different way of thinking and proving can change the way we think about everything, because it's only when a new way of thinking comes along that we can really understand the strengths and weaknesses of the ways that we decide what's true. Without a basic collection of different ways of thinking, we make choices without seeing – and therefore without understanding – all of our options. What makes a truly autonomous, freethinking mind possible is perspective. Our intellectual independence depends not on what we know, but on the breadth and depth of our ability to think in different ways. The ability to think for ourselves is limited unless we are able to step out of the frame that other people try to place around our reality with their own ways of thinking. Philosophy is what teaches us to step back and see the fact *that* ways of thinking differ by showing us *how* they differ. Thinking for ourselves is impossible without perspective, and philosophy is what gives it to us.

It is something of a modern tradition to see science as the saviour of mankind. The historian Yuval Noah Harari writes that 'modern-day science is a unique tradition of knowledge, inasmuch as it openly admits ignorance regarding the most important questions.' In this observation, he is contrasting science with religion. When The Enlightenment popularised the scientific way of thinking, it began to eat away at the authority of religious thinking that had hitherto both dominated and predominated. But science is not philosophy: it doesn't step back to take in the full perspective of different ways of think-ing. Scientific thinking and religious thinking are both methods, but neither is the *method of methods*; the *subject of subjects*. And yet in spite of science's inability to help us step back and see the whole spectrum, in providing at least one alternative to religious thinking it provoked enough perspective to change the course of history. If it's true that there is wisdom in crowds, then providing the crowd with a new way of thinking will pro-duce new discoveries, and this is exactly what happened as a consequence of the birth of the scientific method. Humankind became able to understand, explain, predict and control the physical world in a way that had previously been impossible. Scientific thinking gave us the power to do many things, but the power of science was itself created by philosophy. Science cannot drop the assumptions that make it science, and when it considers its own assumptions it becomes no longer science, but the philosophy of science. Neither science nor religion can step back from themselves to take in the full, broad and magnificent horizon of different ways of thinking. The road to autonomy is paved only with philosophy.

It does need to be said, however, that though religious thinking and scientific thinking are each a method unto them-selves, both of them under the perspective of philosophy, their effect on our ability to think for ourselves is not equal. I shall just come out and say it: *religious thinking narrows the mind.*

Whether religious thinking seeks to explain the natural world, history, beauty, justice or indeed anything at all, it sees everything through the lens of God. God is the assumption to which every idea must be tethered. Instead of setting us free to consider the magnificent array of completely different types of things that we can investigate and know in different ways, religious thinking demands that even the tiniest fragments of knowledge include some concept of God, his desires, his plan or his properties. Where an absence of religious thinking gives you physics, biology, history, economics, art, ethics and so many other different ways of thinking, religious thinking subsumes them all under itself. In our efforts to open ourselves to new possibilities, we must be cautious about a way of thinking that insists that every explanation about every part of the world be made to dance to the ever-present melody of the divine.

Consider, for example, the way that religious thinking changes through time; or rather, how in one respect, it never changes. When religious thinking is confronted with new facts that don't fit with its understanding of the world, it will rearrange all of them except for one: the existence of a thinking god. In this refusal to give up an assumption that can never be dispensed with, it reveals why its nature is inimical to the development of truly open thought. The habit that religious thinking inculcates in us is that of accepting assumptions and of finding new explanations that allow old assumptions to persist unchanged rather than questioning them. Since religious thinking teaches us to begin with, or at the very least, include in every explanation the same assumption – God – it repeatedly drives our thought into a deep groove from which it is hard to escape.

The full notions of evidence, meaning and reality are – sometimes deliberately – concealed by religious education, and this leads to the absence of true autonomy. The perspective of philosophical thinking gives us the opportunity to frame problems in different ways by learning to sit 'outside' of different ways of thinking. To think in a truly unbounded way, with no path of potential future knowledge prohibited, and to stand tall in order to take in the whole vista of competing ways of thinking, we must be attached to nothing. We must not cling to a collection of beliefs that admit no questioning or compromise, and around which everything else must be made to revolve. Philosophy, by contrast with religion, insists on nothing as its foundation, other than the questioning of foundations. Philosophy is willing to throw out, replace or play with any assumption just to see what happens. That is true freedom of thought.

As long as it is one method among many, religious thinking doesn't limit our ability to think freely and I'm tempted to suggest that it even expands our range of options. But the larger and more exclusively the tenets of religious thinking loom in the minds of those who are taught to think through its method, the more it inhibits the philosophical reflex that allows us to think in different ways. Religious thinking is only an obstacle to an understanding, freethinking society when it dominates, but when it does dominate, it draws the curtains of our options tight such that only the narrowest shaft of light may enter. Were a parent to half-blind a child by poking out an eye, we would object. And yet, the intellectual equivalent – ensuring that some children are denied the opportunity to see the world in particular ways by instilling in them only one way of thinking, and one that inculcates a habit of telling new stories to protect old ones at that – arouses little if no objection. There are parts of the world where, if you ask children why earthquakes happen in California, you will be told that it is God's punishment for liberal attitudes towards homosexuality. This way of thinking eclipses and excludes so many others: the physical science that explains fault lines in the earth, and the mathematical thinking that shows the lack of correlation between earthquakes and those liberal attitudes, to choose just two. Religion can conceal straightforward scientific knowledge, but it is at its most insidious when it fails to teach its children to think inductively. By doing so, it narrows our capacity to make the judgements of causality through which we fundamentally understand the world, and the life-changing decisions that we make based upon that understanding.

The power of philosophical thinking to fundamentally change our understanding of whole bodies of knowledge, to make us aware of the depth of our political misunderstanding, and to help us to spend less time fruitlessly shouting at each other comes from its vocabulary. *The way* that we learn to think philosophically is vital because the currency of our mutual political and philosophical understanding is the language that we use to trade our ideas. Philosophical thinking is more than a pile of ideas: it's the ability to label them so that we can exchange them with as much precision as possible. Without a shared vocabulary that makes clear the fundamental concepts of reality, evidence, meaning and reasoning that all of our truths are built on, we are reduced to complaining about 'liars', 'charlatans' and 'demagogues' while being completely powerless to point out what we believe makes them those things. A vocabulary of ideas that makes clear our beliefs about what's true and why is what stops us from being politically powerless because it makes it possible to point out the fragility or the dishonesty that we sense but cannot always put into words.

If we believe that the goalposts of an argument are being moved before the eyes of our fellow citizens by those we consider dishonest, we should learn to point out how, and we should learn to do it in such a way that makes it possible to do more than just call them liars. If we're lucky, we can do it well enough to embarrass those who hope we won't catch them red-handed with their hidden premises, assumptions, contradictions, probable reasoning, dishonest inductions or bad analogies.

When we fail to find the words to point out something fundamental and substantial, we say nothing that convinces anyone who does not already agree with us. And yet, to become less tribal, we must be able to convince the other tribes. In order to achieve greater success in that endeavour, we need to jettison the vagueness of the pseudointellectual terms that we've only recently adopted. When people complain about a post-truth world or fake news, we should ask them if they believe that the politicians of ancient Greece – or those of any other time or place – were any more truthful than ours are today. There never was a golden age of truth, and so there is no age of post-truth. The solution to the manipulation of what we see as truth is not to call our opponents liars. The solution is a small vocabulary of fundamental concepts that give us the ability to notice that manipulation, to describe it and to point it out. Only words can bridge the gap of misunderstanding – the words that lift our minds up to the abstract concepts that give us perspective on everything that we claim is true, and which make it possible to share that experience with others. What reveals and sharpens the abilities on which stable politics, intellectual freedom and our capacity to understand depend are six simple concepts: *deduction*, *induction*, *analogy*, *reality*, *evidence* and *meaning*, as well as the education that shows us how to make use of them.

In troubled times, when the process of politics fails and we find ourselves walking back into the darkness of killing fields, gas chambers and crusades of violence, we remember why the happiness, peace and prosperity of the human race depends on us finding the words to understand each other. If we continue to fail to harness our miraculous awareness of the elements of our own truths, we'll corrode the unavoidable and essential foundation of intelligent, freethinking societies and we'll leave future generations to pay the terrible price.

The Silver Bullet: Why Schools Don't Teach Us to Think

The fundamental and unavoidable concepts that define the way human beings think and argue are better understood and explained today than at any other time in history. Yet despite the towering piles of ideas about thinking that we've amassed and honed in the centuries since Aristotle's death, in our age we fail to use them with significantly greater frequency or clarity than did Alexander the Great: a fourteen-year-old boy who lived in the 4th century BC. But if the fundamental ideas are not only still around but more highly polished than ever, then why are they not the public currency of discussion and debate? Why are they not the fuel of our private freedom, range and subtlety of thought? The answer lies in what we teach our children – or rather, in what we fail to teach them.

Education is supposed to be a silver bullet – a productivity-inducing saviour of the economy, a mind-expanding bringer of creativity, a solution for the problems that drag societies down and even, in some cases, an intrinsic good with little obvious practical benefit. But in their attempts to achieve all these things, Western schools have lost their way. It's easy to say that education is a good thing, and in an age of soundbites, slogans, memes and other short and shallow affirmations of what we believe, there are many ways to signal our support for it. It's easy to wax lyrical about the value of education, but it's hard to define it: to say *what should be on the curriculum* and *why*. Concerned voices argue for better funding for schools, fewer tests, different tests, civic education, the resurrection or destruction of grammar schools, charter schools or private schools and countless other suggestions. But the most important question is the one we ask least often and answer with the least conviction. When teachers are asked that question by their students – 'why are we learning this?' – it strikes fear into their hearts. If you're a teacher of business studies or economics, at least you can claim that your subject is a ticket to job opportunity; but what do the other teachers say when their pupils ask why they're studying mathematics, Spanish or geography if they've got no intention of being an engineer, a translator or a professional geographer?

The answer is this: the reward for studying a subject is not the facts you end up with at the end of the course; it's the way of thinking that produced them. Most discussions about what to do and why – in business, in politics, in family life – don't map in any way on to the subjects that we learn at school. We rarely face problems that are uniquely 'scientific', 'mathematical' or 'literary'. More often, they are a mixture of different ways of thinking. Life is nothing like school; it isn't divided into subjects. Life forces us to use different types of thinking to make sense of all the angles of complex problems. A true education in thinking does not teach us to absorb a collection of facts that we can't make use of; it teaches us to apply an arsenal of different ways of thinking and problem-solving to life itself.

Today we conceive of the subjects that modern culture values and teaches in schools – the subjects that shape the way we think – primarily as their end product. What we take away from our study of subjects is not a way of thinking, but facts. When subjects are not overtly taught as ways of thinking, they can become not even limited *sets* of facts, but misguided, disorganised and confusing *piles of facts*. The way we learn can prepare us to amaze at a pub quiz or pass the exams of a subject, yet be of limited use to us the moment we walk out of the school gates for the last time. Without a clear conception of different types of thinking, it is hard for us to see their relative strengths and weaknesses in finding different kinds of truths, and to decide when to use them. Every subject, when taught as a way of thinking, has the potential to be a goldmine of fundamental and general ideas.

The most methodologically baffling subject is, unquestionably, geography. One minute, geography studies rocks and rivers in the way that a natural scientist might, and the next it theorises about human choices and activities like a social scientist. Geography might give us a lesson in the statistical analysis of the physical world only to follow it with a lesson about cultural or economic trends. Geography – in its physical and human guises – can be akin either to chemistry or to anthropology, and when it's not moving between these two completely different ways of thinking, proving and explaining, it can be something even worse: an archetypal pile of facts about the length of rivers or the height of mountains. We don't think of geography as a 'hard science', and yet that's exactly what physical geography is. Human geography – which explains the relationship of a landscape and the humans that live in it – is a mind-boggling and wonderful mixture of psychology, archaeology, anthropology and other disciplines too. When you boil geography down to reveal the essence of its method, it turns out to be a complex mixture. This melange of methods isn't a problem for professional geographers – the crossover and potential for collaboration between disciplines is what makes it so intellectually fruitful – but for teaching children to see the differences between different ways of thinking, a mess of methods is a dangerous thing.

A subject that moves between methods runs the risk of making those methods unclear, but it's the opinion of some professionals that their subjects are taught in a way that completely misrepresents and misunderstands them altogether. The British poet Michael Rosen recently complained of a poetry exam in which students were asked to choose the 'right' alternative title for a poem. He argued that the question completely misunderstands the point of poetry. He went on to suggest that poetry exists in opposition to the aims of science or political debate; that it 'uses the sounds of words to express feelings without actually saying what those feelings are', that it's a way to 'suggest things without necessarily coming to a conclusion' and to 'play with language without it having to be literal'. Even when we find a type of thinking that is deliberately less precise than most, we teach and test it as if it were otherwise. We should teach and test subjects like poetry and art in a way that is intrinsically connected to their nature. We should aim to conceive of poetry and art more like poets and artists, and less like examiners whose job is to quantify whatever is within their reach – even the things that cannot easily be quantified.

Not only do we place insufficient emphasis on the methods that make each subject what it is, and that teach us to think in different ways, but we also misunderstand the types of thinking they involve. In foreign languages, we're stuck deep in the idea that, because its main and most obvious ingredients are words, it must be the cousin of English and couldn't be further from mathematics. But dig beneath the surface of this simplistic idea and you'll see that the grammar – the formulaic structure of a language – has as much in common with mathematics or chemistry as it does with English. The agreement of gender between nouns and adjectives or between pronouns and verb endings is a similar sort of thinking to the balancing of a mathematical or chemical equation: what you do to one side you must do to the other.

The questions of order and structure without which no human being can learn to speak a second language are less often the central pillar of foreign language teaching today than they used to be. The laborious memorisation of verb tables can be extremely dull, but verbs are the unit around which every sentence that we utter is organised. If you fail to teach the principles that allow us communicate *who did what* and *when they did it*, you teach in denial of the nature of human language. As the Greek grammarian Dionysius Thrax explained, grammar is what 'permits us to speak a language or to speak about a language', and when we teach languages without due emphasis on it, we make what must inevitably be central only peripheral. Lofty ambitions for the study of foreign languages are embodied in the inspirational posters you see on classroom walls – such as Goethe's claim that: 'he who does not speak a foreign language knows nothing of his own', or Charlemagne's that: 'to have another language is to have another soul' – but before we are able to achieve such aims, we must return to teaching the basic and intrinsic principles that define human language.

To think of subjects primarily as piles of knowledge rather than the method that created them is to make it hard to apply what we learn at school to the problems of real life, and this has been the fate of science. It's a common complaint of scientists that most of us don't understand the scientific method, and yet to merely concentrate on a veneer of clever-sounding facts remains an approach that holds sway in the modern world of educational theory. In the battle to decide whether education should revolve around knowledge or ways of thinking, it is the educational philosopher E.D. Hirsch who carries the flag for facts. Here he is, defending his 'knowledge-based curriculum', in full awareness of the bemusement of scientists:

> Some scientists may feel that we are trying to combat scientific illiteracy in an inappropriate way. Lists of facts and concepts just don't reflect the true character of science. Granted, but a large part of any science can be learned without mathematics, and that part is precisely the content that is likely to be most important to the general public.

The part of the scientific method that we can put to use most often and to the greatest effect in our everyday lives is science's understanding of induction and statistical thinking. It is this training that makes scientists able to notice causes and connections in everyday life that the rest of us habitually miss. When Hirsch encourages today's teachers to teach science 'without mathematics', he pushes modern culture deeper into the pile of facts that obscures our understanding of scientific thinking and a true scientific education.

English is not really about novels, science is not really about molecules or space and history is not really about the dates of battles or the deaths of kings. Each and every subject can do more than give us cold, dead facts that we can only apply to the subject itself. Education should give us more than knowledge that impresses at a pub quiz. It should teach us to understand that the real power of subjects is to be found in the way of thinking that defines them – because without that, it's almost impossible to see the connection between those countless thousands of hours of lessons and the mixed and complex questions of life itself.

This move away from teaching the ability to think about any subject, topic or thing by sharpening the fundamental tools of thinking towards an emphasis on the concrete facts of particular subjects has long been derided as counterproductive. More than half a century ago, the novelist Dorothy L. Sayers, in her 1948 essay 'The Lost Tools of Learning', wrote that 'Modern education concentrates on "teaching subjects", leaving the method of thinking, arguing, and expressing one's conclusions to be picked up by the scholar as he goes along.' The medieval curriculum whose passing she regrets taught logic, grammar and rhetoric. It was called the 'Trivium', and was 'intended to teach the pupil the proper use of the tools of learning, before he began to apply them to subjects at all'.

Aristotle's conception of education starts with thinking and moves towards how we might apply it in order to find the thing we call knowledge. Today, our curricula work in reverse: they revolve around bodies of knowledge in the hope that we'll absorb their methods. The classical view of education – influenced heavily by Aristotle's work on reasoning and systems of thinking – emphasised the general instead of the particular, and it was the approach that endured through the age of the Romans and the medieval Catholic Church. Today, as modern cognitive psychology returns to the idea that abstract and general ideas teach us far more than particular facts, we have the chance to return to a golden age of powerful and general ideas. Changing the way we think, though, demands that we conceive of education as the teaching of *methods*, and not as the teaching of facts about the things that those methods investigate. As Northrop

Frye put it: 'Physics is an organised body of knowledge about nature, and a student of it says that he is learning physics, not that he is learning nature.'

The allure of concrete facts is great. The sweet taste of the finished product satisfies us, but taught without due emphasis on the methods that produce them, they are like bowls of sweets at a children's party. If we don't consume them judiciously, we end up running around on a didactic high, carried away by the saccharine appeal of our apparent cleverness. We're so used to thinking about subjects as the study of *things* that it can be difficult to free ourselves from this idea. Instead we should aim to be like Alexander, who when the conversation changed to unfamiliar topics, would simply have started to think about the best way to approach the question, if indeed he believed it was one of those questions that can be meaningfully answered.

For the avoidance of doubt: I am not denigrating facts in themselves. I am not arguing that we could or should throw out facts; far from it. If you don't know the dates of history, what reasoning could you perform about what caused what? If you don't know the Spanish word for 'drink', what will you do? Be 'creative' and make one up? Without the vocabulary of languages, the facts of history or the facts of natural science, it's impossible to teach the styles of thinking that make those subjects what they are. We learn to think *through* the facts, as long as we remember that they're grist for the mill that is thinking.

⌐

A tyranny of superficial knowledge is a dangerous thing, but in a well-intentioned attempt to move away from the piling-up of facts, modern education careered into a different obstacle:

vague ideas about thinking. Einstein's definition of education was 'that which remains, if one has forgotten everything he learned in school', and this vision of thinking is the holy grail of education. The facts fade from our memory, but the intelligence that we honed *through them* is the real goal. It's easy to say that because facts don't truly educate us, we should concentrate on teaching the magic glue of thinking that connects all the things we can argue about and know – but it is hard to describe thinking in a way that makes a difference. It's easier to teach facts than it is to teach the concepts that really constitute general intelligence, and it is hard to express what those concepts are in a way that is concrete, practical and effective. But today, this is exactly the problem we face: a modern urge to jettison facts, only to replace them with a simplistic collection of buzzwords that not only fails to explain the fundamental structure of different ways of thinking, but also actively conceals the differences between them.

The variety of intellectual colour that we are able to summon depends, in large part, on the richness of our vocabulary of ideas – but the modern age's lexicon of thinking is limited and vague. When we want to describe what is going on in the minds of intelligent people, we use phrases like 'critical thinking', 'analysis' and 'creativity', but these labels make it harder to see the thinking that they're supposed to help us to understand. In the same way that you could describe elite athletes who specialise in completely different sports all with the word 'athletic' – and compress all of the differences in their athletic abilities into that one word – labelling abilities with vague words doesn't help us to see what others can do that we can't. A concrete vocabulary of ideas is one that clearly shows us all the distinctions we can't yet see; a vague one only covers them up.

The roots of our modern struggle to describe the subtle differences we want to notice go back more than half a century. In 1956, an American educational psychologist by the name of Benjamin Bloom put his name to a book called *Taxonomy of Educational Objectives: The Classification of Educational Goals.* Education has always been obliged to tell us where it's taking us, and for decades it is Benjamin Bloom's educational goals that schools in the Western world have been aiming for. The six words that have shaped the modern Western mind more than any other – the vocabulary of ideas that's supposed to help us reveal the mysteries of human thinking – are these:

> *Creating*
>
> *Evaluating*
>
> *Analysing*
>
> *Applying*
>
> *Remembering*
>
> *Understanding*

These six words are supposed to describe – and help us to master – various types of thinking that we could understand and use to improve our lives. It's a scale of six words that tries to describe what one person can do with their mind that another cannot. The scale is organised by complexity, with the most complex at the top, and on the face of it, this appears quite a sensible and common-sense way to talk about thinking. After all, creating seems harder than just remembering, doesn't it? And you do have to understand something before you can analyse or evaluate it, don't you? But is it really that simple?

Take *analysing*, for instance. The analysing of literature is completely different – incomparable – to the analysing of science. They are fundamentally different ways of analysing. To call both of them 'analysing' is to cover up the difference between them. It tells you that two ways of thinking are the same, when they are not. In the same way, evaluating a poem isn't the same as evaluating a set of data or a newspaper article, and the analysis of music is nothing like the analysis of football. *What* we evaluate and analyse makes all the difference to *how* we do it.

The aim of talking about thinking is to reveal the differences between all the ways we can think so that we can use any of them when we need to. A framework of words about thinking that conceals those differences cannot teach you to think; it can only confuse you. As a way of teaching us to reflect on our own thinking, and when and where we should use it, the list of words that underpins modern schooling in the Western world creates more problems than it solves.

You can't make people smarter by telling them to 'think critically' or, as the Sophists did, by telling them that 'making sense' was a revolution in ideas. Both Bloom and the Sophists were on the right track: they understood that without talking about thinking, it's difficult for one human to teach another to see the angles that they miss. Bloom wanted us, like Aristotle did, to have a powerful menu of ideas that we could apply to everything we think about. He said we should be able to 'apply the appropriate abstraction without having to be prompted as to which abstraction is correct or without having to be shown how to use it in that situation'. But the fact is that his vocabulary of thinking isn't enough to teach us how to think like a scientist, a lawyer, a poet or a philosopher, and instead it has become a comforting set of labels we use to reassure ourselves that we've taught kids something useful about thinking. We need a framework of thinking – a vocabulary of ideas – but it's not Bloom's that transforms what we notice and how we think, it's Aristotle's.

Philosophers have, for centuries, rightly held up Socrates as the prototype of the questioning, independent and critical mind. But in the attempt to help us reach this goal, educators – even those of profound thought and lifelong dedication – have not managed to describe the ideas that make it possible. The philosopher Martha Nussbaum, after citing a roll-call of dedicated, sincere and influential educators, concedes that in practical terms, we still do not have much of a recipe for how to teach critical and independent thought:

> The examples of [the educators] Pestalozzi, Alcott, and Tagore are helpful, but extremely general. They do not tell today's average teacher very much about how to structure learning so that it elicits and develops the child's ability to understand the logical structure of an argument, to detect bad reasoning, to challenge ambiguity ... Indeed, one of the great defects of Tagore's experiment – shared to some degree by Pestalozzi and Alcott – was that he prescribed no method that others could carry on in his absence ... Dewey, however, never addressed systematically the question of how Socratic critical reasoning might be taught to children of various ages.

But look! A new and shiny tablet! An interactive webpage! Today, we spend far more time talking about how to present information than we do asking whether it can teach us to think. A bad textbook with shoddy, confusing and vague ideas piled up into a disorganised array of facts that leads nowhere doesn't suddenly become useful by turning the book into an app, a web-page or pixels on a screen. Utility, convenience and the capacity to hold our attention do not intrinsically educate us. Education depends on the quality of its ideas. Technology has the power to enhance education in countless ways, but it also has the power to make us fetishise style over substance – and *that* is the educational, cultural and political mode of the modern age.

Today's schoolchildren have grown up in a rhetorical age that educates them to believe that intelligence is not the ability to think with philosophical, rational or conceptual skill, but rather the ability to sound good. If we are troubled by the vapid pronouncements of politicians, poor-quality political debate, gullibility in the face of polarised media outlets, a deluge of meaningless management-speak, susceptibility to the emptiness of advertising slogans, the regressive rise of pseudoscience and the inability of young people (and, in turn, adult citizens) to make sense of the things that other people tell them are true, we need look no further than the schooling that fuels it all.

Rhetorical culture is what you get from a rhetorical education, because instead of a *vocabulary of ideas*, modern education emphasises a *vocabulary of vocabulary*. The school closest to where I live has more than 60 books on its recommended reading list for fourteen year olds. Only two of them are non-fiction. We live in an educational culture that, through novels and poetry, focuses on teaching us words like 'verdant' instead of 'green', 'discombobulated' instead of 'confused', and 'subterranean' instead of 'underground'. The vocabulary we learn – and therefore the ideas that we can use to analyse the world and what other people claim is true – is centred on style at the expense of substance. For thousands of years – alongside the cultural essentials of fiction and poetry – we used to teach the fundamental ideas of reasoning, as well as concrete and practical concepts about evidence and truth. Our education used to teach us to think philosophically, through powerful concepts like *deduction*, the *hidden premise* and *analogy*. Today, we've narrowed our education to focus on an artistic, literary and rhetorical way of thinking and arguing that puts sounding good ahead of thinking deeply. We learn pleasant, even beautiful prose, but not clear argument. The result is that we're more familiar with beautiful language and beautiful ideas than precise language and precise ideas, and when we come to talk about things other than stories – like politics or science – it shows.

How much mental energy and attention we expend dressing ideas up, polishing them instead of deconstructing them! Today we 'leverage' things that we used to merely 'use'. In the past, we didn't have the 'time' to do things, but now we don't have 'the bandwidth'. This faux-cleverness – this dressing up of simple ideas that everyone understands in longer and more stylish words – comes from learning to call things verdant rather than green.

Today, we offer children the style of poets, novelists and orators, but not the necessary counterweight: the substantial precision of philosophers. This lack of attention to the way we use words and the way that they are combined in argument is the result of an imbalance in our education, our culture, and consequently, in our politics.

Of course, it would be a mistake to dismiss fiction, poetry or any other art. We shouldn't dispose of one imbalance only to replace it with another. You might have the arguments of both sides of any important issue well understood, but have your mind changed by reading a novel (or watching a TV programme) about how others live – others whose lives you had imagined to be totally different until you *saw* them or *experienced* them.

Reasoning and argument aren't, by a long shot, the sum total of the human thought process and experience, but they are its essential foundation because every one of us shares and cannot avoid them – and this is especially true in politics. The end result of a school system that teaches style over substance is a culture that learns not *ideas and concepts themselves*, but rather how to coat them in a veneer of erudite vocabulary, and to mistake this process for education.

Today, education is trapped between the extremes of a dedication to the concrete but limiting comfort of facts, and a menu of vague and meaningless ways of describing human thinking. The everyday vocabulary that we use to talk about thinking – in school, and consequently in Western society in general – is philosophically and psychologically naïve. As a result, it struggles to help us either to understand, refine or add to the ways we think. Our conception of education and intelligence in the early 21st century has pushed us further into a rhetorical age – one that's unable to grab hold of what is fundamental and eternal. Swept away by our inability to think, talk and therefore understand both the world and each other in a philosophical way, we have had to settle for rhetoric. When Aristotle wrote that 'The duty of rhetoric is to deal with such matters as we deliberate upon without arts or systems to guide us, in the hearing of persons who cannot take in at a glance a complicated argument, or follow a long chain of reasoning,' he presaged the intellectual tenor of the modern age. To change the way we think, we need to be able to talk about thinking. Moreover, we need ways of describing thought that are specific and helpful. It means very little to say 'I don't agree with your analysis', but to say that the person you're talking to hasn't defined the thing they're discussing, that they've changed their definition midway through a debate, that their argument relies on questionable assumptions or premises, that their reasoning is just probable rather than certain, or that they've been fooled by a loose analogy or infallible signs ... *that* is saying something about the way human beings think.

If we want our children to give us an opinion then we have to teach them the concrete ideas that allow them to see the structure of arguments, theories, analogies and different ways of thinking, proving and explaining. Education's challenge is to show us the possibilities of our own minds with a vocabulary of ideas that lives or dies by its quality, its clarity and its utility. A curriculum that teaches us facts about everything other than the unchanging facts of the way we think, and a vocabulary of ideas that makes it harder to see the distinctions that constitute subtle and precise thought is a curriculum that fails those whose minds it seeks to open. That which leaves us statistically, linguistically, logically, conceptually and philosophically unaware is not worthy of the name of education.

The Limits of Thinking

The Sophists were right: skill in the art of argument is power. The ability to see the fundamental structure of arguments, theories and different ways of thinking not only gives us more options in our search to find our own truths; it also makes us better at persuading other people that we're right. Thinking, in a sense, is arguing with yourself. With every angle that we notice for ourselves, we add to our power to pick and choose which angles to show other people in our attempts to bring them round to our point of view. But what do we do with that power? Do we always use it to honestly explore the contradictions and counter-considerations of our own beliefs, or do we use what we know simply to win as many arguments and persuade as many people as possible?

The answer, of course, is often that we are easily tempted by the prospect of victory, and this is particularly true when we're young. For Aristotle, what happens when you combine youth with training in words and reasoning is that you get intelligent kids with the ability to refute and to ridicule. He says: 'while they love honour, they love victory still more; for youth is eager for superiority over others ... they are fond of fun and therefore witty, wit being well-bred insolence.' Here, Aristotle comes across as the teacher who is patient with cocky youngsters experimenting with what they can do with their growing intelligence. He seems happy to accept a little of the desire to dominate or to have fun, if it's a stage on the road to a sincere search for truth. Plato wasn't quite as laid-back about honing young intellects and putting up with the consequences. He was worried that those young egos would run wild, complaining that 'when young people get their first taste of arguments, they misuse it by treating it as a kind of game of contradiction. They imitate those who've refuted them by refuting others themselves, and, like puppies, they enjoy dragging and tearing those around them with their arguments.'

Plato's description of the young reminds me of my youthful self. When I first came across some of the concepts that make up the vocabulary of ideas promoted in this book, I realised that I could make things sound persuasive even when I didn't believe them. The arrogant, teenage me would dishonestly disclose only the angles that were convenient – and even now, in the heat of an argument about something I *want* to be true more than I *believe* is true, I still catch myself doing it. A little bit of argumentative skill makes us feel clever and in control, and sometimes it feels so good that it tempts us into deceiving even ourselves. Do we not all still suffer from some of the same youthful ego-gravity that drags us down to the level of wanting nothing more than to win?

All of us actively look for the evidence that suits us, and if we find any that doesn't fit, we have a talent for twisting it so that it does, or ignoring it altogether. Charles Darwin – who undermined the belief of a greater number of people than perhaps anyone in the course of human history when he put forward the theory of evolution by natural selection – was more than aware of the dangers of being attached to what you believe, or want to believe, simply because it's more comfortable than contemplating the alternative. Describing his own search for truth, he wrote:

> I had, also, during many years, followed a golden rule, namely, that whenever a published fact, a new observation or thought came across me, which was opposed to my general results, to make a memorandum of it without fail and at once; for I had found that such facts and thoughts were far more apt to escape from the memory than favourable ones. Owing to this habit, very few objections were raised against my views which I had not at least noticed and attempted to answer.

Darwin's solution to what we today call *confirmation bias* (our tendency to ignore or wilfully explain away any observation that appears to contradict what we hold to be true) was intellectual: he made a system of notes that made it harder for him to ignore inconvenient ideas. Today, we often think of confirmation bias in exactly that way: as an intellectual problem that demands an intellectual solution. But while it's true that an intellectual approach to arguments, logic, language and numbers can help us to understand the way we think, to consider more possibilities, and thus avoid our own mistakes, its success is limited by the hunger of our egos to protect what we already believe. Of all the assumptions that we could question, the ones we rarely examine with complete honesty and openness are our own. What stops us from being able to clearly see our options is not a lack of intellectual strategies or ideas. The foundation of the intellectual process by which we make every new observation or bit of data 'fit' into what we already believe and dismiss the rest isn't intellectual; it's emotional.

When we consider a premise that we disagree with, or when someone points out to us that a part of our reasoning doesn't add up, we feel a pang of emotion, a jolt of stress, a twinge of pain. We have an emotional aversion to being proven wrong – and especially so in public – because our egos unrealistically tell us that we should have everything figured out and arranged in perfect harmony. Damage caused to one part of our structure of beliefs causes the others that rely on it for support to wobble and crack, and the process of reorganising and rebuilding that structure can cause us to suffer acute psychological distress. When others put a crack in our argument, instead of studying the crack and putting some thought into building ourselves a new argument, we lash out and try and smash everyone else's. We hope that this will serve as an effective distraction to mitigate the panic we feel when we realise that sometimes, our beliefs don't add up.

A wave of emotion is very often the underlying cause of poor argument and clouded thinking; it's what causes us to say the most hurtful thing or go straight for the most extreme comparison. It explains why the Hitler Analogy is so common: because the more emotionally desperate we get, the weaker our ability to argue fairly becomes. The moment when we're least likely to treat our own arguments the same as those of others and genuinely question them is when we feel emotionally stretched; when the foundational cornerstones of our systems of belief and identity are threatened. Ultimately, it is not a lack of intellectual tools that stops us from questioning our own beliefs; it's a lack of the emotional strength to use them on ourselves.

This strength – the ability to ignore that rising feeling of discomfort or even panic, and to honestly and openly entertain new and distressing ideas – can't really be learned from a book. It isn't like a fact. It can't be quickly googled and memorised. It can't easily be shared like a story or even a vocabulary of ideas. We should heed the words of Socrates, who lamented that wisdom is not 'like water, which always flows from a full cup into an empty one'.

To exceed the limits of the way we think, we have to think of the shaping of the intellect as being more than the pouring of ideas into heads. Socrates berated people for agreeing with him just to be polite, and he amazed his pupils with his devotion to examining his life openly and honestly. He was one of those people who leaves you staggered by their ability to do – emotionally – what you aren't currently capable of doing. Perhaps that's what Steve Jobs meant when he said he'd give up all his technology for an afternoon with Socrates: he didn't just want Socrates' *ideas*; he wanted *the experience of* Socrates.

Ideas alone do not educate. Without a living example that we respect deeply enough to learn from, ideas alone can be cold and lifeless. We need more than teachers with ideas; we need mentors who show us what's possible: a strength not just of intellect, but of intellectual character. The effect of one person on another, which is education at its most basic level, depends on the magical point of contact that's a product of both of their personalities. Strength of intellectual character doesn't exist in the ideas or the values we learn; it exists in living form as those from whom we learn it.

The relationship between a mentor and their pupil is one that can instil the emotional bravery on which true intellectual exploration depends. When successful, it does what few human connections achieve: it overcomes the love we have for ourselves and our own ideas. The living human force of education is why our most powerful educational influences are family, friends, and the teachers who transcend the pouring of knowledge from one head into another as if it were water, and become mentors, lighting a great fire that powers us to perfect our nature from within. In the words of Goethe, 'we only learn from those we love'. Both education and intelligence are products of not only how we think, but also how we feel. No matter how much we know – even about thinking – what makes us truly wise is the emotional ability to withstand that feeling of rising panic and to think again; and that takes more than a library of ideas. The final irony of the mind is that it's built on the guts.

Part V

A School of Thought

The Way it is: On The Intelligence, Education and Happiness of Human Beings

The Minds We Have, The Lives We Live

The basic predicament of all living creatures is to be born into a game whose rules they did not decide, and to play it with a mind they did not create. The mind is every animal's primary means of interacting with the world and surviving in it, and this is especially true of one animal in particular: human beings. Of all the tools that we rely on in the course of our time on Earth, the most important is one that we are born with.

The divine spark of mind inside us – the god in our machine – is what allows us to make sense of, understand and control reality. Our minds create *possibilities*. The more that we understand the tool that orients us in the world and allows us to survive in it, the easier and the richer our lives become. The happiness of human beings – as individuals, as societies and as a species – depends on our ability to use the minds we have to master the lives we live.

In the pursuit of that happiness, we wield a mind that, were they able to understand it, would make us the envy of the animals. The unparalleled depth of our self-awareness and our capacity to share our thoughts through speech give us the ability not only to shape our lives, but also *to sharpen the tool that we use to shape our lives*. When our synapses fire, they can do so in the contemplation of firing synapses. What is truly special about the human mind is neither the depth nor the power of its thought, but the fact that it is aware of itself. We are the only living creatures who are born with the ability to understand and upgrade the very thing on which their survival and happiness depend.

What defines the human mind, though, is not just its awareness of its patterns, but the patterns themselves. Deductive, inductive and analogical reasoning are universal. Either we use a rule to tell us what's true of examples, we use examples to work out what might be true as a rule, or we use the similarities that we notice between things to consider in what other ways they might be similar. When we think, when we argue and when we describe, we deduce, we induce and we analogise.

To create something meaningful, however, we need more than just reason: we need truths. In the absence of unprovable starting points in the search for knowledge, the logical operations which form the basic mechanisms of thought would have no material to work on. They would start with nothing and produce nothing. Almost every truth is built on the method that produced it: a system of assumptions about reality, evidence and meaning. No culture has *The Answers*, but every culture has ways of finding them. There is no truth without a system of truth.

The structure of the mind that we all share is the reason why – despite the differences in our languages and our cultures – we are able to make sense of the ideas of other humans who are separated from us in space and time. It is due to our intellectual inheritance and the written word that we can still hear and understand the voices of men and women who have lain dead in the ground for thousands of years. Our minds are all cut from the same cloth. The knowledge of our species is woven in threads of words and numbers onto a common fabric of reason, and to think like a human being is to be stuck with *deduction, induction, analogy, reality, meaning* and *evidence*. The six secrets reflect something deep and universal about the nature of the human mind. This is the way it is. This is the human intellectual condition.

It is easier to make out the similarities that define us – such as our self-aware, rational, linguistic and systematic minds – than it is to make out a common outline of the human condition: *the shape that our lives must take* because of those similarities. We are characterised by so many drives, desires and instincts that a common blueprint of our nature is a difficult thing to sketch, and yet our lives do have broad and unmistakable similarities. We can debate which of our instincts is the stronger – say, to cooperate or to compete – but without *other people*, there is no possibility of either. As Aristotle observed, man is a social animal. Few of us want to live in a lonely wilderness, existing amid the splendour of our own Walden instead of in the company of others. It is overwhelmingly the case that we do not live alone. We desire each other's company, approval and support, and as our species became more numerous – forcing us to cooperate or compete with ever-larger groups of people – we became not just social animals, but political animals too. This is the lot of human beings: we are stuck with each other.

In addition to the inevitable social and political situation in which we find ourselves, we are very often faced with problems that can appear less practical – even frivolous – but which are no less a part of our human condition. Instead of expending our limited resources solely in search of shelter or food, or other essentials like peace, we have always lifted up our gaze to tackle less immediate problems. We feel the pull of our curiosity dragging us towards certain questions, some of them abstract and theoretical, with no immediate prospect of material gain. Perhaps we evolved a philosophical curiosity because it eventually leads us back to some practical insight and advantage, but for whatever reason we feel it, we are compelled to try to understand. Our lives are shaped not just by our social and political condition, but by a philosophical condition that draws us to knowledge through the feelings of curiosity and wonder. As Aristotle says: 'all men by nature desire to know.'

It is fashionable to say that such and such an aspect of human nature is what defines us: music, art, sport, meditation, worship ... even intoxication and madness. We explore many things that express the complexity of the human mind and spirit, but the substance of our everyday lives is the social, political and philosophical challenges that they present us with. We each embellish our lives in a myriad of different ways, but our common foundation is the same.

It is a tenet of evolutionary biology that the human mind must have evolved in such a way as to prepare us for the kinds of problems that we inevitably encounter. When education fails to teach us about the fundamentals of the minds that we have evolved in order to solve the problems that are unavoidably the substance of human life, it undermines the foundation of human progress and happiness. But to what extent have we taken the opportunity to understand and upgrade the intelligence on which our survival and our happiness depend? How well has humanity risen to the challenge of conceiving of and providing an education that harnesses the minds we have, in order to make the most of the lives we live?

The Spirit of a Society, The Mind of a Species

In the mountains of northern Colombia there is a tribe called the Kogi. The Kogi take their future leaders – as young children of three or four – into the darkness of secluded temples, or into caves that represent 'the womb of the Great Mother'. Away from all family and social life, eating sparingly and fasting regularly, they rise at sunset and go to sleep before dawn. In the temple and in the cave, they learn the myths, singing, dancing, botany, dreams, signs, spells and symbols of their people. They do not emerge during the hours of daylight until they are ready to be 'reborn', eighteen years later. To be a Kogi is to value Kogi culture – a particular understanding of the world and a particular way of life – and it is this journey into the darkness that keeps it alive.

This passing down of culture – this *social education* – might seem extreme to the Western mind: a quasi-magical exception to what happens in Western minds and Western schools. But, in essence, it is no different. Just as the Kogi educate – or indoctrinate – their children, so do we. Education, for the entirety of human history, has been dominated by the teaching of culture. Every community of human beings that has ever lived has sung a different melody, but none of us has ever been silent. Social education is inevitable. Intellectual education is not.

The social education we get is essential, but it is also largely arbitrary. Every category of culture – our art, jokes, food, drink or music – is configured in a particular way, but could just as well be almost any other way. Alcoholic drinks are no more universally human than non-alcoholic drinks. One way of telling jokes is no more intrinsic to humans as a whole than any other way of telling them – but the same isn't true of thinking. The patterns of thinking are not arbitrary. Induction – which has become the foundation of Western science – allows a human being to successfully reveal the workings of the physical world in a way that objectively produces incomparable results. Ideas that are truly universal reward human beings equally, regardless of their place in space, time or the social hierarchy.

Intellectual education transcends the particular. It connects us to what is universal in man in a way that social education intrinsically cannot, but until the Greeks, it was impossible. The human beings who preceded them left no evidence of a comparable insight into the way we think. When the Greeks discovered a host of elements of our reality that seemed not to be specific to a culture, but universal – like the properties of triangles, the ratios of musical scales, the psychology of religion and even the concepts of nature and convention themselves – they opened a doorway that led them to a place outside of their own particular culture. In trying to understand the limits of their own perspective, they were led to question their political system, their gods, their minds and their assumptions in a way that had never been done before. They reached out beyond their own boundaries and managed to grasp something eternal.

This early glimpse of the eternal – and the proliferation of ideas that followed it – made it possible for the ancient Greeks to see the culture into which they had been born (and which they still held in great affection) in a new light. This thought crystallised in the mind of Plato, whose *Republic* encouraged his fellow Greeks to think again about the nature of the 'caves' of culture into which we are born. For the first time, an exclusively social education no longer represented something wholly positive. Plato saw that we are all born into a cave of cultural assumptions, tied to our society's values, its ideas, and its way of thinking, and he imagined the possibility of something new. What he imagined was an education that introduces us not only to the spirit of a society, but also to the mind of a species.

It was the inspirational electricity of Socrates that jolted Plato into giving up his career as a playwright and devoting his life to the art of thinking, but it was Plato's student who truly made intellectual education possible. We owe a great debt to Aristotle of Stagira, for building a mirror into which any human being can stare if curiosity moves them to lay eyes on the structure of their own mind. The principles of human psychology and epistemology that can be seen if we peer into that mirror for long enough are what make the sharpening of reason and the widening of perspective possible. Aristotle left us an education that made it possible for one human being to teach another not just what to believe, but how to think.

Out of the womb we all tumble, into the whorl of a ceaseless present. Bewildered by a cascade of dizzying experience, we scream protests of incomprehension and fear as if we might endlessly fall. But we don't. We land softly in our mother's arms. Held in the wide embrace of our community, the world begins to make sense. The whispered advice of the elders blows through every generation like a song, and that song is *culture*. Culture, like education, is a single word that struggles to capture the breadth of an idea. It contains multitudes – a vast and intricate portrait of an ideal of human life; a vision of what a human being is and what a human being should be. But until Aristotle, social education was the limit of our mental horizon. To make it possible to be more than 'a creature of accident, chained to and formed by the particular cave in which he is born', man *needs* intellectual education. The cave of culture is essential for the unity on which we depend, but just as humanity outgrew its infancy, none of us are children for long. It is only the second stage in our education that 'completes' us, or rather, makes it possible for us to complete ourselves.

The Principles of Intellectual Education and the Modern Misunderstanding of the Mind

Intellectual education is built on the belief that some ideas are more fundamental than others, and that we do not discover the very best of them alone. When one human being introduces another to the fundamental concepts inherent in their mind in a way that harnesses their metacognitive and metalinguistic ability, the effect is profound and unique.

But if we want a genuine intellectual education, we need more than the six secrets of intelligence themselves; we need the principles behind them. We should continue to refine the definitions, explanations and examples of fundamental ideas – and perhaps even the ideas themselves. But we cannot do without the philosophy that supports them.

The psychologists whose work explores *how we think* and *how we learn to think* – the Modern School of Thought – can teach us to think in a new (or rather, a classical) way about our minds and how we sharpen them. In Daniel Kahneman's faith in the power of language, in Richard Nisbett's experimental evidence of our capacity for abstract learning, and in James Flynn's belief in the potential of general concepts rather than particular knowledge to improve our minds, the spirit of Aristotelian and classical education has begun the process of rebirth. This is the understanding of intelligence and education to which we must now return.

Today, however, the principles on which a genuine intellectual education depends are neglected – or even dismissed out of hand. In their absence, modern education has fallen prey to misleading ideas that have shaped – and continue to shape – our culture's understanding of intelligence. The fundamental and universal principles of intellectual education that develop our minds are in conflict with the forces, theories and individuals that dismiss them, and so before we come to each principle – the ideas that we need to value if we are to make the best use of the six secrets – we must understand the main misconceptions and obstacles that are working against them. The way we're taught to think and what we're taught to believe about intelligence are so ingrained in us that we don't notice them. If we don't clearly see what is broken in our modern vision of intelligence and education, then how can we hope to fix it?

Obstacle 1: 'Traditional' Education – Knowledge, Style and Great Books

Modern education, though it feels the effect of intellectual fashions that have taken hold in recent decades, is still rooted in ideas that come not from the classical era, but from the 19th and early 20th centuries. This 'traditional' education misleads us in two equally dangerous ways: in what it teaches us to believe about intelligence, and in the way it encourages us to develop it. The first of these – our perception of intelligence – is a common, if not prevalent misconception: that intelligence is not the way in which we think, but rather *a particular kind of knowledge*.

The modern age's basic understanding of an intelligent person is someone who has *a large vocabulary, a certain erudite style, knowledge of culturally prized writers like Shakespeare or Homer*, and *particular areas of general knowledge.* The person who sounds elegant and erudite, who shines at a pub quiz and whose grammar is faultless is widely lauded as not just educated, but *intelligent* too.

Despite the fact that these types of knowledge often coincide with intelligence, they should not be mistaken for what intelligence truly amounts to: the way we think. As we have seen, the educational philosopher who represents and defends the traditional education that prizes this kind of culturally approved knowledge is E.D. Hirsch. Hirsch's book *Cultural Literacy*, published in 1987, defends a vision of traditional education defined by knowledge – but though it is a laudable attempt to outline the kind of education that produces eloquent citizens capable of mutual understanding, clear communication and the ability to reason their way to successful cooperation, it epitomises our modern misconception of what intelligence is and how we develop it.

One passage from *Cultural Literacy* has Hirsch explaining that, in a former age, his father could succinctly drop allusions to Shakespeare into his business letters. In more modern times, Hirsch argues, you could write 'there is a tide' to let someone know that there's a window of opportunity that's about to close, but you'd be wasting your time because they wouldn't understand your Shakespearean reference. He claims that 'to persuade somebody that your recommendation is wise and well-founded, you have to give lots of reasons and cite known examples and authorities. My father accomplished that and more in four words, which made quoting Shakespeare as effective as any efficiency consultant could wish.'

But ask yourself if, in quoting the Shakespearean metaphor 'there is a tide', Hirsch's father genuinely achieved any of

Hirsch's criteria. Does a metaphor count as either a reason to take the opportunity, an example of a time when an opportunity was missed, or even an authority? Why should we consider Shakespeare – a 17th-century dramatist – an authority on the factors affecting the costs of business expenses? Quoting Shakespeare is not a reason, not an example, doesn't count as evidence and lends no relevant authority. The idea of 'taking an opportunity before it passes' is no better or worse when we dress it up in Shakespearean metaphor. So why quote Shakespeare? The answer is no more profound than the application of a rhetorical sheen: it makes a common-sense idea – 'don't waste an opportunity' – sound more pleasant to the ear and therefore more persuasive.

This idea – that a literary veneer of persuasive poetry amounts to evidence, rational argument, example or authority – demonstrates the limitations of Hirsch's philosophy of communication and the understanding of intelligence that powers it. It is very close to the vision of intelligence on which the Sophists built their education in the art of rhetoric – but pleasant-sounding words combined with a shared repertoire of literary phrases and allusions do not amount to the intelligence that is at the root of good communication.

Whether the knowledge we mistake for intelligence is literary metaphor, geographical and historical 'basic' general knowledge or a larger, more literary and supposedly more impressive vocabulary, its failings are the same. Like social education, the knowledge of any culture is more arbitrary than it is universal. Instead of teaching us to think with the ideas that connect *every* culture's knowledge, 'traditional' education believes that intelligence arises naturally from the study of the knowledge that has been prized by a *single* culture. Because we mistake a veneer of culture for intelligence, we think that we can make people intelligent *through* culture: *through* the facts or *through* great books. Traditional education does not, and has never, taught us to think directly. Instead of universal ideas about a potentially infinite horizon of different types of knowledge, traditional education comprises *only* the learning of the arbitrary and conventional facts and vocabulary of a particular time and place.

What 'traditional' (or what is sometimes called 'liberal') education both have in common is their unwarranted claim to be truly classical in origin. Trying to connect one's product to an ancient lineage is an old marketing technique, and it is one to which traditional education is drawn by its nature. In *Cultural Literacy*, Hirsch invokes the august figure of Cicero. He claims that to achieve a 'Ciceronian ideal of universal public discourse' (to create a society of educated citizens who are able to take part in politics) we should educate ourselves as Cicero intended. Cicero, who was part of the classical tradition, recommended rhetoric, which Hirsch takes to mean cultural literacy – a knowledge of shared facts, vocabulary, metaphors and allusions. But if you read Cicero's book on rhetoric, you will discover that it is little concerned with knowledge. It is, as the introduction to the Loeb Classical Library edition calls it, 'a technical manual, systematic and formal in arrangement ... presenting methods and principles'. The traditional education that is inspired by Hirsch has misunderstood and misappropriated the classical model, and the result is an education of great – often classical – books, but without the systematic, technical education in thinking that was always its foundation.

We should not believe that knowledge suffices to set us on the road to intelligent communication, or that it ever did. In our desire to capture ancient wisdom, we cite the names and works of intelligent people from the past, and we hold up the books themselves as the road to intelligence rather than the systematic and universal education of principles that produced them. Yes, our classical and medieval forebears read 'great books'. Yes, they shared a common currency of historical and geographical facts – but the education that provided the foundation for those things was a technical analysis of language and logic. The reason that the Trivium worked – the classical curriculum that taught grammar, logic and rhetoric – was because it was a systematic endeavour focused on the foundations of thinking, and because it had universal and general principles.

The inability of traditional education to see the fundamental logical and linguistic foundation of classical education has led it to an over-reliance on literature. As C.P. Snow argued against F.R. Leavis in the middle of the last century, the 'traditional culture' of the West is literary culture. Snow and Leavis fought a public battle over the relative influence of scientific and literary culture at a time when scientific progress was beginning to usher in the technological age. And yet the increasing share of science's contribution to the way we live never resulted in equilibrium. In Snow's words, 'it is the traditional culture, to an extent remarkably little diminished by the emergence of the scientific one, which manages the western world.' Even now, more than half a century later, so advanced into the technological age, the way we talk, think, argue and educate is shaped to a far greater degree by literature than it is by science or philosophy.

The misunderstanding and the misappropriation of the vital, universal ingredients of the classical model of education is a trend older than Hirsch. The 19th-century cultural critic

Matthew Arnold argued that education should revolve around 'the best that has been thought and said': in other words, the 'great books' approach. To his credit, Hirsch understands the arbitrary nature of culture: he argues that we need culturally shared knowledge not necessarily because it is *best*, but because it is *ours*, and it therefore binds us together. But irrespective of whether we think of culture as having some objective value, or being merely ours, any approach that focuses our understanding of intelligence (and therefore, our education) on knowledge at the expense of thinking limits our ability to develop that intelligence.

Traditional education teaches us to think of intelligence as a superficial veneer of erudite knowledge and style, and it never attempts to teach us to think directly. The result is a culture that yearns either for the comfort of knowledge or the elegance of poetry, but not the precision and reason of philosophy. We need not just 'the best that has been thought and said', but also – and foremost – the best that has been thought and said *about thinking and saying*. Classical education was built not on learning knowledge, but on honing the intelligence that produces it. That intelligence is the energy that pulls against the inertia of our admiration for the knowledge we have already acquired, and it is what reinvigorates both the knowledge and the culture of the generations to come.

Principle 1: Intelligence is How You Think, not What You Know
Intelligence is less tangible than knowledge. It is both harder to define and harder to teach – but we shouldn't be satisfied to aim at an easier target just because we see it more clearly. The modern age teaches us to believe that what constitutes and cultivates a freethinking, intelligent mind is rhetorical

style, a familiarity with culturally prized writers and a general knowledge of facts. Instead, it should teach us to conceive of intelligence as the depth of our ability to understand different ways of thinking, proving and explaining. It should teach us to conceive of intelligence as the ability to make out the structure of an argument, a theory or an analogy in such a way that it illuminates any conversation or debate on any subject. It is only when you conceive of intelligence as how you think rather than what you know that this conclusion becomes inevitable: the fundamental and unavoidable principles of reasoning and truth develop our minds like no other education can.

Obstacle 2: A Vague and Ineffective Vocabulary of Ideas

Considering the scientific and philosophical progress of the almost 2,500 years since Aristotle's death, it would be reasonable to assume that the ideas upon which modern Western education has been built cannot be fundamentally misguided. The intelligence researcher James Flynn, who sees that our view of intelligence and education revolves not around 'a cluster of interrelated concepts that collectively create a method of analysis' but around a 'knowledge trap' in which concepts 'get lost in the sheer volume of that knowledge', exemplifies the difficulty of pushing against the inertia of modern education. He wrote: 'despite the scores of lectures and tutorials, the hours of marking and feedback, that I lavished on each of my students, I do not believe I gave them what I value most in thinking my way through life.' That an academic and teacher of international standing should reach the peak of their career and their influence, and yet have been unable to incorporate into their teaching what they believe to be truly valuable illustrates the massive weight of that inertia.

Despite the unprecedented depth of our modern understanding of the fundamental concepts on which philosophy,
economics, social science and natural science are based, our
education system is still conceptualised and designed with an
intellectual and philosophical sophistication that's unworthy
of the modern age. If our education is to keep pace with the
forefront of knowledge, we must periodically return to it and
dispassionately examine the foundations of the way we are
taught to think – but were we to do that now, we would find
a worrying lack of depth. Almost every school in the Western
world refers to the complexity of human thinking with the
label 'critical thinking', or an equally vague synonym like 'analysis'. Critical thinking, when it describes no concrete set of
ideas but merely *the idea of intelligence*, amounts to the claim
that you can make people more intelligent by telling them to
think more intelligently. This empty husk of a concept spawns
further vague ideas, like '21st-century thinking', as if the nature
of human intelligence fundamentally changed in the year 2000.
The way we describe intelligence in the 21st century is the result
of a philosophy of education that speaks in the inspiring-but-
vacant advertising language of modern consumerism.

To change this, we need to produce a curriculum of concepts, and one that is concrete enough to be put into practice
and make a difference to our everyday lives. The phrase 'critical thinking' is no more than a general label for a precise set of
ideas. It is too vague to be the *content* of education. The broad
concept of critical thinking, if it is to be more than a euphemism
for intelligence, must deepen our understanding of the words
on which every argument and theory turns: words like 'truth',
'proof', 'evidence', 'scientific', 'real', 'logical' or 'fact'. A curriculum of fundamental concepts – a vocabulary of ideas – could be

a modern Trivium that would make a worthy foundation on top of which to build modern education. Such a foundation would transform the way we are able to think and talk about what's true, and it would make us the envy of the ages – if only we could summon the courage to re-examine and rebuild it.

Principle 2: Education Demands a Concrete and Practical Vocabulary of Ideas

We live in an age that holds up the Socratic spirit of curiosity, self-examination and intelligent public debate as an ideal, but does so in the absence of the philosophical methods that show us how to do it. What we need is a framework for understanding the principles of reasoning and argument, rather than a collection of buzzwords that we use to sound cutting-edge; but as long as our vocabulary of thinking is built from ideas that are too vague to be meaningful or practical – like 'critical thinking' or 'analysis' – we'll continue to find ourselves trapped by the way we think about education and intelligence. The longer we battle through an education that never explains the fundamental ideas in a concrete way, the more convinced we become that all structure, all logic, all patterns, all technique and all thinking about thinking are 'academic' and 'unnatural'.

If we want to be able to reason about anything, to understand the way that other people think and argue, and so to produce a subtle understanding of the broad horizon of truth rather than just a part of it, we need a practical and concrete set of ideas that is truly fundamental. Around six fundamental principles – *deduction, induction, analogy, reality, evidence* and *meaning* – we could build a universe of ideas. Concrete and practical terms like 'premise', 'hidden premise', 'quantifier', 'probable reasoning' or 'fallible sign' are the elements that allow us to recognise and understand what is going on in each other's minds. If we were to follow the example of Kahneman, Nisbett, Flynn and Aristotle, the result would be transformative. What makes possible intellectual education – the sharing of fundamental and unavoidable patterns of thought – is a concrete and practical conceptual vocabulary that we can relate to real-life problems. That is what determines the quality and the utility of the ideas that teach us to think.

Obstacle 3: The Formless God of 'Creativity' and the Disempowering Fatalism of 'Talent'

In the same way that 'critical thinking' can be a phrase we use to convince ourselves that we have taught children something fundamental about thinking, the same is true of 'creativity'. Modern education has a tendency to define creativity in a way that cannot be put to use: to call for its adoption in a way that's very much inspirational but not at all practical.

In the hands of educational theorists like Sir Ken Robinson, creativity has become a deity that we're encouraged to worship in the hope of reinvigorating both schools and society with the promise of new ideas and the injection of some Dionysian human energy – but this creativity-god has no concrete form, and amounts, in practical terms, to nothing more than the concept of inspiration. Whenever you try to make it into something practical – to pick it up in your hands and do something with it – it vanishes back into an ether of ungraspable abstraction. Once the glow of creativity speeches wears off, we're left with the same abilities we had before, and only a feeling of disappointment.

What makes the inspiring but shapeless notion of creativity so insidious, though, is not just the vagueness of the idea itself, but also the *rhetoric of creativity* with which it is delivered. Inspirational but ineffective creativity sermons are delivered with waves of seductive anecdotes about talent, scare stories about the 'factory model' of education and fridge-magnet platitudes of psychology like 'we don't grow into creativity, we grow out of it'. Statements like Robinson's 'creativity is as important as literacy' are facile, seductive and needlessly divisive – and they are made exclusively by those who are already literate. Those whose educational philosophy is to conjure *only* an idyllic vision of rewarding, absorbing and valuable creative flow have little more to say than this: 'the arts are neglected'. And in that, they are undoubtedly right. However, the fact that the arts are neglected does not necessitate or justify the creation of an 'academic' bogeyman. Is creativity a unique quality of drama, dance, music, sculpture or any other art? Does creativity exclude physicists, mathematicians, linguists, lawyers or historians? The call to value and to teach the arts should not be delivered with a divisive rhetoric whereby everything that is not an art is deemed less creative or, worse, said to 'kill creativity'. To do so is to imitate and invert an academic snobbery towards the arts.

The vendors of vague creativity promises are themselves rarely talented artists, musicians or athletes. If you ask those who are widely lauded as creative, they will tell you that the path to creativity is an arduous one built out of technique, patterns and practice. Principles and techniques capture the objective structures of activities from musical improvisation to football to life drawing. Instead of living the experience of the effort (and even the pain) of structured learning, and discovering for ourselves the effect of internalising each of the components of creative skill to such a degree that we can conjure them almost without thinking, we picture the journey to ability as an effortless unfolding of our innate talents. The genuine self-belief that transforms what we believe we can learn does not come from other people *telling us* that we are talented, but from our own sense of amazement when *we realise* that we are able to do things that we previously thought impossible – and *that* grows out of patterns and practice.

We are far more comfortable with the idea of finding our talent than we are with developing it, and this lack of respect for and faith in structured learning is deeply counterproductive. Instead of the belief that, through patterns and practice, we might achieve almost anything, we are taught to focus on the idea of innate abilities that are fixed at birth. This unhelpful story produces a disempowering fatalism, and it fixes our mindset into a brittle and fragile form that begins to crack whenever learning becomes difficult. The irony of inspirational visions of creativity – and especially an emphasis on creativity in the form of innate talent – is that they inspire us while making it harder for us to develop the artistic, musical or sporting ability that we desire.

Principle 3: The Foundation of Ability, Self-belief and Creativity is Patterns and Practice, not Talent

What we are able to achieve is deeply affected by what we are taught to believe about intelligence and talent. When we dismiss the creativity that grows out of patterns and practice, we limit the flowering of our artistic, musical and sporting potential. Every ounce of energy and focus that we devote to the *expectation* of our talent diminishes our faith in the structured learning from which creativity genuinely emerges. The foundation of ability, self-belief and creativity is patterns and practice, not talent.

Obstacle 4: Romanticism

In spite of the enduring influence of 'traditional' education, the modern age's philosophical gravity is pulling us mostly in another direction: towards Romanticism. A vague conception of 'creativity' is part of a wider basket of Romantic ideas, all of which have an intuitive appeal, but which, like creativity, demand a resolutely cautious scepticism. Romanticism is just as great a cause of the modern neglect of a true education of the mind because, despite its differences from more traditional ideas, its instincts are just as inimical to an education worthy of the name.

The influence of Romanticism in education is due in large part to the 18th-century philosopher Jean-Jacques Rousseau, who wrote *Emile, or On Education*: a fictional account of the education of a young boy. In search of a better balance between the educational course that each of us might follow were we allowed to choose it for ourselves and that which society would dictate for us, Rousseau painted a portrait of education that sought to shift the balance towards the former. His portrait of Emile's education was the birth of *discovery learning* and it was driven by a particular rationale: the emphasis on individual differences.

The more you assume and emphasise the individual differences between human beings, the more it follows that there should be differences in their education, and this *personalisation* or *individualisation* of learning is returning to fashion. Out of the political changes of the Enlightenment – the slow advance of individual freedom and individual rights – grew the idea that 'what is personal is right and best for each individual'. The mistake we have made in the modern age is to have confused the extent of the truth of this axiom in politics with the extent of its truth in psychology and education.

Today, for the better, we pay greater attention to the rights of the individual, but this has led to the suspicion of any one-size-fits-all policy – even when it does genuinely fit. We believe that what is personal is best and are suspicious of the universal and the general. And yet, too much fetishising of individual experience diminishes the value – to us, the *personal* value – of what we can learn from other people and demotes it to a lowly position in a misconceived hierarchy. We all get to choose our morals, but not the basic shape of our minds.

Perhaps the greatest difficulty in finding the right balance of Romantic ideas in education is their intuitive and sometimes dangerously seductive nature: Romanticism has an obvious psychological appeal. Intellectual education demands particular fundamental and abstract ideas. Traditional education presents us with particular weighty tomes and particular piles of facts. Romantic education, however, offers us an incomparable amount of freedom. This openness to our own feelings about what we would rather do in the moment has a natural appeal – just as freedom itself does. But the easy promise of an unstructured education can be as self-defeating as it is seductive.

Freud captured the need for a tension in the process of education with which Romanticism is deeply uncomfortable when he wrote that 'education has to find its way between the Scylla of non-interference and the Charybdis of frustration'. To give us the best chance of developing ability, the way we are taught must balance inhibition and control with free play and exploration. Education need not be unnecessarily arduous. The ability that grows out of systematic instruction doesn't have to be forged in an endless misery of scale practice, verb conjugation or practice in reasoning and arguments, but it cannot do without it as a foundation. There is a balance to be found that depends on our age, the developmental state of our brains and the type of activity we want to learn. Too much drumming of structure into a brain that is too young to absorb it leads to misery and disenchantment. Too little at the right age, and the lack of challenge and progress limits our development. When our education fails to take us to new levels of skill, it risks leading us instead to boredom. Mastery depends on motivation, but motivation does not arise from freedom alone.

We must step back and admire the confident humanism of the classical world alongside the humility of Romanticism and be able to appreciate the proper balance between them. At its best, Romanticism is an openness to ideas and experience that we either do not know how to understand within some sort of a structure, or which will always elude our attempts to do so because of their very nature. At its worst, it is a capitulation to the easy option: a resigned sigh that accompanies the claim that everything is fundamentally uncertain, mysterious, subjective, irreducible, individual and unteachable. Romanticism sometimes lures us into its 'boundless desire for things that are uncertain' and makes it easy to justify falling back into the armchair of life without doing very much thinking at all.

Perhaps Romanticism's attraction to mystery was humanity's escapist response to the truths of the Enlightenment that it didn't want to hear. Perhaps Romantic ideas are the world's answer to Copernicus displacing the Earth from the centre of the universe and Darwin dislodging man from the centre of creation. Perhaps it was a childish rebellion against having to grow up – a clinging to the rock of pure imagination in the face of powerful currents of change. Many educational experiences are personal, unique and joyously enigmatic, but that does not mean that everything we might learn is an inscrutable riddle. Unlike so many secrets that cannot be truly communicated from one person to another, the fundamental elements of our rational mind are no impenetrable mystery: it is in our nature to understand them.

Principle 4: A School of Thought is no less natural than The School of Life

The Romantic love of exploration and individuality brings with it the risk of dismissing the deliberate passing down of an objective and universal heritage in favour of a seductive ideology: a 'natural' discovery through play and experience alone, or an excessive emphasis on them. We need to return to the confidence of the humanist possibility of education and self-knowledge, not the comforting resignation of mystery or the seductive call of freedom.

We don't just mature according to a plan, like a rose, a butterfly or a cow. It is in all of our natures not just to unfold alone, but to be formed by one another. We are animals of a special kind, born with an intellectual aptitude to shape and to be shaped. The ability to pass on an intellectual heritage – to think and talk about thinking in an abstract way – is uniquely human. The passing down of an intellectual inheritance of reasoning is not some artificial construct of a society imposing its will on its children and citizens. In so far as it harnesses our nature and is unique to us, a deliberate intellectual education is just as 'natural' as what we discover for ourselves at the 'school of life'. A school of thought – as opposed to a school of life – introduces us to what is fundamental and unchanging in the mind, not merely what holds our attention in the moment; and it does it in a way that is uniquely human.

Sounding the Alarm: Consequences

It is not always easy to see education's effects on the culture of the modern age, but two of them are impossible to ignore. It should come as no surprise that the average person who lived 100 or 200 years ago had, through their lack of education, no defence against the army of aura-vendors and snake-oil salesman who depend on society's ignorance of science to make a living. But today's absence of a usable everyday understanding of the scientific way of thinking means that even those who have received better educational opportunities than most still fail to see through the same kind of pseudoscientific ruses that fooled medieval peasants. The improper teaching of methodology has brought us a retrograde attitude to science that is out of keeping with the modern age.

The age of science will not dissolve into ignorance because a slightly higher percentage of people than would otherwise be the case believe in homeopathy or any other pseudoscience. Science is now so specialised that it is carried forward by only a relative few. Most of us don't need to be experts (nor could we be) with the depth of specialist knowledge that's required to understand the cutting edge of science – but the public understanding of science affects the wisdom of the crowd, and it is the crowd that drives large-scale progress. To erode that understanding is to erode confidence in a tool of undeniable utility.

Science, which has provided us with everything from medicine to environmental solutions on a global scale, is not a human endeavour that we can afford to ignore. If we do not engage seriously with the scientific method – the method that, in essence, created the modern world – we jeopardise it. We could, with this special way of thinking that we have created and passed

down from one human being to another, think our way to a better world: one that that can feed everyone without consuming
itself. If we are to continue, as a culture, to save not just souls,
but lives too, and to manage and understand our physical reality
in a way that countless millennia of witch doctors never could,
we must not fail to pass on the thinking that makes it possible.

The second detrimental – maybe even catastrophic – effect
of an education that doesn't prepare us well for the lives we lead
is that it causes us to turn the volume of politics all the way up
to screaming point without teaching us to notice that we still
don't hear each other.

All of us, for reasons of cultural background or perhaps even
of intrinsic psychological makeup, have wildly divergent feelings and opinions about human nature, ethics and politics. For
this reason, *people will always disagree*, but this inevitable disagreement – this natural and ineradicable spectrum of opinion
– is made wider and worse by our inability to understand how
the extreme ends of every argument are exaggerated. Citizens
who are skilfully educated in logic and language, however,
are harder to manipulate. They are steadier under the assault
of extreme ideas. To the mind of the truly philosophical citi-
zen, the fringes of arguments always seem frayed. If we are to
become harder to manipulate and more understanding of other
people, we need to be brought up in the habit of being able to
interrogate what others believe and why they believe it. In the
absence of philosopher-kings, let us all be philosopher-citizens.

The importance of a philosophical style of thought to
successful states has been noted by philosophers since Plato.
Martha Nussbaum continues this tradition in her observation
that 'logic is real, and it often governs our human relations.
Lots of slurs and stereotypes work in exactly this way, through

fallacious inference. The ability to detect fallacy is one of the things that makes democratic life decent.' Modern education, being built on a foundation of literary style rather than philosophical substance, prepares us badly for the task of being discerning citizens. A lack of philosophical skill makes us easier to persuade and to manipulate – and the result is a rhetorical style of public life that sweeps us up and suffocates us in an avalanche of empty platitudes.

But it is not only politicians who are to blame, for we too have our part to play. For all our passion for our ideals of justice and equality, we fail to persuade our fellows: those on whose agreement we depend if we want to change the way we live. We struggle to point out why some arguments don't add up. Without the shared ideas, without the language to make ourselves understood and to make clear the manipulation that we believe is the tool of our political opponents, all we can do is shout 'fake news' or 'post-truth' at those we disagree with. If we aren't taught to reflect on the way we use words – to consciously think and talk about meaning – can we be surprised at how difficult we find it to picture the structure of other people's arguments and beliefs; and to explain what we see, clearly and concisely, to others?

As a culture, we don't directly introduce children to the concepts and techniques that teach them to think and argue. All of us, being less skilful in understanding and exchanging ideas than we could be, end up afraid to have difficult conversations. While the failure to teach the techniques of thinking, understanding and arguing is itself detrimental to democratic societies, so too is the attitude that is often a consequence of their absence: a fear of open debate. We learn to hold our tongues because we don't systematically learn to clearly and calmly speak our minds, but no truly functioning relationship is based on polite smiles. When we maintain too much respectful distance from each other because we are afraid to have difficult conversations, we find it hard to see, let alone fix, society's cracks.

What little common currency we have to trade at the market of ideas! The lack of a public vocabulary of debate inhibits our ability to forge the consensus on which political progress depends. A society that's unpractised in reasoning cannot be surprised by the unenviable quality of its politics. It's not enough to only persuade people to examine their lives, or to call people to virtue or peace or love, as figures philosophical and religious since Socrates have done. What we need is a collection of ideas that helps us to do it: the fundamental concepts of reasoning and truth – and the philosophy of education and intelligence that supports them. The power of our yearning for a better world is, alone, not enough to create one.

If we want to understand each other better, to be able to expose the manipulations of politics, and to see the structure of everything that we and other people claim is true, we must return to teaching what is fundamental. Real political progress does not come easily, but if we choose easy and cheap emotion – if we choose to shout at each other rhetorically instead of talking to one another philosophically – we'll convince no one, find little or no progress, and despite all our efforts and intentions to make the world a better and more peaceful place we'll end up with nothing to show for them.

What is Worth Learning, or A Theory of Education

Education can be many things. It can be what we are each forced to learn by the time, place and circumstances of our birth. It can be whatever we choose to learn for pleasure, for personal development, or even for its own sake. What we call education is really many different types of activity carried out by many different people – but there is a common thread. A middle-class gentleman on a London train, a miner's daughter in rural China, and the boy we know as Alexander the Great are all connected by the unchanging and unavoidable elements of a human mind and a human life. Those elements are the starting point of a theory of education.

To ask the question *what is worth learning?* is really to ask a cascade of questions. A theory of psychology alone – an understanding of the mind – is not enough to support a theory of education. To suggest *what* is worth learning, *how* we might learn it and *why*, we must paint not just a scientific picture of a human mind, but also a philosophical vision of a human life. What we should learn depends not just on the way things are, but also on the way we would like them to be.

The educational decisions that we make – either for ourselves or for our children – matter: because education is the womb of culture. We must not accept our education simply because it is what has survived, because it is the norm or because it is ours. We can build the cultures of the future on a new and better foundation.

Throughout human history, it is social education that has always ruled, and the modern age is no different. We teach our children about tolerance, gender, racism, bullying and citizenship. We teach them to play the sports and instruments of our culture and to sing songs that shape their attitudes, their morals and their ability to be part of a group. Education has two sides, and our age is mostly concerned with only one of them. What we worry about most is not whether education teaches us to think; it's what it teaches us to believe, and this is the way it has always been. For thousands of years, parents, teachers, religious leaders, politicians and kings have suggested and imposed countless visions of a way of life, and they will continue to do so until the world stops turning. But while social education is ever-present, an education for our minds is rare. Social education is the essential and inevitable glue that binds us into a functioning whole: it is what structures our early lives and gives us a place in society from which to become our adult selves. But we do not remain children for long.

In our journey to the independence of adulthood, we do not enjoy the luxury of being able to choose any path. Education must make a special place for reasoning and for language, because they are the elements out of which our minds are made. An inability to deal with their opportunities and dangers leaves us unable to say what we think or to clearly understand our fellow humans. It leaves us mute, powerless, and distanced from the nature of our own minds. Whether we are confronted by a newspaper article, a political debate, a medical decision, a business proposal or a family argument, our lives revolve around our ability to decide, to cajole, to persuade, and to judge the opinions of others. You might disagree, but you could only do so by providing a reasoned argument of your own.

The call to rebalance and rebuild the foundation of education is no appeal for a tyranny of words, numbers and reason over the depths of experience that are more difficult to describe. We can't always explain everything, and the emotional response that dance, drama, art, music or sport produces in us is also a deep and vital part of the human experience. Sometimes we can't put things into language, let alone exact language: we have to represent or experience them. But most of life is not like this. No work of art or spiritual experience can replace words, numbers and reason. We can learn to dance or sing or pray or weep to express our pain or our joy, but not to forge the laws that guarantee our freedom. To shape our world is to argue, to distinguish meanings and to point out manipulation. Our ability to live with each other and to achieve our goals depends on our ability to reflect on the words we use, the arguments we make and the logic of the solutions we offer. Necessity dictates that we build our world before we embellish it.

Our social and political nature and our communal obligations – *what we owe to each other* – must, however, be held in balance with the fact that it is also part of our experience to each be set adrift in our own little boat. Ultimately, we are all, first and foremost, individuals with the power to make up our own minds and decide for ourselves. But if we can't clearly see the structure of an argument or a theory, if we don't notice the depth of the analogies, comparisons and examples that we're offered, or if the alarm bells don't go off when we hear the words 'proof', 'evidence' or 'truth' then how easily can we decide for ourselves?

It is the right, but not the good fortune, of every human being to be introduced to the fundamental principles inherent in their own mind. We live in an age of unprecedented intellectual and political freedom, but the irony of the age of individualism is that we do not teach – and only rarely mention – the unchanging ideas that reveal the broad and magnificent horizon of different kinds of truth. We have both the knowledge and the resources to teach the fundamentals of thinking and argument, and not just to the sons of kings or to some special class of philosophers or politicians, but to everyone. The way we think is the intellectual heritage of mankind as a species, and everyone deserves a share in it. No education worthy of the name denies us a glimpse of the constellation of possibilities inside the human mind.

To deny another human being the education upon which their autonomy depends is to deny them a central principle of human existence: that our lives are our own, and that we have the right to make of them what we will by the force of our own conviction. It is to deny us our human right to the education on which meaningful freedom is based: not just the right to choose, but the right to be educated in such a way that the choices we make are not those of our parents, our religion or our society, but *ours*. The only true route to individual autonomy – the only way to ensure we decide for ourselves – is to be taught to think for ourselves. The most disempowering education and the one that is the greatest affront to our inalienable right to true autonomy isn't indoctrination; it is never having been shown the ideas we all use to decide what's true for ourselves. In the words of Hannah Arendt, 'the aim of totalitarian education has never been to instill convictions, but to destroy the capacity to form any.' That capacity is based on the philosophical ability to distinguish different kinds of truths, and the principles that describe something fundamental and unavoidable about the human mind.

In every waking moment, we depend on our intelligence. We live on the crest of a wave – an endlessly surging moment we call the present – and suddenly we're face to face with a choice that matters and it cries 'THINK!' But time doesn't stop. The logic twists, the language turns, the numbers dance and all of a sudden it's too late; the moment's gone. The way we think in every one of those moments is what shapes our lives – but unlike so many things that we experience but can't explain, it is no impenetrable enigma. It is hard to grasp what we cannot see, but we were born to capture the ideas that matter most. The reward is something that no one can take away from you: the power of your own thought.

Acknowledgements

To the friends and family without whose support I would not have been able to write this book: thank you. In so many ways, I have relied on Leigh and Melissa Adams, Keenan Probst, Dad, Richard Tibber, Paul and Marlene Norton, Adam and Alicia Adams, and Andrea and Julian Margolin. Any embarrassment that I might feel in thanking, above all, the unwavering and limitless source of patience and trust that is my mother pales in comparison to the scale of her contribution and the depth of my gratitude. I owe you more than I could ever repay.

David Ashley and Charles Freedman – thank you, both of you, for your long-standing friendship and encouragement. Daniel Simon – thank you for enduring a barrage of analogies and analysis, and for your scepticism. I am indebted to Milo Bird and Amy Winchester for their kindness at an important time, and to Thalia Suzuma and Emily Labram for their wisdom and encouragement. Alexander Margolin – from the beginning until the end, your support has been invaluable.

To Shai and Amélie Shotts, in whose wonderful home I wrote so much of this book, thank you for understanding my obsession. I could not have done it without you. Jeremy and Carole – for your advice, on manuscripts and life, thank you, too.

To my agent, Andrew Gordon – without whom this book would have remained in my head rather than been set in print – and to my editor Tom Webber, I will be forever grateful. As the writer Jon Ronson put it, authors can hand over their manuscript and then defend themselves by 'exuding a silent mix of defiance and despair'. That defiance met its match in Tom's patience and his resolve, and were it not for his skill, I would have been left with far more to regret. For the shortcomings that remain, the responsibility is mine.

Finally, given the affinity that I feel with Aristotle, I have been lucky to find a modern-day Socrates and Plato. Jack Lewis and Emad Akhtar, for the countless hours of conversation in which so many ideas crystallised, thank you. May the philosophical fires never cease to burn.

Bibliography

Arendt, Hannah. *The Origins of Totalitarianism*. London: Deutsch, 1969.

Aristophanes. 'The Clouds'. In *Lysistrata and Other Plays: The Acharnians, The Clouds, Lysistrata*. Translated from the Greek by Alan H. Sommerstein. London: Penguin, 2002.

Aristotle, and Jonathan Barnes (ed.). *The Complete Works of Aristotle: The Revised Oxford Translation*. Princeton, NJ: Princeton University Press, 1984.

Arnold, Matthew. *Culture and Anarchy: An Essay in Political and Social Criticism*. New York: Macmillan, 1882.

Bump, Philip. 'Palin: "This Isn't Racist," but Debt is "Like Slavery"'. *The Atlantic*, 11 November 2013. [online] Available at: https://www.theatlantic.com/politics/archive/2013/11/palin-isnt-racist-debt-slavery/355165/ [Accessed 11 March 2019].

Darwin, Charles and Nora Barlow (ed.). *The Autobiography of Charles Darwin*. New York: W.W. Norton and Company, Inc., 1969.

Barrow, Robin. *Plato and Education*. London: Routledge and Kegan Paul, 1976.

Bloom, Allan. *The Closing of the American Mind*. New York: Simon and Schuster, 1988.

Bloom, Benjamin S. *Taxonomy of Educational Objectives: The Classification of Educational Goals*. New York: Longmans, Green, 1956.

Bradsher, Keith. 'In China, Families Bet It All on College for Their Children'. *The New York Times*, 16 February 2013. [online] Available at: http://www.nytimes.com/2013/02/17/business/in-china-families-bet-it-all-on-a-child-in-college.html?_r=0. [Accessed 11 March 2019].

Brumbaugh, Robert S., and Nathaniel M. Lawrence. *Philosophers on Education: Six Essays on the Foundations of Western Thought.* Boston: Houghton Mifflin Company, 1963.

Burnyeat, M.F. 'Enthymeme: Aristotle on the Logic of Persuasion'. In Furley, D.J. and Nehamas, A. (eds.), *Aristotle's Rhetoric: Proceedings of the Twelfth Symposium Aristotelicum.* Princeton: Princeton University Press, 1994, 3–55.

Cheng, P.W., and K.J. Holyoak. 'Pragmatic Reasoning Schemas'. *Cognitive Psychology* 17 (4): 391–416, 1985.

Cicero. *Rhetorica Ad Herennium.* Translated from the Latin by Harry Caplan. Loeb Classical Library 403. Cambridge, MA: Harvard University Press, 1954.

Consigny, Scott. *Gorgias: Sophist and Artist.* Columbia, SC: University of South Carolina Press, 2001.

Davidson, Thomas. *Aristotle and Ancient Educational Ideals.* New York: Charles Scribner's Sons, 1907.

Davis, Wade. *Light at the Edge of the World.* Vancouver: Douglas and MacIntyre, 2007.

Dobson, John Frederic. *Ancient Education and its Meaning to us.* New York: Longmans, Green and Co., 1932.

Dillon, John and Tania Gergel. *The Greek Sophists.* London: Penguin, 2003.

Dodds, Eric Robertson. *The Greeks and the Irrational.* Berkeley: University of California Press, 1951.

Dweck, Carol S. *Mindset: The New Psychology of Success.* New York: Ballantine Books, 2008.

Einstein, Albert. *Ideas and Opinions.* New York: Crown Publishers, 1956.

Flynn, James R. *How to Improve Your Mind: Twenty Keys to Unlock the Modern World.* London: Wiley-Blackwell, 2012.

Fong, Geoffrey, David Krantz, and Richard Nisbett. 'The Effects of Statistical Training on Thinking About Everyday Problems'. *Cognitive Psychology* 18 (3): 253–292, 1986.

Freeman, Kenneth J. *Schools of Hellas.* London: Macmillan and Co., 1907.

Freeman, Kathleen. *Ancilla to the pre-Socratic Philosophers: A Complete Translation of the Fragments in Diels, Fragmente der Vorsokratiker.* Oxford: Blackwell, 1948.

Friedländer, Paul. *Plato I: An Introduction.* London: Routledge and Kegan Paul, 1958.

Freud, S. 'New Introductory Lectures on Psycho-Analysis. Lecture 34. Explanations, Applications and Orientations.' In Strachey, J. (ed.), *The Standard Edition of the Complete Psychological Works of Sigmund Freud*, Vol. 22. London: Hogarth Press, 1964, 136–157.

Frye, Northrop. 'The Archetypes of Literature. *The Kenyon Review.* Vol. 13, No. 1, Winter 1951, 92–110.

Galloway, J. 'Herman Cain and Donald Trump tilt at West Coast Windmills'. *The Atlanta Journal-Constitution*, 25 October 2016. [online] Available at: https://www.ajc.com/blog/politics/ herman-cain-and-donald-trump-tilt west-coast-windmills/ qtcOrU27zdU5SrB9516M1I./ [Accessed 11 March 2019].

Guthrie, W.K.C. *A History of Greek Philosophy.* Vol. 3, Part 1. *The Sophists.* Cambridge: Cambridge University Press, 1971.

Hinks, D.A.G. 'Tisias and Corax and the Invention of Rhetoric'. *The Classical Quarterly*, Vol. 34, No. 1/2, January–April 1940, 61–69.

Hirsch, E.D., Joseph F. Kett, and James Trefil. *Cultural Literacy: What Every American Needs to Know.* New York: Vintage Books, 1988.

Hirsch, E.D. *Why Knowledge Matters: Rescuing our Children from Failed Educational Theories.* Cambridge, MA: Harvard Education Press, 2016.

Hitchens, Christopher. *God is Not Great: How Religion Poisons Everything.* New York: Twelve, 2007.

Hofstadter, Douglas. *Gödel, Escher, Bach.* 20th anniversary edition. London: Penguin Books, 2000.

Hofstadter, Douglas and Emmanuel Sander. *Surfaces and Essences: Analogy as the Fuel and Fire of Thinking.* New York, NY: Basic Books, 2013.

Homer. *The Iliad.* Translated from the Greek by E.V. Rieu, D.C.H. Rieu and Peter Jones. Edited by Peter Jones. London: Penguin, 2003.

Homer. *The Odyssey*. Translated from the Greek by E.V. Rieu, D.C.H. Rieu. Edited by Peter Jones. London: Penguin, 2003.

Jaeger, Werner. *Aristotle: Fundamentals of the History of his Development*. Translated by Richard Robinson. Oxford: at the Clarendon Press, London: Humphrey Milford. 1934.

Jaeger, Werner. *Paideia: The Ideals of Greek Culture*. Vol. 1. *Archaic Greece. The Mind of Athens*. Translated from the second German edition by Gilbert Highet. New York: Oxford University Press, 1939.

Jaeger, Werner. *Paideia: The Ideals of Greek Culture*. Vol. 2. *In Search of the Divine Centre*. Translated from the second German edition by Gilbert Highet. New York: Oxford University Press, 1943.

Jaeger, Werner. *Paideia: The Ideals of Greek Culture*. Vol. 3. *The Conflict of Cultural Ideals in the Age of Plato*. Translated from the second German edition by Gilbert Highet. New York: Oxford University Press, 1944.

Jarratt, Susan Carole Funderburgh. *Rereading the Sophists: Classical Rhetoric Refigured*. Carbondale: Southern Illinois University Press, 1991.

Kahneman, Daniel. *Thinking, Fast and Slow*. London: Penguin, 2011.

Kerferd, G.B. *The Sophistic Movement*. Cambridge: Cambridge University Press, 1981.

Kitzmiller v. Dover Area School District. 400 F. Supp. 2d 707 (M.D. Pa. 2005). [online] Available at: https://ncse.com/files/pub/legal/kitzmiller/highlights/2005-12-20_Kitzmiller_decision.pdf [Accessed 11 March 2019].

Kravitz, David. *The Dictionary of Greek and Roman Mythology*. London: New English Library, 1975.

Leavis, F.R. *Two Cultures? The Significance of C.P. Snow*. Cambridge: Cambridge University Press, 2013.

Lakoff, George, and Mark Johnson. *The Metaphors We Live By*. Chicago: University of Chicago Press, 1980.

Lane Fox, Robin. *The Search for Alexander*. London: Little, Brown and Co., 1981.

Lear, Jonathan. *Aristotle: The Desire to Understand*. New York: Cambridge University Press, 1988.

Lehman, Darrin R., Richard O. Lempert, and Richard E. Nisbett. 'The Effects of Graduate Training on Reasoning.' *American Psychologist*. Vol. 43, No. 6, June 1988, 431–442.

Leroi, Armand Marie. *The Lagoon: How Aristotle Invented Science*. London: Bloomsbury, 2014.

Lodge, R.C. *Plato's Theory of Education*. London: Routledge, 2001.

Macmillan, Harold. 'Oxford Remembered'. *The Times*, Issue 59530, 18 October 1975.

Marrou, Henri-Irénéé. *A History of Education in Antiquity*. Translated by George Lamb. Madison: The University of Wisconsin Press, 1982. Originally published as *Histoire de l'Education dans l'Antiquité*. Paris: Editions du Seuil, 1948.

Mayhew, Robert. *Prodicus the Sophist*. Oxford: Oxford University Press, 2011.

McComiskey, Bruce. *Gorgias and the New Sophistic Rhetoric*. Carbondale and Edwardsville: Southern Illinois University Press, 2001.

Natali, Carlo. *Aristotle: His Life and School*. Princeton: Princeton University Press, 2013.

Nickerson, R.S., D.N. Perkins, and E.E. Smith, *The Teaching of Thinking*. Hillsdale, NJ: Lawrence Erlbaum Associates, 1985.

Nisbett, Richard E. *Intelligence and How to Get It: Why Schools and Cultures Count*. New York: W.W. Norton and Co., 2009.

Nisbett, Richard E. *Mindware: Tools for Smart Thinking*. London: Allen Lane, 2015.

Nisbett, Richard E. (ed.). *Rules for Reasoning*. Hillsdale, NJ: Lawrence Erlbaum Associates, 1993.

Nussbaum, Martha C. *Not for Profit: Why Democracy Needs the Humanities*. Princeton, NJ: Princeton University Press, 2010.

Orwell, George. 'Politics and the English Language'. *Horizon*, 13 (76): 252–265, 1946.

Perkins, David N. and Gavriel Salomon. 'Are Cognitive Skills Context-Bound?' *Educational Researcher*. Vol. 18, No. 1, January–February 1989, 16–25.

Plato. *Complete Works.* Edited by John M. Cooper. Cambridge: Hackett Publishing Company, 1977.

Plato. *Gorgias.* Translated by Robin Waterfield. Oxford: Oxford University Press, 1994.

Plato. *Phaedrus.* Translated by Christopher Rowe. London: Penguin, 2005.

Plato. *Protagoras and Meno.* Translated by Adam Beresford. London: Penguin, 2005.

Plato. *The Republic.* Translated by Desmond Lee. London: Penguin, 2007.

Plato. *The Symposium.* Translated by Peter Gill. London: Penguin, 1999.

Plutarch. 'Life of Alexander'. In *The Age of Alexander: Ten Greek Lives by Plutarch.* Translated by Ian Scott-Kilvert and Timothy E. Duff. London: Penguin, 2011, 279–364.

Reichel-Dolmatoff, Gerardo. *The Sacred Mountains of Colombia's Kogi Indians.* Leiden: E.J. Brill, 1990.

Robinson, Ken, and Lou Aronica. *The Element: How Finding your Passion Changes Everything.* New York: Penguin Group USA, 2009.

Robinson, Ken. 'Do Schools Kill Creativity?' *TED: Ideas Worth Spreading.* [online] Available at: https://www.ted.com/talks/ ken_robinson_says_schools_kill_creativity?language=en [Accessed 11 March 2019]

Robinson, T.M. *Contrasting Arguments: An Edition of the Dissoi Logoi.* New York: Arno Press, 1979.

Rosen, Michael. 'Dear Ms Morgan: your guidance is a mini-syllabus on how to wreck poetry'. *Guardian,* 7 April 2015. [online] Available at: https://www.theguardian.com/education/2015/ apr/07/key-stage-1-poetry-assessment-wrecks-poems-for -children [Accessed 11 March 2019].

Ross, W.D. *Aristotle.* London: Methuen and Co., 1923.

Saul, H. 'Andrea Leadsom wants British broadcasters to be more "patriotic" in Brexit coverage'. *i,* 24 June 2017. [online] Available at: https://inews.co.uk/news/politics/andrea

-leadsom-wants-british-broadcasters-patriotic-brexit
-coverage/ [Accessed 11 March 2019].

Sayers, Dorothy. *The Lost Tools of Learning*. London: Methuen, 1948.

Scheffler, Israel. *Conditions of Knowledge: An Introduction to Epistemology and Education*. London: Routledge and Kegan Paul, 1965.

Scheffler, Israel. *Reason and Teaching*. London: Routledge and Kegan Paul, 1976.

Sharpe, Matthew. 'Hunting Plato's Agalmata'. *The European Legacy: Toward New Paradigms*. 14:5, 2009, 535–547. DOI: 10.1080/10848770903128422.

Skidelsky, Robert. 'Post-crash Economics: Some Common Fallacies About Austerity.' *The Guardian*, 21 November 2013. [online] Available at: https://www.theguardian.com/business/2013/nov/21/post-crash-economics-austerity-common-fallacies [Accessed 11 March 2019].

Snow. C.P. *The Two Cultures*. Cambridge: Cambridge University Press, 2013.

Sprague, Rosamond Kent. *The Older Sophists: A Complete Translation by Several Hands of the Fragments in Die Fragmente der Vorsokratiker*. Columbia, SC: University of South Carolina Press, 1972.

Stone, Jon. 'Labour Antisemitism Row: Read the Ken Livingstone interview transcripts in full.' *The Independent*, 28 April 2016. [online] Available at: https://www.independent.co.uk/news/uk/politics/labour-anti-semitism-row-full-transcript-of-ken-livingstones-interviews-a7005311.html [Accessed 11 March 2019].

Strassler, Robert B. (ed.). *The Landmark Thucydides*. Translated from the Greek by Richard Crawley. New York: Free Press, 2008.

'The Classroom of the Future'. *Newsweek*. 28 October 2001. [online] Available at: https://www.newsweek.com/classroom-future-154191 [Accessed 11 March 2019].

Tversky, Amos, and Daniel Kahneman. 'Judgment Under Uncertainty: Heuristics and Biases'. *Science*. Vol. 185, No. 4157, September 1974, 1124–1131.

Wardy, Robert. *The Birth of Rhetoric: Gorgias, Plato and Their Successors.* London: Routledge, 1996.

Wolfsdorf, David Conan. 'Sophistic Method and Practice'. In W. Martin Bloomer, (ed.), *A Companion to Ancient Education.* Chichester: Wiley-Blackwell, 2015, 63–74.

Woolf, Virginia and Mitchell A. Leaska (ed.). *A Passionate Apprentice: The Early Journals 1897–1909.* London: Hogarth Press, 1990.

About the Author

Craig Adams studied Linguistics and Modern Languages at Oxford. He worked in publishing as an editor of non-fiction before hearing the inspirational call of teaching. Disillusioned by being made to follow a curriculum that taught his students everything apart from the most important ideas, he left to write this book. He lives in London.